THE LONDON EXTENSION
of the
MIDLAND RAILWAY
St Pancras - Bedford

Stanier Jubilee 45648 WEMYSS leaves St Pancras with the 16.30 semi-fast to Nottingham on 25 August 1948. *E.D.Bruton.*

THE HISTORY OF THE St PANCRAS - BEDFORD ROUTE

by

Geoff Goslin.

Copyright Irwell Press

ISBN 1-871608-47-3
First published in the United Kingdom
1994 by Irwell Press,
P.O.Box 1260,
Caernarfon,
Gwynedd, LL55 3ZD
Printed by The Amadeus Press, Huddersfield

IRWELL PRESS

PREFACE

The London Extension of the Midland Railway has always possessed its own identity. Built southwards from Bedford to provide the Midland with an independent route to London its present configuration of quadruple track was envisaged from the time of its planning and produced a line with characteristics of neatness and orderliness which still persist.

In contrast the layout at Bedford presented continuing operating problems and the development of the Extension with the existing route to Hitchin culminated in a sprawl of lines over a wide area of railway land. It was probably the complexities of train movements at Bedford which gave the author, tutored from an early age by a railway enthusiast father, a lasting interest in signalling and traffic operation. These features of the extension have been given due prominence in the descriptions which follow.

The Extension can be regarded as having three phases of existence. The first, as a conventional double line of railway, dated from the initial trains of 1867 to the completion of quadrupling in 1895. During the second phase, which lasted from 1895 until 1960, the line was a four track trunk railway with long distance freight and passenger services but with comparatively little emphasis on internal passenger traffic. The introduction of diesel suburban trains in 1960 began a long transition into a third phase as an electrified suburban railway carrying additionally a much reduced freight traffic and a much-simplified express service. From 1988 the Thameslink services have connected the extension to a variety of destinations south of the Thames.

Bedford is now a northern outpost, both of electrification and of Network Southeast and it is quite possible that a future generation will come to regard the Extension more as a northwards projection of services from the south rather than as a gateway to London from the Midlands.

The documents of the Midland, London Midland & Scottish and British Railways have been used as primary sources in the preparation of this book with assistance being given by a wide variety of other published matter, too numerous, alas, to be listed individually. Indispensable assistance has also been given by Peter Holmes and John Osgood with much invaluable information being provided by Mike Christensen, Alec Crawley, John Gough, Roger Newman, John Parker, Stephen Summerson and Geoff Woodward. Their co-operation is greatly acknowledged. I am greatly indebted to the late Geoffrey Webb who read the draft, making many corrections and helpful suggestions, although responsibility for accuracy rests with the author. The staff of the public Record Office at Kew, the National Railway Museum at York, Bedford and Flitwick public libraries and the Bedfordshire County Record Office have all been most helpful. Thanks are also due to my daughter, Alison, for the design of the jacket.

Finally the Bedford Railwaymen who provided the author, some 50 years ago, with an insight into the operating practices of the time are remembered. To them and their successors, this book is dedicated.

CONTENTS

1. PRE-EXTENSION BEDFORD

The Leicester and Hitchin line first brought the trains of the Midland Railway to Bedford in 1857. All the original installations of the Midland at Bedford were located along the course of the line to Hitchin, to the south of the final site of the station and the eventual junction with the Extension. The Bedford station was originally intended to be sited to the south of the Ouse and the level crossing with the LNWR's Bletchley to Bedford branch provided an opportunity for a joint station to be built. To this end the Leicester and Hitchin Powers included the closure of the eastern end of Ampthill Road where the railway crossed its course. In substitution, a deviation, Britannia Road, was to be constructed so that traffic from the Ampthill direction could enter Bedford via the Kempston Road. This was actually carried out and negotiations were opened with the LNWR for the building of a joint station. Heads of Agreement were produced in May 1856 but, at the level of the respective Boards, the terms were not acceptable and the agreement was not ratified. So when passenger traffic commenced between Leicester and Hitchin on 8th May 1857, the Midland had no station between Oakley and Cardington and its trains had to use the LNWR station at Bedford. A single line spur was laid from the LNWR station to a junction on the Midland line, facing for up trains and crossing the western connection to the LNWR goods yard. Up trains could run straight in, but they had to propel out again. Down trains had to set back to reach the station but could depart normally. This arrangement gave no pleasure to the Board of Trade but was sanctioned reluctantly as a temporary measure.

In October 1857, after trains had been running for five months, a meeting took place between Midland directors and the Mayor and townsmen of Bedford. Agreement was reached on a site for a station to the north of the river, where Cox Pit Lane crossed the railway on the level. There was much opposition to this from residents south of the river, probably led from behind by the Duke of Bedford with an eye on the value of his land in that area. The views of the Midland and the Mayor prevailed, however, and the station, eventually to become Bedford Midland Road, was opened on 1st February 1859. This was the beginning of a love-hate re-

Believed to be the only surviving photograph of Bedford station as originally built, this view looking north from Cox Pit Lane level crossing shows the original through platforms which were truncated into sidings and bays when the extension platforms were built to the left of the picture. The bookstall and refreshment room were built over the old formation. *Beds County Record Office*

Engineering works during the early stages of the Extension which shows rows of columns in the background waiting to be incorporated into the structure of St Pancras station where they were used to support the floors and platforms. *NRM*

lationship that was enjoyed, if that is the right word, between the Midland and the Bedford Corporation over the next few years. The station was built with two platforms, each 300 feet long, to the north of the level crossing. Between the crossing and the platform on the down side was a crossing keeper's house with a pointed bay window. This was almost certainly built with the railway in 1857, rather than with the station in 1859. A similar building still exists at Little Bowden crossing, near Market Harborough. The crossing had separate gates for up and down lines, overlapping when closed against the narrow road. The main station building on the up platform remained substantially unaltered until its demolition in 1980. Serving the most important intermediate town on the line, it was given some distinctive touches, including a large *porte cochere* and a lantern roof to the booking hall. At the north end of the up platform was a vehicle turntable with connections to both up and down lines and with spurs to a loading bay and three short sidings. The turntable was small, 14 ft. in diameter, scaled from an early plan.

A coal yard situated south of the river had been opened with the railway in 1857. The goods yard was established between Cox Pit Lane and the river, and was opened on 1st February 1859. The original goods shed was 135 ft. 6 ins. long and its front wall stood 22 ft. 6 ins. from the near rail of the then up main line. Although facing points in the running lines were avoided, there was no provision of catch points to safeguard trains on the main lines from movements out of the yard.

Now, two years after the opening of the line, the Midland had their passenger station and goods and coal yards established. Not everything was quite right, however. In 1861, a petition was made by the inhabitants of Bedford to the LNWR and Midland Companies for a joint passenger station. Furthermore, the stopping up of Ampthill Road had been authorised for the purpose of building a station there and this had not been achieved. The LNWR had provided a properly gated level crossing for the Ampthill Road over the lines to their goods yard but since 1857 it had not led anywhere. On 7th August 1861, the

Midland Board recorded that there had been an indictment against the Company for nuisance caused by the stopping up. The jury had found the case proved and the Midland had been fined forty pounds. It was noted that the Powers to build a bridge to carry Ampthill Road over the line had expired and that it was requisite to renew them. On 2nd October 1861 it was noted that a clause to build a bridge would be included in the Bill for the next session. On 17th April 1862, the Mayor, John Howard, wrote to the Chairman, Samuel Beale - the Town Council had plans for a new road and a bridge over the Ouse to connect the Midland station with the proposed new LNWR station. The proposal would lessen the Midland expenses in opening up Ampthill Road as the LNWR rails would be taken up. [This referred to the lines to the LNWR yard; their proximity at the Ampthill Road level crossing to the parallel Midland line to Hitchin meant that bridges over both railways would have to be built by the Midland, no doubt the real cause of the latter's procrastination.]

The Mayor requested a meeting between

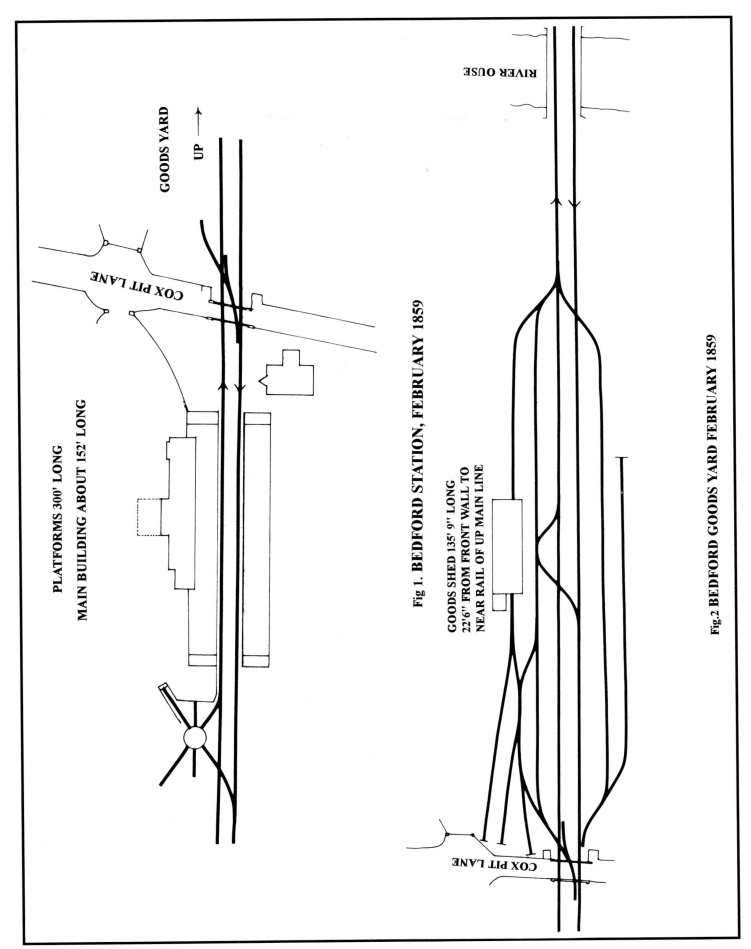

PLATFORMS 300' LONG

MAIN BUILDING ABOUT 152' LONG

GOODS YARD

UP →

COX PIT LANE

Fig 1. BEDFORD STATION, FEBRUARY 1859

GOODS SHED 135' 9" LONG
22'6" FROM FRONT WALL TO
NEAR RAIL OF UP MAIN LINE

RIVER OUSE

COX PIT LANE

Fig.2 BEDFORD GOODS YARD FEBRUARY 1859

the Midland and a Committee was appointed to negotiate. A Board minute of 4th June 1862 records an interview with the deputation from Bedford Corporation. The latter's proposals would save £3,000 on the cost of the Ampthill Road bridge. It was noted that LNWR co-operation was necessary to achieve this. In view of the saving, the Midland undertook to contribute £3,000 towards the cost of the new road and the bridge over the Ouse. The Bedford deputation passed a vote of thanks to the Midland - marking the high water mark in the Midland/Bedford relationship. Later it was recorded that LNWR co-operation had been refused. No doubt the Council thereby lost their £3,000.

On 3rd December 1862, the Board of Trade forwarded a letter from the Town Clerk of Bedford regarding the stopping up of Ampthill Road. The Midland Board ordered that the Secretary write to the Town Clerk in terms that the Midland's plans for the Extension to London gave another opportunity for a joint station, "an object the Corporation is much interested in" and that the achievement of such a station would probably be prevented by a bridge at Ampthill Road. A former attempt to agree on a joint station failed due to lack of LNWR co-operation. Here it must be interposed in fairness to the LNWR, who were first in the field, that only the Midland stood to gain commercially from a joint

station. The essentially branch line nature of the LNWR route through Bedford meant that an improved interchange would only result in more of the LNWR's traffic being fed on to the Midland. But having spent money on a station to the north of the river, the Midland Board were probably no more than lukewarm in making the proposals. The Town Clerk replied on 13th December 1862 that the plan of the proposed line had been examined. The Council appreciated the advantage of a joint station; "it was not considered that such a station would be proper compensation for the injury caused by the closing of Ampthill Road". Here was a further indication, in addition to their involvement of the Board of Trade, that the Council's attitude was hardening. The prospect of a joint station for Bedford seems to have been undervalued in the quest for a bridge. Nevertheless nine months passed before the next move.

On 2nd September 1863, the Board noted a resolution of the Town Council that the Town Clerk "take immediate steps to compel the Midland to re-open Ampthill Road." The Board replied that: "the delay is due to proposals for a joint station to the general convenience in which case Ampthill Road can be dispensed with. The Chairman is at present on the Continent and there will be further communication when he returns." On 4th November 1863, the Board at last ad-

mitted defeat. It was resolved "to have a bridge to carry the Ampthill Road - to be constructed under the direction of the Way and Works Committee who are to take steps to purchase any land required." The subject was finally discussed by the Board on 2nd November 1864. It was recorded that an application to the Courts had been made by Bedford Corporation for a fine due to non-completion of the bridge in due time. Counsel's advice had been taken and it had been recommended that £100 be paid "to the proper parties to finally stay the threatened proceedings and in full satisfaction of any costs against the Midland." It was approved that a cheque be drawn and paid to the proper parties through the hands of Messrs. Berridge & Morris. So, for some seven years, Bedfordians had lost the use of Ampthill Road while the Will o'the wisp of a joint station had been pursued and the Midland Board had fought a model delaying action. Although not recorded, it was doubtless the final extinction of the prospect of a joint station that led to the decision in 1864 to commence the Extension to the north of the Ouse rather than to the south of the LNWR crossing. The avoidance of a railway level crossing for the future main line had to be weighed against the convenience of a single passenger station.

The winding drum and engine house for the temporary lines over the top of Belsize tunnel. Wagons of spoil await a controlled descent. *NRM*

2. PLANNING AND CONSTRUCTION

The opening in 1857 of the Leicester and Hitchin line brought the Midland to within 32 miles of London. In less than a year running powers had been granted and Midland trains were running to King's Cross. The delays that eventually arose due to congestion on that 32 mile section of the GNR have been well detailed in other works. Given the volume of traffic that converged on Hitchin, it is difficult to see how the situation could have been resolved, even with the best of goodwill on the GN side. The expense of a complete quadrupling of the track between Hitchin and King's Cross would have been enormous. To this day, the section of the Great Northern between Digswell and Woolmer Green has defied widening, by-passed only by the inconvenient Hertford loop.

There is no doubt that the congestion south of Hitchin was the last straw that drove the Midland Board to decide on the construction of the Extension. There was also another, less often mentioned but highly significant, commercial advantage to be gained from an independent route. Much of the coal traffic carried south through Leicester by the Midland was handed over to the LNWR at Rugby. With its own line to London, the Midland would be able to transfer some 75 miles of haulage of this traffic from the LNWR to itself. There is evidence that the Midland had independent access in mind long before the difficulties with the GNR came to a head. The Act for the goods station at Agar Town (later St Pancras Goods) was passed as early as 25th May 1860, and from 1st July 1862 coal, routed via the GNR, was transferred at the London end to Agar Town. The layout of the station

A view taken on 20 June 1867 of Kentish Town station, looking south. The Islip Street overbridge presents a very different aspect today although the building on the extreme top left is unmistakeable. A contractor's engine is working on the down goods line. *NRM*

leaves little doubt that it was intended from the start for it to be served from an independent line.

By 1862, the capitalised value of the annual payment the GNR was demanding for Midland use of a quadrupled line from Hitchin was at least comparable with the cost of a new line from Bedford. The Great Northern's terms for the granting of running powers in perpetuity from Hitchin to King's Cross were a rent of £60,000 per annum and 5 per cent per annum of the cost of the additional works required. (This second item was likely to be considerable in view of the Welwyn Viaduct and the large numbers of tunnels involved). The intermediate towns between Bedford and London, - Luton, Harpenden and St Albans - were already served by GNR branches. The new line would, however, offer a more direct route to London from these three places and there would be no difficulty in obtaining a major share of the passenger traffic. The solution was becoming clear and, on 14th October 1862 the Board, with Samuel Beale in the Chair, resolved that: "The necessary surveys be made and plans prepared for a Line of Railway from some point on the Leicester and Hitchin Railway at or south of the Town of Bedford to London and that the necessary notices be given of a Bill to be introduced in the next Session of Parliament for the purpose and that the Engineers Messrs. Barlow and Liddell and So-

table 1		LONDON EXTENSION CONTRACTS
Distance (m.ch)	Area	Contractor
0.60 - 1.70	Dock Jcn - Kentish Town	A.W. Ritson
1.70 - 4.0	Kentish Town - West Hampstead	J. Firbank
4.00 - 6.20	West Hampstead - Brent	J. Firbank
6.20 - 14.40	Brent - Radlett	Waring Bros
14.40 - Bedford	Radlett - Bedford	T. Brassey & S. Ballard

pected opposition of the GNR, the Bill was passed and received the Royal assent on 22nd June 1863. The authorised capital was £1,750,000 in shares with an additional £583,330 in loans, a total of £2,333,330. From Bedford, the course of the planned line passed close to Ampthill where a tunnel was required. It then touched the towns of Luton, Harpenden and St Albans. After another tunnel at Elstree, the Edgware Road was reached at Hendon. The line kept company with the road until an easterly change of direction took it to the Belsize tunnel, nearly a mile in length. After this tunnel the line swung southwards again to approach the Agar Town goods station. It then crossed the Regents Canal to reach a passenger terminus on the New Road.

The original proposals included a connection to the Metropolitan Railway, diverging 200 yards north of the New Road (now Euston Road)

descending to the junction. So the clauses proposing the branch were deleted from the Bill before it was presented. A revised, and ultimately successful proposal was included in a separate Bill in 1864.

The divergence was now planned to be at St Paul's Road Junction and the branch, just over a mile in length, would descend in tunnel to join the widened Metropolitan line to the west of King's Cross station. This Bill was sanctioned on 25th July 1864. A further Act of 1864 authorised a change to the location at Bedford of the junction with the Leicester to Hitchin line. This was originally intended to be made to the south of the Elstow Road overbridge, itself to the south of the level crossing with the LNWR, but the new site was at Bedford station. A later Act of 1866 provided for the deviation of 32 chains of the GNR's Welwyn to Luton branch where both lines skirted the northern end of the Luton Hoo estate.

The two engineers who had carried out the survey for the Extension were appointed to supervise its construction. William Henry Barlow had charge of the section from St Pancras to mile post 14 1/2 and Charles Liddell looked after the remainder. The Midland's resident engineer was Mr Campion. The Contracts eventually let are shown in Table 1.

The Ampthill tunnel was the subject of a separate Contract with John Knowles of Shefford, who had previously built Warden tunnel on the Hitchin line. Contract No.1. was re-let to John Ashwell on 11th April 1866, after Ritson had failed. The unfinished portion of their No.4 Contract was relinquished by Warings and re-let to Joseph Firbank. However, Warings were also occupied on the final 60 chains, let to them as the St Pancras Extension Contract on 12th February 1866.

The elderly Thomas Brassey was the most celebrated of the railway contractors, his reputation having been made by his work on the Grand Junction and Great Northern Railways. He was also the builder of the Leicester and Hitchin. While his name lent prestige to the partnership, it is Ballard whose name is mentioned in Liddell's progress reports and correspondence. Ballard was also called from time to time to account for delays, mainly towards the end in connection with the stations.

Barlow and Liddell outlined their joint estimate of the required timescale to Samuel Beale on 5th January 1864. The most difficult portions of the line were identified as follows: London Goods station to the Brent: 800,000 cu. yds. of excavation would be required, most to be taken out in one direction and half of it through the tunnel. 50 million bricks would be used. A great part of the ballast would have to be brought in for 12 miles after the tunnel had been finished.

The country portal of Belsize tunnel during the early stages of boring. Note the rural nature of the locality in comparison with the urban sprawl which the railway later generated. *NRM*

licitor Mr Carter, be instructed accordingly, and that the Engineers and Solicitor confer upon the subject when they consider it necessary to do so, and take instructions from the Chairman, Deputy Chairman and Mr Barwell."

The Midland Railway (Extension to London) Bill was presented to the Commons Select Committee on 3rd March 1863. Despite the ex-

and crossing over it to a junction east of King's Cross Metropolitan station. It must be remembered that this station was then on a site adjacent to that of the present day King's Cross Thameslink. Both John Fowler, Engineer in Chief of the Metropolitan, and Col. Yolland of the Board of Trade had reservations about the scheme which included a gradient of 1 in 30

On top of Belsize tunnel, near No.4 shaft. *NRM*

Time required, not less than 4 years. Elstree tunnel and cuttings: 2 1/2 years. As there was no gravel or ballast on the London side of the tunnel, the works ought to be completed in time to allow 15 months for ballasting the line and building the stations on the south side. Cutting at Chalton and cuttings and tunnel at Ampthill: the time required, "with economical execution", would not exceed three and a half years.

There was no ceremonial cutting of the first sod. Instead, on 27th January 1865, W P Price, then Deputy Chairman, laid a brick, bearing his initials, about 5 feet below ground level at the site of one of the shafts of Belsize tunnel. According to Williams, the ceremony took place in a driving snowstorm with a foot depth of half melted snow. Eventually, after sinking by the undermining process, the brick was destined to

take up its final position at the foot of the shaft where it joined the top of the tunnel.

The minute books of the Bedford to London Extension Committee (which also contain the minutes of the practically synonymous South Construction Committee) contain a wealth of information on the progress of the construction work. They also include the text of a letter, dated 27th January 1865, from Charles Liddell to James Allport, the General Manager, advocating the construction of stations and overbridges in such a way as to admit one or two additional lines eventually to be added.

On 11th February 1865, the South Construction Committee resolved that: "The letter be referred to the Board with the recommendation of this Committee that Mr Liddell's suggestion for the eventual construction of four lines of Railway be adopted and carried out and that the necessary land for the purpose be obtained and the overbridges constructed and stations arranged for 4 lines". The recommendation was agreed by the Board, thereby ensuring that the first steps were taken to achieve the quadrupling, finally to be completed in 1895. A general impression which emerges from the minutes is that the major difficulties were encountered at the London end. That this was foreseen is reflected in the division of responsibilities into unequal lengths. Liddell's progress reports for his thirty-five and a quarter miles were less detailed than Barlow's for his length of fourteen. Very soon the latter was concentrating his attention upon the southern end of his section. Here, clearance of the site had involved the eviction of thousands of tenants of slum properties in Agar Town, a district which was completely destroyed in order to make space for the railway and its terminals. That in itself was no great loss, but the unfortunate inhabitants, with no compensation whatsoever, caused even greater overcrowding in the adjoining areas to which they were forced to move. The resulting scandal did, however, have the effect that future Acts for railways made provision for re-housing those whose dwellings were demolished.

The minutes of the Board mentioned for the first time on 4th November 1863 the new scheme for what was later known as the City branch. The Board considered a proposal for a junction between the Midland Extension and the Metropolitan Railway, "suggested by the Engineer [John Fowler] of the latter Company". It was referred to the Chairman and Deputy Chairman with authority, "should they decide upon advisability, to instruct the Engineers to make surveys and the Solicitor to give notices". The line was included in the Acts of 1864. As initially surveyed, the tunnel for the City branch was to pass under the Old St Pancras churchyard leaving at least 12 ft. between ground level and the crown of the brickwork. It was confidently expected that it could be bored without disturbing interred remains. It was, however, found that for hundreds of years burials had been made in successive layers, extending much more than 12 ft. below the later level of the ground. The tunnel was to pass beneath the churchyard for a length of 145 yds. The plan of construction had to be changed; the ground was excavated, the corpses removed and re-interred at Kensal

Haverstock Hill station under construction, looking south towards Lismore Circus tunnels on 15 June 1867. The retaining walls were originally buttressed by girders with intermediate support from columns on the down platform. *NRM*

Green and Highgate cemeteries and the tunnel built by the cut and cover method. With clinical detachment, Barlow's progress reports in the 1866/7 period give details in linear yards of "bodies removed from the burial ground" in much the same way that he recorded the progress of brickwork. The press got wind of stories of coffins broken open and human remains lying about. Much adverse publicity was thereby incurred.

Barlow's main concern was doubtless the erection of the roof of St Pancras station. Even though he delegated the detail design, its conception and, most certainly, the responsibility for its successful completion was his alone. Today it has become so familiar a sight that it is easy to take it for granted - it has always been there! But with a span of 245 ft., a height above the rails, themselves at first floor level, of 100 ft. and a length of 689 ft., its erection even today would be a major undertaking, in an age when tower cranes can appear, it seems, at the snap of a finger. The problems that were faced over 120 years ago have, now, to be imagined. The Butterley Company, who produced the iron-work, undertook its actual erection. An immense moveable timber stage was constructed on which, one by one, the 49 wrought iron ribs were built up. Although today there can only be admiration for the achievement, at the time the Butterley Company were being harried by the Midland to adhere to the programme. On 15th October 1867, a Board minute recorded that: "Barlow, being much dissatisfied with the Progress made by the Butterley Company, the Contractors for the Ironwork of the roofing of St Pancras station, appointment was made for Mr F Wright and Mr Alleyne to attend a meeting of the Board to-day".

The outcome of the meeting was a Memorandum of Agreement under which the Butterley

The covered way for the Hampstead Junction line taken on 15 June 1867, later the site of Carlton Road Junction. *NRM*

Company agreed to construct a second stage to a design approved by Barlow. The Agreement provided for the roof to be erected, slated, glazed and completed for a length of 450 ft. from the northern end, including the northern gable, on or before 1st May 1868, and the remainder, including the southern gable, on or before 1st October 1868. In the event of non-completion by that time, the penalties laid down in the original Contract would apply.

With construction in progress, applications for the provision of additional stations were received. On 6th August 1867, agreement to a request for a station between Ampthill and Harlington was deferred. There was a further request for a station at Kempston Hardwick. It was minuted that "Millbrook would be the proper site for the latter station". As Kempston Hardwick is nearer to Bedford than it is to Millbrook, this conclusion can only be translated as "there is more potential revenue from the occupants of Ampthill Park House than from the cottagers of Kempston Hardwick".

The question of a station for Flitwick was reconsidered on 17th June 1868. Liddell produced a plan of the proposed station. He believed that if an agreement could be made with a Mr Baker for a supply of sand from that place [Flitwick] to his brickworks at Hendon, the land for the station might be obtained free of cash. It was resolved to refer to the General Manager's Department to report as to the expediency of constructing a station on the terms stated. On 16th September 1868, a plan was produced showing the required alteration to the road to make space for the goods accommodation on the east side of the line. (This was never achieved, and Flitwick was unique on the Extension in having the goods yard on the west side). Allport produced a plan on 6th October 1868 of land proposed to be given to the Company by Major Brooks, a member of a prominent Flitwick family. There was also a small strip of land which Mr Goodman proposed to give. On 3rd November 1868, it was ordered that possession of the land be taken, the diversion of the road be made and crossover points be put in. Finally, on 2nd March 1869, it was ordered that a station "somewhat similar to the one at Harlington be erected". The provision of signalling equipment was con-

The south portals of Camden Road Tunnels near completion on 15 June 1867. The route bisected a fashionable residential area and the stone-faced portals and retaining walls were provided as a match for local aesthetic sensibilities. *NRM*

Looking towards St Pancras from Belsize tunnel through the retaining arches which still exist. The interlaced track can be seen, diverging in the background as goods lines on the right and passenger lines through Haverstock Hill station on the left. *NRM*

sidered by the Committee. Although the Midland was reluctant to adopt interlocking it was to the forefront in the use of the block system which was installed from the first on the Extension. On 20th February 1867, the Stores Department were requested to supply 50 semaphore signals, 100 distant signals and 20 signal boxes, "the heights of the semaphores to be furnished by the General Manager".

Although, at least in the case of the signals, these obviously were round numbers, the two to one ratio in favour of distant signals is interesting. At the time, rotating boards or discs were used for distants and it is possible that they found other uses in addition to the present understanding of the term. On 30th April 1867, it was minuted that: "The General Manager be reminded to give as soon as possible the necessary particulars to the Stores Department of the signals required".

Charles Liddell's report for 18th December 1867 gave details of the progress with the signal boxes. Leagrave, Luton, Chiltern Green, Harpenden and St Albans were "fixed". Ampthill, Harlington, Radlett and St Albans Junction (Park Street) were "not yet fixed". Pre-

viously it had been resolved, on 2nd July 1867, that: "The General Manager be authorised to arrange with Mr Crossley to have the Telegraph Apparatus necessary to carry out the block system of Signalling Trains constructed on the Extension wherever the General Manager may consider it necessary; and also to provide any further telegraphic arrangements for the purpose of repeating signals or otherwise". On 20th May 1868, it was minuted that: "Catch Sidings at several stations required by the Government Inspector are in progress".

Tank houses to provide a water supply for engines were built at Leagrave and Radlett. On 31st March 1868, it was ordered [rather late in the context of the other works] that: "The Engine Houses are to be built at Bedford and St Albans to hold 4 engines each with an engine turntable at each place".

An official pre-opening journey from Bedford to London was made on 7th September 1867. The train, hauled by two goods engines, stopped at various locations for inspections to be made of the works. Messrs. Barlow, Liddell, Campion, Ballard, Firbank and Ashwell travelled on the train. Two days, or rather, nights,

later, through goods trains commenced using the lines to reach St Pancras Goods station. The contractors had possession during the day and, as ballasting was incomplete, only restricted speeds were possible initially. Goods and coal yards and goods sheds were ready for use from 15th October 1867 at Ampthill, Harlington, Leagrave, Luton and (without the shed) Chiltern Green.

Liddell reported on 20th November 1867 on his length to the north of mile post 14 1/2 that: "The works of the line are for the greater part complete - little now remaining to be done but trimming and finishing". There was concern about the unfinished state of the works at Aldenham station (at that time quite randomly referred to as Aldenham or Radlett) but the Committee required the Engineers to give notice to the Board of Trade that the line from Bedford to London would be ready for opening to passenger traffic "on 1st January next" [1868]. In the event it was not opened until over six months later. Ballard was taken to task about the delays in completing the stations. As late as 20th May 1868, Liddell reported that at all stations, the down line [main] buildings required the roofing, rafters and glazing finishing. The [subsidi-

Work at St Pancras on 5 August 1867, the focus being upon the excavations for the City branch; the Midland Railway's connection to Moorgate Street. *NRM*

ary] up line waiting rooms had to be floored and glazed. Painting also had to be finished.

On 2nd June 1868, it was ordered that; "Mr Campion be authorised to fit up the Temporary Passenger Station at St Pancras after having a conference with Mr Needham [the Traffic Manager] on the subject". The establishment of a temporary station must have proved impractical as the first passenger trains six weeks later,

used the City branch and the Metropolitan Railway to Moorgate Street.

Meanwhile, as the works approached a successful conclusion, the directors were concerned with the financial position. The Extension had proved to be far more costly than the original estimate and there were other commitments which also required additional capital. At the second half-yearly meeting of 1867, the

shareholders were warned that there had been an overspend. Before the first meeting of 1868, a circular, dated 14th December 1867, was sent to the shareholders by the Board. The additional expenditure on the Extension was given as £2,150,000 [this made the total cost £4,483,330, nearly double the original estimate]. In addition there were overspends on the Sheffield and Chesterfield and other new lines to a total of £1,350,000; to cope with an increase in traffic, engines, plant and rolling stock had been built to a value of £960,000 and, finally, £540,000 was earmarked for future requirements, making a total of £5,000,000. It was proposed to raise £3,750,000 by shares and £1,250,000 by borrowing. A Special General Meeting was called for 15th January 1868 "in advance of the usual half-yearly meeting to give an explanation of the circular".

At the meeting, Mr Hutchinson said that in the case of the London Extension, the cost of the work originally planned had not increased so much but the scope of the works had been enlarged. The value of property had risen very considerably after 1862 when the plans had been deposited. Other factors were:

4 lines instead of 2 for 7 miles from London.
Land and overbridges for 4 lines for the remainder.
Gradients improved from 1 in 176 to 1 in 200.
4 acres instead of 2 for St Pancras.
Cellarage and shops under St Pancras instead of earth fill.
Expensive Parliamentary requirements had to be met.
The overspend on the original estimate only amounted to £200,000, due to the rise in the cost of labour and materials since 1863.

The meeting agreed to the appointment of a Committee of Consultation with 9 members, to confer with the directors and to report to the half-yearly meeting to be held in February. The report was presented on 19th February 1868. After paying a tribute to the integrity of the Board, it regretted that the Company had overstretched itself, resulting in "an amount of liability which cannot be met without great inconvenience to the shareholders". The extra items listed by Hutchinson were confirmed, the use of steel rails instead of iron (double the cost but a much longer life) was added. "All these things, no doubt, account for the independent access to the metropolis being likely to cost several millions beyond the original estimate". The additional expenditure due to the change of location of the junction at Bedford was not mentioned. Extra land purchases, a bridge over the Ouse and an increase in the total length of the line were all involved. Together, these items must have resulted in a significant addition to the cost.

The Committee went on to propose that an agreement be reached with the LNWR for the use of their Lancaster to Carlisle line which would enable the Settle and Carlisle, authorised but as yet unbuilt, to be abandoned. At the half-yearly meeting it was stated that there had been a large increase in traffic, averaging £4,700 per week. So the Committee's report and the oppor-

One of the earliest views of St Pancras and its magnificent roof, neither of which has changed greatly over the years. Note that the well-known clock has yet to be put into position. *NRM*

The extravagence of the extension and the grandeur of St Pancras contrast strangely with the rather motley carriage stock seen in this very early view of the station.

tune revenue increase vindicated the Board to some extent. There was now, however, a much more cautious policy. Work on the Midland Grand Hotel at St Pancras only proceeded slowly. It was still incomplete when it was opened in 1873. The House of Commons Committee did not agree to the abandonment of the Settle and Carlisle, a course which would not have found favour with the North British and Lancashire and Yorkshire Railways. The decision has been to the benefit of the generations of passengers who have appreciated the magnificent scenery of the route. For much of its existence, however, it has been a doubtful commercial asset to its successive operators.

The Extension was formally inspected on behalf of the Board of Trade by Lt.Col. Rich R.E whose first report was dated 25th April 1868. As a result of his recommendations the B.O.T directed the Midland to postpone opening the line for passengers for one month. Lt.Col. Rich

noted that the St Albans branch (the connection with the LNWR at Park Street which had been used to convey constructional materials) had not been inspected: "the Company states that it is not intended to open the line for passenger traffic". The first 5 miles 8 chains were laid with steel rails weighing 82lb/yd, the remaining rails were iron, weighing 83lb/yd. The rails were 20 ft. long. The track had inside wooden keys and was ballasted with burnt clay and gravel. "Aldenham or Radlett" was among the stations mentioned. A turntable had been installed at the London end and others were proposed at St Albans and Bedford. It is noticeable that St Pancras passenger station was not mentioned by name, it was still the "station in London". There were recommendations for interlocking at junctions and connections from the main line to sidings.

With the London terminus and the connections to the City branch both incomplete,

Lt.Col. Rich found cause for postponement of the opening. He made another inspection on 2nd July 1868, finding the St Albans branch and the London station still incomplete but sanctioned opening "between Bedford and Camden Road stations and thence by the St Pancras branch to the King's Cross station of the Metropolitan Railway". The B.O.T passed on the good tidings to the Midland the next day.

The St Albans branch (to the LNW at Park Street) was inspected on 1st August 1868. The reason is not clear for there seems to have been no intention to arrange for a passenger service or even to keep the line open permanently for goods. Not surprisingly, in view of the nature of the line, Lt.Col. Rich found details that needed attention, the most important being a weak cast iron bridge girder. The junctions at both end were unsuitable for passenger trains. At the Midland end there was a trailing connection to the down main line and a trailing crossover between the main lines. At Park Street there was a single line junction with a loop on the branch. The loop would have to be extended to form up and down junctions with the St Albans to Watford line. No undertaking had been received as to the proposed method of working the branch and in view of this and incompleteness it could not be opened.

On 3rd August 1868, the opening of the line from the junction of the St Pancras branch to the London terminus (i.e from St Paul's Road Junction to St Pancras) was once again postponed for a month. Lt.Col. Hutchinson then took over the inspecting. On 22nd September 1868 he recommended the postponement for one month of the opening of "The London Extension from St Pauls Junction to St Pancras station - the signal arrangements and station buildings and approaches are as yet by no means complete". He did permit himself the observation that "The station is a very handsome structure and appears to have been erected with great skill and rapidity". There were two departure and three arrival platforms, with arrival and departure of trains controlled by two signal boxes in telegraphic communication with each other. A great effort must

Cambridge Street coal depot, located a short distance to the north of St Pancras. Note the horse-drawn traverser. *P. Holmes collection*

4-4-0 No. 1750 with an up express in Bedford at the turn of the century. Rebuilt several times 1750 (renumbered 370 in 1907) enjoyed a long life and was not withdrawn until 1951. *NRM*

have been made to complete the works, for, on 1st October 1868, Lt.Col. Hutchinson reported favourably to the B.O.T and on the same day the Midland was permitted to open its fine terminus on condition that the recommendations were attended to; the latter were now mainly concerned with protection of passengers from the work still in progress on the roof.

A final tidying up was necessary. Near St Pancras the passenger lines had been diverted from a direct course over the tunnel for the City branch. Now 17 arches of brickwork and two girder bridges enabled 9 1/2 chains of line to be completed on the permanent alignment. The temporary passenger lines over this length became the goods lines. Lt.Col. Hutchinson inspected on 24th February 1869 and, finally with approval, on 8th March 1869. "A crossover road and siding leading from a proposed carriage shed to the down line must be taken out or properly signalled". One last comment was that, although outside the bounds of the inspection, it was worth mentioning that "The Company shortly intend to cross the passenger lines on the level with two goods lines leading to the canal basin. It is a very great pity that this most objectionable arrangement cannot be avoided especially after the great expense that has been incurred in keeping separate the Goods and Passenger lines from Hendon to London". This must have been a reference to the connection from the goods lines to the east side at Dock Junction. It was installed with a single crossing only. It may be difficult now to understand the force of the objection, but it must be remembered that at the time the development of brakes, interlocking and general signalling practice were all at a comparatively primitive stage.

After the opening of St Pancras station on 1st October 1868, it might be thought that the Bedford to London Extension Committee would have been dissolved. Instead it turned its attention to George Gilbert Scott's Midland Grand Hotel. The Midland, in a period of financial stringency, found themselves building a most expensive, even extravagant, edifice. There is little doubt that if the competition for its design had been held in 1866, after the Overend and Gurney banking failure, the hotel would have been a more modest undertaking altogether. But in 1865, when Scott's entry was successful, the financial outlook was good and the extent of the eventual overspend on the Extension was not appreciated. The Midland was looking for a building of distinction to emphasise their new found prestige as a trunk line from London. The design matched their requirement to perfection. But in the late 1860s and early 1870s, expenditure had to be limited and progress on the hotel was necessarily slow. The opening of the first part to be completed did not take place until 1873. In the meantime Scott had been knighted, in 1872.

At times the Committee appeared to find communication with Scott somewhat difficult. The great architect was renowned for undertaking many commissions simultaneously and, in pre-telephone days he was often inaccessible. When Mr R Etzensburger, previously manager of the Victoria Hotel in Venice, was appointed as Hotel Manager, the Committee found themselves involved with a more volatile personality, with a background far removed from that of the stolid contractors, skilled in earthmoving and brickwork, with whom they had mainly been dealing. Once again, a propensity for spending money had to be kept in check. There were teething troubles with the hotel, including a lift accident, fortunately without fatalities. At last, however, with the hotel open, if only partially complete, the work of the Committee was concluded. Latterly it had become involved in trivial matters. From supervising the construction of 50 miles of main line railway and a great terminus, it had turned its attention in anticlimax to such details as the purchase of extra crockery and the problems of smoking waiting room chimneys.

3. THE ROUTE: St PANCRAS TO St ALBANS

The approaches to St Pancras as seen from the platform end in 1936 with the station box prominent. This view remained unaltered until 1959 when a new signalbox was opened on the down side of the station. In the left foreground is the lift shaft down which wagons were transferred to the ground-floor storage area. *Photomatic*

A description of the Extension which commences with St Pancras and proceeds northwards must not be allowed to mask the fact that the line was a southwards projection of a Derby based enterprise. There was, it seems, a realisation that a provincial newcomer to London had to make its presence known. The next new arrival, the Manchester, Sheffield & Lincolnshire, despite its change of title to the grandiose Great Central Railway, crept somewhat shyly into Marylebone. The Midland advertised its arrival in town with a unique combination of an engineering masterpiece, William Barlow's huge, beautiful, but strictly functional, train shed and George Gilbert Scott's Midland Grand hotel which was one of the finest achievements of Victorian gothic architecture. Not long before St Pancras was built, the comparatively modestly styled facade and precincts of King's Cross had been criticised by GNR shareholders for being too lavish. Later, Scott, who apparently did not suffer from a surfeit of modesty, wrote that he believed that the hotel was possibly too good for its purpose. Train shed and hotel together must have announced to Londoners in general and the GNR in particular that here was a competitor who meant business. Now, for well over a century, St Pancras rampant and King's Cross gardant have been rivals,

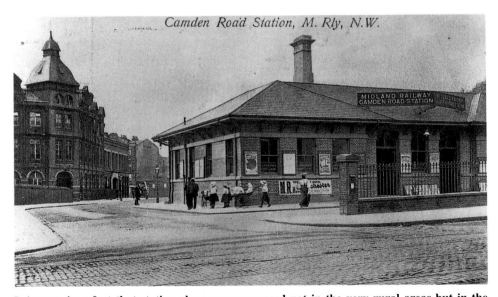

It is a curious fact that station closures commenced not in the very rural areas but in the heart of the metropolis as trams, buses and the underground stripped away demand from the cross-London main line routes. The stations affected included Camden Road, the first station out of St Pancras and having a frequent service of trains both to the Midland terminus and across the Widened Lines to Victoria. After a considerable struggle to survive the station closed, along with Haverstock Hill on 1 January 1916. *Lens of Sutton*

St. Paul's Road Passenger Junction signalbox which controlled the junction between the main lines and the City branch. *A. Vaughan*

separated only by the Pancras Road. St Pancras has been well described previously, notably in Alan A Jackson's *London's Termini,* but a summary of its features cannot be omitted here. In 1846, a Royal Commission had recommended that railways from the north should enter London no further than a boundary defined by what are now the Marylebone, Euston and Pentonville Roads. As with the GNR at King's Cross, the Regents Canal, eventually to be of insignificant importance compared with the railways, defined the level at which the Midland could approach the boundary set by the Commissioners.

In order to duck under the canal, the exit from King's Cross had been lumbered with the dip in Gasworks tunnel and the subsequent 1 in 105 of Holloway bank. The St Pancras approach lines crossed over the canal with the result that the platforms had to be built some 20 ft. above street level. Necessity was turned into virtue by establishing an enormous storage space for beer beneath the station. Although the tortuous subway from the Underground disguises somewhat the climb required to reach platform level, access to St Pancras has always only been really convenient for passengers arriving by cab. In

times when escalators are provided in comparatively small provincial shops, their installation here is long overdue.

Above the beer store, the station floor provides a tie for the single span roof. The visual impact of the roof on entering the station is impressive enough today and it must have been even more so when it was new. Then it stood alone as the hotel was still at the foundation stage when the first trains used the station. Dominated by the 270 ft. clock tower, the hotel is one of London's most familiar buildings. As late as 1963, H P White could write "Twentieth century taste regards it with aesthetic horror, though the avant garde are rediscovering merit in it." It is to be hoped that the views of the 1963 avant garde have now become those of the majority. By 1935, the lack of the modern comforts then expected in a first class hotel was becoming serious. Also, an interior which now would be appreciated as a fine example of Victorian art and design, was then considered merely old fashioned. As at the time of its building, economics dictated policy, and the cost of modernisation was deemed to be prohibitive. The Midland Grand closed its doors and was converted to offices. It has recently been announced that there are plans to re-open the hotel.

In the station, five platforms were originally provided. These were West and East Departure, later Nos.1 and 2, and Main, East and Excursion Arrival, later Nos.5,6 and 7. Between the Main and East Arrival platforms there was a 25 ft. wide road for cabs and mail vans. Six carriage lines separated the departure and arrival platforms. A new double faced platform was brought into use on 15th May 1892. This replaced three of the carriage lines. A week later all the platforms were numbered from west to east as Nos.1 to 7, the new pair becoming Nos.3 and 4. For many years after 1892 there was little change at St Pancras. For the remainder of the Midland's existence, the station was adequate for its traffic. The LMS was so beset by falling revenue that by the late 1920s the general aspect of the station had become rather dowdy. Grouping had led to St Pancras playing second fiddle to Euston, not that much money was spent there either. Badly in need of some fresh paint, Barlow's great roof resonated to a medley of bulb horned taxis and the occasional exchange of whistles followed by the sonorous bark of the banker as an express departed.

The Second World War brought damage by bombing and St Pancras had to be closed temporarily in October 1940 and again in 1941, when a bomb fell at the inner end of Platform No.3. Some coaches were destroyed and the inner ends of Nos.2 and 3 were shortened for some time. The hydraulic wagon hoist which provided access to the storage vaults saw progressively diminishing use until it was finally removed in the 1960s. Some improvements were made by BR, especially in the years that included the introduction of diesel services. The fine booking hall was refurbished, the refreshment rooms were revised and new barriers were erected at the platform entrances. More recently, much of the brickwork has been cleaned to great advantage; the roof, too, has benefited from repainting. The station has regained an appearance that welcomed a much earlier generation of travel-

Engine Shed Junction signal box at Kentish Town looking north along the fast lines. On the right the Kentish Town curve climbs towards Mortimer Street Junction. The top of a ventilating shaft for North Curve tunnel No.1 can be seen above the down line of the curve. The girder bridges carry the Tottenham South Curve to Highgate Road Junction. Immediately beyond are the elongated bridges over which the LNWR Hampstead Junction Railway crosses the Extension. Carlton Road Junction can be seen through the fast line bridges. *A. Vaughan*

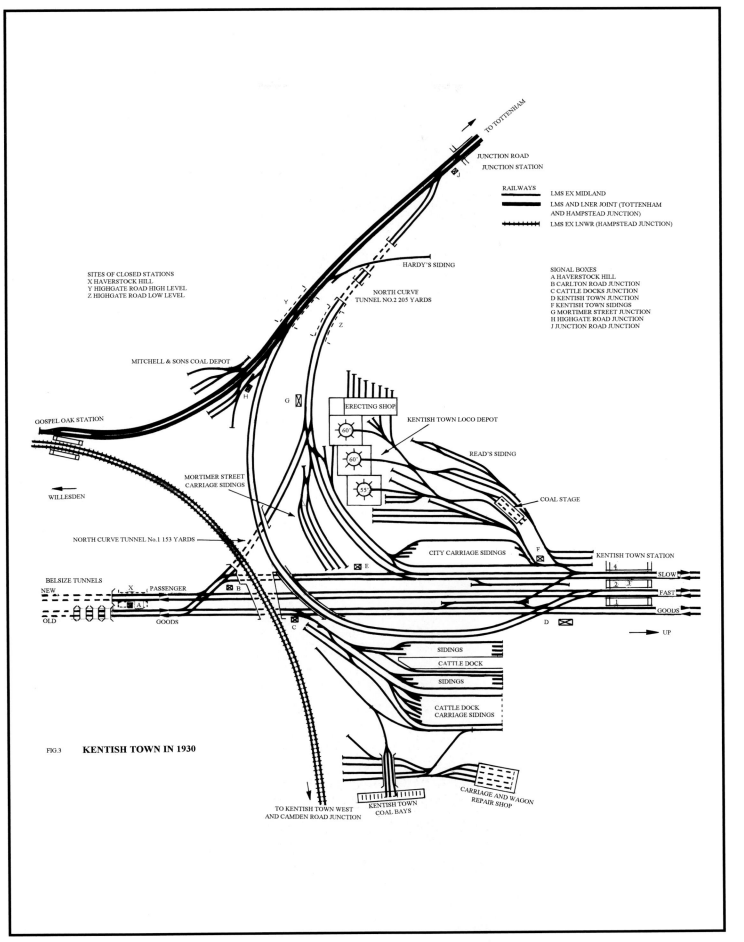

TO TOTTENHAM

JUNCTION ROAD
JUNCTION STATION

J

HARDY'S SIDING

SITES OF CLOSED STATIONS
X HAVERSTOCK HILL
Y HIGHGATE ROAD HIGH LEVEL
Z HIGHGATE ROAD LOW LEVEL

NORTH CURVE
TUNNEL NO.2 205 YARDS

SIGNAL BOXES
A HAVERSTOCK HILL
B CARLTON ROAD JUNCTION
C CATTLE DOCKS JUNCTION
D KENTISH TOWN JUNCTION
F KENTISH TOWN SIDINGS
G MORTIMER STREET JUNCTION
H HIGHGATE ROAD JUNCTION
J JUNCTION ROAD JUNCTION

Y

Z

MITCHELL & SONS COAL DEPOT

H

G

ERECTING SHOP

KENTISH TOWN LOCO DEPOT

60'

GOSPEL OAK STATION

60'

READ'S SIDING

55'

WILLESDEN

MORTIMER STREET
CARRIAGE SIDINGS

COAL STAGE

NORTH CURVE TUNNEL No.1 153 YARDS

CITY CARRIAGE SIDINGS

F

KENTISH TOWN STATION

E

4

BELSIZE TUNNELS

SLOW

NEW

X   PASSENGER

B

2 3

FAST

A

1

OLD

GOODS

GOODS

C

D

UP

SIDINGS

CATTLE DOCK

SIDINGS

CATTLE DOCK
CARRIAGE SIDINGS

FIG.3   **KENTISH TOWN IN 1930**

CARRIAGE AND WAGON
REPAIR SHOP

TO KENTISH TOWN WEST
AND CAMDEN ROAD JUNCTION

KENTISH TOWN
COAL BAYS

Access to St Pancras Goods station (originally known as Agar Town) was first obtained from the GNR's King's Cross goods yard. Coal wharves were opened on the site as early as July 1862, the first independent Midland presence in London - the goods and locomotive facilities at King's Cross were only held on lease from the GNR. The massive red brick bulk of the goods station was an early symbol of the advancing Midland. It was opened on 2nd January 1865 and 2 1/2 years later the initial commercial use of the Extension was made when the first goods train over the new line from Bedford arrived, on 9th September 1867. The later Somers Town depot eventually handled a large inwards traffic, especially in potatoes and other vegetables and, at least latterly, St Pancras goods was used largely for outwards traffic. Between the goods station and the coal wharves, lines were extended to cross the Regents Canal and reach Bass & Co's ale stores, dating from 1865. The lines from the depot passed with the main lines under the wide NLR viaduct and joined the goods lines at St Paul's Road Goods Junction. Here, at the entrance to Camden Road tunnels, a return must be made to St Pancras to cover the east side of the line.

Prominent from St Pancras platform ends are the gasholders of the one-time Imperial Gas Company. They split the space available for locomotive sidings, the more important of which, "Cambridge Street Loco Sidings" were on their north side. For locomotives which had come off up trains and awaited a return working, the loco sidings saved much time which would have been incurred in running light to and from Kentish Town. The turntable was a generous 60 ft. in diameter. A long siding from Dock Junction gave access first to Cambridge Street Coal Sidings

Although closed to traffic in 1916, the platforms at Haverstock Hill remained more or less in tact until very recent times. The station building, of the usual Midland solidity, disappeared much earlier. *Lens of Sutton.*

lers. A nice touch has been the installation of a replacement giant clock, carefully modelled on the original.

No.1 Platform, the shortest and therefore the least useful, quietly disappeared in 1982. The rapid contraction of tracks from the platform ends to the four single lines over Pancras Road has always limited train lengths. In 1937 the rubric stated that no up train into St Pancras was to exceed 797 ft. in length, this being interpreted as eleven 57 ft. vehicles, one 65 ft. restaurant car and one engine. With two engines, only ten 57 ft. vehicles and one 65 ft. restaurant car were permitted.

A rising gradient of 1 in 103 commences at the platform ends. This changes to 1 in 132 near the quarter milepost and continues past the site of Cambridge Street box to the half milepost. The connections from Somers Town goods depot joined the main lines at St Pancras Junction. Located to the west of the passenger station, the Somers Town depot possessed freight facilities of a remarkable size for a single site so close to the centre of London. Opened on 1st November 1887, it was known as St Pancras New Goods depot until 1892. Final closure was as late as 4th June 1973. The main frontage was at right angles to the Euston Road on Ossulston Street. One side, however, adjoined the Euston Road itself. In addition to the general goods station, there was a potato market, a milk and fish depot and a coal depot. The coal depot alone could accommodate 579 wagons; as with the goods station, two levels were involved. The first mile of line to Camden Road tunnels contained so many features of interest that it is worth describing the two sides, east, or passenger, and west, or goods, separately. Commencing with the goods side, Pancras Road coal bays were situated to the north of the Junction box. They could accept 90 wagons. Access was from a head shunt which crossed the running lines leading to Somers Town and terminated immediately north of St Pancras Junction box. This remarkable arrange-

ment stemmed from the fact that the head shunt preceded the goods depot and the method of access was never changed. Churchyard goods sidings, the name a grim reminder of the notorious clearance of the burial ground, were on the west side of the goods lines, connected, at the south end, to Somers Town coal depot and, at the north end, to St Pancras Goods station and the goods lines at North London Incline box. Between Churchyard sidings and the goods station the line crossed over the Regents Canal.

Carlton Road Junction looking south. The branch to the left is the connection to the Tottenham & Hampstead Junction Railway. On the right are the 1899 slow lines to Kentish Town and St Pancras. *A. Vaughan.*

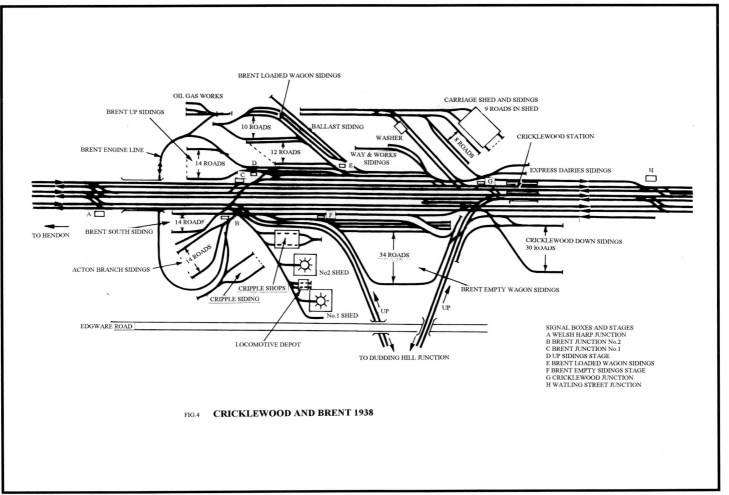

BRENT LOADED WAGON SIDINGS

OIL GAS WORKS

BRENT UP SIDINGS

CARRIAGE SHED AND SIDINGS
9 ROADS IN SHED

10 ROADS

BALLAST SIDING

WASHER

CRICKLEWOOD STATION

BRENT ENGINE LINE

12 ROADS

8 ROADS

WAY & WORKS
SIDINGS

EXPRESS DAIRIES SIDINGS

14 ROADS

D

E

G

H

A

TO HENDON

BRENT SOUTH SIDING

14 ROADS

B

F

CRICKLEWOOD DOWN SIDINGS
30 ROADS

ACTON BRANCH SIDINGS

14 ROADS

34 ROADS

BRENT EMPTY WAGON SIDINGS

No2 SHED

CRIPPLE SHOPS

CRIPPLE SIDING

UP

UP

EDGWARE ROAD

No.1 SHED

LOCOMOTIVE DEPOT

TO DUDDING HILL JUNCTION

SIGNAL BOXES AND STAGES
A WELSH HARP JUNCTION
B BRENT JUNCTION No.2
C BRENT JUNCTION No.1
D UP SIDINGS STAGE
E BRENT LOADED WAGON SIDINGS
F BRENT EMPTY SIDINGS STAGE
G CRICKLEWOOD JUNCTION
H WATLING STREET JUNCTION

FIG.4   **CRICKLEWOOD AND BRENT 1938**

5XP 45565 VICTORIA (Holbeck) approaches Elstree on 28 July 1951 with the 21.50 Edinburgh (Waverley) to St Pancras. *E.D. Bruton.*

and then, after the canal crossing, to coal bays and coal drops situated on Camley Street which, as the one-time Cambridge Street gave its name to the adjacent signal box. The rear of the King's Cross goods yard and Top Shed was then in sight, the offices of the latter proudly capped by a weathervane in the shape of a GN large Atlantic.

The City branch to the Widened Lines of the Metropolitan Company at King's Cross diverged at St Paul's Road Passenger Junction. The branch, an integral part of the Extension, commenced on the east side at the junction. After a short distance it descended at 1 in 58 to enter the tunnel, 1396 yards long, under St Pancras. This has been referred to variously as St Pancras tunnel and King's Cross tunnel. It was St Pancras tunnel when the intermediate signal box was opened in 1889 and again it was so named in the 1960 WTT Appendix. Early working notices and Midland Distance Diagrams termed it King's Cross tunnel and as such it has been referred to since electrification. The course of the branch in the tunnel lies under the main lines, swinging west until, at a point roughly under Midland Road, a sharp left handed curve takes the line towards the now derelict alignments of the curves from the GNR. The down Great Northern line was the first to be encountered, at the foot of the latter's difficult ascent at 1 in 35, 48 and 52 through Hotel Curve tunnel. Within a short distance a trailing junction was made with the up GNR line which had descended at 1 in 46 through the Up Metropolitan tunnel from York Road. From the junction the route continued to Moorgate Street over the Widened Lines of the Metropolitan Railway.

A major widening operation was completed on 13th November 1898 when up and down slow lines were opened from St Paul's Road Passenger Junction through Kentish Town station to Kentish Town Sidings box. The previous passenger lines over this length were re-designated fast lines. Heavy civil works were involved as for much of the length the line ran in cutting with retaining walls. The Camden Road tunnels, immediately north of St Paul's Road Passenger Junction box, are really covered ways. They were a Parliamentary requirement of the Act for the Extension. The lengths are 306 yards for the fast lines and 311 yards for the goods. The slow line tunnel of 1898 was permitted to have an intermediate opening. The name of St Paul's Road, from which the passenger and goods boxes took their titles, has been changed to Agar Grove, thereby commemorating the district destroyed when the line was built. There is, however, still a St Paul's Crescent nearby. The tunnels open on to the site of Camden Road station, a casualty of a combination of tram competition and wartime economies on 1st January 1916. The slow line platforms had existed for only 18 years but those for the fast lines dated from the opening of the Extension.

Just through the Islip Street overbridge is Kentish Town station. Short distance passenger traffic built up to a large volume; by 1903 over half a million passengers were booked annually. The opening in 1907 of the adjoining station on the Charing Cross, Euston and Hampstead tube eroded this number but bookings still exceeded 134,000 in 1922. Despite its proximity to the tube station, Kentish Town has never achieved the interchange status for business travellers of stations such as Finsbury Park. This has been partly due to the limited number of trains from the outer areas which were booked to stop. In the 1920s and earlier, some stops made by up trains were primarily intended for ticket collecting purposes.

A complex system of lines, junctions and various ancillary installations was located on the country side of Kentish Town station. This signifies to the west rather than to the north, as the Extension gradually turns through nearly a right angle on its course from St Pancras. The first railway on the scene had no connection locally with the Midland for many years. This was the Hampstead Junction Railway, promoted by the LNWR and opened on 2nd January 1860 from Kentish Town Junction on the NLR to Old Oak Junction at Willesden. (Kentish Town Junction, NLR, was at Camden Town station and should not be confused with the Midland's Kentish Town Junction box). There were three curves connecting the Extension to the Tottenham and Hampstead Junction Railway. The first connection was opened from Kentish Town Junction to Highgate Road for freight traffic on 3rd January 1870. This was variously known as the Highgate Incline or Tottenham South Curve. At Kentish Town Junction, the curve commenced on the down side of the goods lines and climbed at 1 in 48 to pass over the main line. There were facing

West End station shortly before it was re-named West Hampstead in September 1905. The view was taken from the original footbridge which connected the Iverson Road entrance with the platforms. On the left construction work is in progress on the station buildings and the local line platforms. *L&GRP.*

West Hampstead in the 1930s, with passengers waiting on the up local platform. *Lens of Sutton.*

A 4-4-2, No. 27, passes through Cricklewood - then known as Childs Hill & Cricklewood - with an up express prior to the station's extended development in 1905. *L&GRP.*

connections from the down passenger (later down fast) and down goods lines. Up goods trains had to stop for brakes to be pinned down before descending the incline, unless the load was less than 16 wagons, in which case the initial speed had to be less than 4 m.p.h. Banking was authorised for down goods trains between the yard of St Pancras goods station and Highgate Road.

For thirteen years there was no further development, then, on 2nd April 1883, the Tottenham North Curve, from Carlton Road Junction on the Midland to Junction Road Junction on the T&HJ was opened to goods traffic. At Carlton Road Junction there were facing connections from both the up passenger and up goods lines. In the 153 yards of North Curve tunnel No.1 it passed under both the Hampstead Junc-

tion and the Highgate Incline, here only a few yards from each other. After a short distance in the open it entered North Curve tunnel No.2, 205 yards long. (Originally designated North Curve tunnels Nos.2 and 3 due to an intermediate gap, the two portions were regarded as one in an amendment to the last Midland Distance Diagram). At Junction Road Junction the new curve joined the T&HJ in a simple double line junction. At that stage in its development, the T&HJ effectively terminated in an end-on junction with the Midland at Highgate Road. There was now an opportunity to install a curve from the up side at Kentish Town to the T&HJ. This was duly opened on 17th December 1900, extending from Engine Shed Junction at Kentish Town to Mortimer Street Junction which was

located between the two North Curve tunnels. The new link became known as the Kentish Town Curve. Not only did it avoid the Highgate Incline but also its junction at Kentish Town was on the up side and, therefore, was more convenient for local passenger traffic. Highgate Road Low Level station, situated between Mortimer Street Junction and North Curve tunnel No.2, was opened with the Kentish Town Curve. The original Highgate Road station then had High Level added to its title.

The City Carriage Sidings on the up side were double ended and comparatively short. They had an extension leading to trailing connections with the up and down Kentish Town Curve lines at Engine Shed Junction and Mortimer Street Junction respectively. The locomotive depot was opened with the Extension in 1868. Originally there were two roundhouses, both with 42 ft. turntables. No.1 was a victim of the 1898 widening. No.2 then became No.1 and was rebuilt with a 55 ft. turntable. The Nos.2 and 3 roundhouses, dating from 1899, possessed 55 ft. turntables initially, although they ended their lives with 60 ft. examples. As usual, the Midland, although favouring the round house layout, disguised them in large square buildings. All three were ranged, slightly staggered, alongside the Kentish Town curve. A connection from No.3 roundhouse provided an alternative outlet at Kentish Town Junction. Beyond No.3 were fitting and erecting shops. At one time major repairs were carried out here. Rationalisation led to the closure of the shops in 1932. They were later used for the repair of road vehicles. In 1939 a mechanical coaling plant replaced the old double coal stage that had been part of the 1899 improvements.

At the rear of the loco yard were Read Brothers Bottling Stores. In addition to the celebrated store beneath St Pancras terminus and the Bass store near St Pancras goods depot, this was a third destination for some of the vast quantities of beer carried up from Burton by the Midland. The Read buildings had pretensions to architectural merit, this was fortunate as they formed the background to countless portraits of Midland and LMS locomotives. Many of these photographs carried an unintended advertisement for Dogs Head Brand Bottled Beers; now, like the engines, long departed. As if to ensure that no stretch of railway land in the area was unused, four carriage roads, Mortimer Street Carriage Sidings, were laid in between the Tottenham South and Kentish Town curves with buffer stops close to the up slow line near Engine Shed Junction box.

The groups of sidings on the down side to which access was obtained from Cattle Docks Junction box were largely concealed from passing trains by the embankment of the Highgate Incline. The box was tucked away, together with the leads to the sidings, between the Highgate Incline overbridge and the wide bridge, practically a tunnel, over which passed the LNWR's Hampstead Junction line. The two connections from the goods lines merged briefly into a single line before commencing to fan out, giving no indication of the large extent of the sidings. Nearest to the main line was the cattle dock. Together with its accompanying sidings there was accommodation for a total of 372 wagons.

Compared to its freight activities, passenger work at Cricklewood was minimal but the Midland nevertheless granted full facilities which included platforms on all four passenger lines. *Lens of Sutton.*

4-4-0 No. 208 (501 from 1907) passing Welsh Harp with an up express. The photograph was taken from the island platform between the local lines which replaced the original two platforms on the passenger lines in 1890. The station closed completely in 1903. *L&GRP.*

Parallel to the cattle dock roads were the Cattle Dock Carriage Sidings, ten roads with a total length of 2,090 yards which could accommodate about 100 coaches. Next to the carriage sidings was a short head shunt from which three private sidings were reached, Constable Hart's, Turner's and Sankey & Sons. Alongside the head shunt was a four road Carriage and Wagon repair shop which was reached after a second reversal. A similar reversal was required in order to reach the Kentish Town coal drops. These, on a higher level, were approached over the private sidings and the second head shunt for the repair shop. They could accommodate 96 wagons. In its entirety this was a remarkable set of sidings compressed within a limited space.

From the country the Extension approached Kentish Town through Belsize tunnel, 1,734 yards long. Here the up line actually heads slightly north of east. The four tracks which were provided initially from Brent North Junction were interlaced into two at Finchley Road to open out again to four at Haverstock Hill. By this means the cost of a second tunnel was saved, at least initially, and the provision of facing points, regarded with some distaste by mid-Victorian railway planners, was avoided. In addition to the conflicting crossings at each end, the spacing of the up goods and down passenger lines in the tunnel did not permit their use at the same time.

Haverstock Hill station was situated in the cutting at the London end of Belsize tunnel. When new, its retaining walls were supported by heavy iron buttresses spanning the platforms and all four roads. The buildings at ground level, with steeply pitched roofs and bargeboarding reminiscent of a GNR signal box, were unusually picturesque for a station in the London area. The bottleneck formed by Belsize tunnel was relieved when the second bore, built to the north of the first, was opened on 3rd February 1884. The passenger lines were diverted to pass through it, the goods lines continuing to use the

old tunnel. The new tunnel was 1 mile 62 yards in length. The difference between old and new lengths is accounted for by the series of retaining arches into which the old tunnel opens at the Haverstock Hill end where the new lines are still underground. Between Haverstock Hill and Carlton Road Junction, the short passenger and goods line tunnels, about 100 yards long, were known officially as Lismore Circus tunnels. It is doubtful, however, if the name was ever in general use.

Having described the build-up of the Kentish Town area, it now remains to chronicle its decline. Highgate Road High Level lost its Great Eastern trains on 1st October 1915 but

the platforms remained open nominally until the low level side was closed on 1st March 1918. In the meantime, Haverstock Hill had been closed on 1st January 1916. The closure of the locomotive workshops in 1932 has already been noted. The running shed lost importance with the introduction of diesels around 1960. By 1962 the remaining steam locomotives were stored and final closure came in 1963. The reduction in freight traffic led to the closure of the Tottenham South Curve and Cattle Docks Junction box in 1964. The Kentish Town Curve was closed in 1981, the passenger service from Barking being diverted to Gospel Oak. The north curve from Carlton Road was then left as the only means of access from the Extension to the T&HJ.

Finchley Road station was located at the country end of the Belsize tunnels. When the second tunnel was opened in 1884, the consequent diversion of the passenger lines required the provision of new platforms. Prominent on the up side for many years was the enormous brick chimney of Hampstead Borough Electricity Works, an early plant, dating from 1894. Less than half a mile from Finchley Road was West Hampstead station with its convenient interchange with the adjacent stations of the Hampstead Junction and Metropolitan railways. Although it survived the 1916 closures, only 5,780 passengers (about 18 each weekday) were booked at Finchley Road in 1922. Not surprisingly, the LMS decided against its retention and trains ceased to call from 11th July 1927. For the first seven weeks only of its 60 year life it was known as "Finchley Road and St Johns Wood'. The full title persisted on the station nameboards. The local lines, which were extended from Watling Street Junction on 3rd December 1905, joined the fast lines at the country end of the platforms. The increase in passenger workings when the Bedford diesel sets were introduced in 1960, and the coincident decrease in goods traffic, produced a marked imbalance

Evidently, from the fact that a local tradesman went to the trouble of marketing photographs of it, Hendon station was once held in high local regard although, in this (probably early Edwardian) view the population do not seem to be providing much in the way of traffic - total demand amounting to no more than a single passenger and a hand-cart. *Lens of Sutton.*

in the usage of the Belsize tunnels. The new (passenger) bore became something of a bottleneck and the old goods tunnel saw comparatively little use. The logical answer, that of transferring the fast lines to the old tunnel, had to await the electrification before the modest amount of required finance became available.

The exchange sidings with the Metropolitan Railway at Finchley Road had some historical importance. A temporary connection was made in 1878 when the Metropolitan was under construction. The permanent opening was on 1st October 1880, by which time the Metropolitan had penetrated into Middlesex as far as Harrow on the Hill. The connection enabled the Metropolitan to accept coal from the Midland and carry it to the new suburban areas. This was the first freight to be carried by the Metropolitan Railway. Within the next ten years the district eventually to be known as Metro-land had been opened up and a valuable traffic in goods and coal was transferred at Finchley Road. The amount exchanged was, however, reduced when the Great Central commenced to bring traffic to Metropolitan stations via Quainton Road in 1898. In addition to the double ended exchange sidings with a capacity of 73 wagons, the Midland yard, counting both loaded and empty sidings, held another 242 wagons. With two companies approaching the exchange sidings from opposite ends, a safety regulation was necessary - *"It must be clearly understood that on every occasion before either Company's engines or trains are allowed to pass on to either of the exchange sidings, the Shunter or Acting Shunter in charge of operations will be held responsible for ascertaining that the line or lines affected are clear and that no shunting operations are in progress by the other Company"*. In other words "Don't come in from both ends at the same time". Exchange traffic was diverted via Neasden from 8th March 1948 and the connection was severed in June 1953.

Camden Road, Haverstock Hill and Finchley Road, all now closed, dated back to

4-4-0 No. 526, which survived until 1956, heads for St Pancras through Mill Hill in this undated view. The smart rake of uniform Bain coaches behind the engine was a trademark of the Midland and contrasted well with some of the other large systems whose trains often bore a rather untidy appearance. *GWG collection.*

the first days of the Extension. The stations still existing at West Hampstead and Cricklewood were later additions. West Hampstead was opened on 1st March 1871 as West End (For Kilburn and Hampstead). West End referred to West End Lane from which access to the station is now obtained. The original entrance was from Iverson Road via a footbridge over the goods lines. A short period as West End and Brondesbury from 1st April 1904 was ended on 1st September 1905 when "West Hampstead" was adopted. At that time rebuilding was in progress to provide two additional platform faces for the local lines. BR added Midland to the name in 1950. On the down side at West Hampstead there were connections for departures in

the up direction from the extensive West End Sidings. The sidings were approached via three arrival roads. These had facing connections from the up goods at West End Sidings signal box. In addition to the arrival roads there were 16 through sidings with a capacity of 754 wagons together with, at the West Hampstead end, a yard capable of holding an additional 156 wagons.

From Kentish Town there is a climb of 1 in 182 for nearly two miles to the west end of the Belsize tunnels. After a short break there is about three quarters of a mile of 1 in 162 up through West Hampstead, continuing on easy and broken grades to a summit at Cricklewood station. From there a fall of 1 in 196 for over a mile to the Brent Viaduct gave engines of down trains their first favourable grade. After West Hampstead the line gradually resumes a northerly or north westerly direction.

Cricklewood station was opened as "Child's Hill and Cricklewood' on 2nd May 1870. The name was changed to Cricklewood on 1st May 1908. The main building on the up platform resembled those of the smaller stations north of Harpenden. The provision of extra goods lines on the up side in 1899 cut off external access and the main building was demolished. A low level booking office was built on Cricklewood Lane with steps providing access to the platforms. When the new lines had finally evolved into up and down local and second up goods, two additional platform faces were provided on the east side. Immediately to the north of the station, the spur, opened on 3rd August 1875, from Dudding Hill Junction on the Acton branch, joined the fast lines. This spur completed a triangle, the other two sides being the main line and the northern, and more important, connection to the branch from Brent South Junction.

The four miles of the Acton branch from Brent South Junction to Acton Wells Junction on the North and South Western Junction Rail-

Belpaire 4-4-0 No. 835 approaches Elstree with a down train in 1906. *GWG collection.*

Radlett, looking towards London about 1960. The extension to the footbridge to reach the up slow platform of 1895 is evident. Old tractor tyres have been whitened and used for flower beds in the centre island. *Lens of Sutton.*

way was promoted by the Midland and South Western Junction Railway in 1864. Although nominally independent at first, it is certain that the Midland considered it an integral part of the Extension. It was opened throughout on 1st October 1868 and was absorbed completely by the Midland on 1st January 1875. The N&SWJR had been opened for goods traffic on 15th February 1853, providing a link between the LNWR at Willesden and the LSWR at Kew. The line was leased to these two railways until 1871. The advent of the branch from Brent made the Midland an alternative carrier of goods and minerals from the north to the LSWR. This was doubtless viewed with more pleasure by the LSWR side of the partnership. In 1871, the N&SWJ passed to a joint committee of the LNWR, NLR and the Midland. The Railway Clearing House occasionally referred to it as the North and South Western Junction Joint.

150 acres north of Cricklewood for the future yards were included in the original purchase of land for the Extension. The site was well chosen, the falling gradient from south to north eased the major part of the sorting carried out, that of loaded wagons despatched in the up direction. Altogether there were six distinct groups of traffic sidings in the Cricklewood/ Brent area. The total nominal capacity was 4801 wagons, equivalent to some 20 miles of sidings. This, however, is a comparative figure, based on the complete occupation of sidings. The prac-

tical working capacity would be considerably lower.

Dealing with the down side first, at the north end two yards handled up traffic. Brent South Sidings, nearest the running lines, with 15 roads holding 498 wagons and, to the west, Acton Branch Sidings with 14 roads holding 320 wagons. Trains could be despatched to the Acton branch from either yard without fouling the running lines of the Extension. LSWR and, later, SR engines were familiar sights here as they waited to set off for their home lines with transfer coal trains. The largest yard at Brent was contained in the triangle formed by the Extension and the arms of the Acton branch. Known as Brent Empty Wagon Sidings there were 34 sidings together with 3 arrival roads. The total capacity was 1766 wagons. To the south of the Dudding Hill to Cricklewood spur were Cricklewood Down Sidings, 30 comparatively short roads holding a total of 547 wagons.

Cricklewood engine shed was located between the Acton branch and the Edgware Road. It replaced a small shed at Hendon in 1882. The estimate for the latter had been accepted by the Way and Works Committee on 3rd August 1869 so for the first two years of traffic there was no local depot. At Cricklewood there were two roundhouses, the original of 1882 and an addition dating from 1893. In 1911, both had 50 ft. turntables. A 55 ft unit was substituted in No.1 roundhouse in 1933. There was a fitting and re-

pair shop with accommodation for six locomotives. The shed was No.15 in the Midland list, becoming 14A in 1934. In September 1963, a diesel depot was opened on the up side as "Cricklewood East". This shed took over the 14A code, the old steam shed becoming "Cricklewood West" with code 14B inherited from the closed Kentish Town. "Cricklewood West", stabling diesels at the end, finally closed on 14th December 1964.

The Brent Engine line came into use in 1905. This was a single line loop from the east side at Brent Up Sidings to the west side near the locomotive depot entrance. It burrowed under the main lines by Brent Viaduct and was worked by tablet between tablet boxes operated by the enginemen at each end. The tablets were later replaced by key tokens. Engines that had worked into Brent on the up side were facing chimney to the north ready for their return journey after using the engine line. Ashpits were provided in the Empty Wagon Sidings so that an engine which only required fire cleaning could go straight to the yard from which its return train departed without having to go on the shed. Wagon repair shops were situated near the locomotive depot. There were four roads under cover, the total capacity was 208 wagons with another 120 in the nearby cripple sidings.

Development on the up side commenced in 1885 with Brent Up Sidings, a group of 14 roads holding 528 wagons. Another large yard,

Napsbury was the Cinderella of the Extension stations and served the slow lines only. The platform buildings were not up to the usual Midland standards whilst the train service was poor. The timber building on the island platform will be noted. *L&GRP.*

Brent Loaded Wagon Sidings, had 22 roads with a capacity of 1142 wagons. The Carriage Sheds were opened in 1901 in a rather remote corner of the site. This was probably in order to leave space for future extensions to the freight yards. Entry was from Cricklewood Junction on up and down carriage lines, both of which terminated as head shunts for the sheds and associated sidings. A carriage washing plant was installed on the down approach line. Under cover there were 9 roads with a total length of 2385 yards. 8 open sidings added another 3000 yards. In all, some 275 carriages could be accommodated. Behind the station on the up side was an Express Dairies depot with two sidings to which much milk traffic was consigned.

Initially, the goods and passenger lines from London merged into up and down main lines at Brent North Junction. This was situated at the north end of Brent Viaduct. The 19 brick arches of the latter had, therefore, to be built expensively to carry four lines. Here the River Brent opened out into the Welsh Harp lake, later known more prosaically as Brent Reservoir. It maintains a head of water for the Grand Union Canal and used to extend under the railway. The demands for building land and space for new roads have encroached on its boundaries - now it covers less than a third of its original area and can only just be glimpsed from the train. In its present concreted surroundings of dual carriageways, crowned by a gigantic road flyover and verged by hideous buildings, it is difficult to

imagine that this was once a place where Londoners flocked for leisure. A now poignant illustration in William's *The Midland Railway, Its Rise and Progress* of 1877 shows anglers by the viaduct in a tranquil scene.

The demand for pleasure travel was sufficient for Welsh Harp station to be opened on 2nd May 1870. Originally it comprised up and down platforms on the main lines. When the local lines were opened between Hendon and Welsh Harp Junction in 1890 the original platforms at Welsh Harp ceased to be used and services were transferred to a new island platform built between the local lines. Competition and the proximity of Hendon station - the platform ends were only 600 yards apart - led to an early closure for Welsh Harp on 1st July 1903. In 1902, the takings at the booking office had only been about one per cent of those at Hendon. The island platform and its buildings had a life of only thirteen years. The head of the disused subway which led to the platform was visible many years after closure.

Hendon station has changed greatly in importance over the years. Before the turn of the century, the Midland made it a terminus for the shorter distance suburban services, then virtually unchallenged by competition. Edwardian travel to the seaside led to the introduction of through summer services between the South Coast and towns on the Midland. Hendon was the engine changing point for these trains, brought by LSWR locomotives through Acton

Wells or by SECR locomotives via the Widened Lines. Passenger traffic at Hendon reached a peak in 1903/4. Eventually the short distance trains were seen off by the trams and motor buses, the through services were cut short by the 1914-1918 war. The rash of new building which converted countryside to suburb in the 1930s was served by bus and by tube from Hendon Central. The infrequent calls at Hendon LMS by St Albans locals had little to offer the newly settled families.

The widenings of 1890 brought two new pairs of lines through Hendon. On the west side were the goods lines and on the east the local lines. To the north, the former rose to fly over both the original main and the new down local to join the eastern pair at Silk Stream Junction. The Midland knew the flyover as the Hendon Crossing. The local lines were extensions of those already noted as being opened from Welsh Harp. From Silk Stream Junction slow lines continued northwards. New platforms were built for both the goods and local lines at Hendon. The former saw little use, although as late as 1937, a special train for RAF personnel was despatched from the up goods platform after the last Hendon Air Display. There was a wide space between the goods and fast lines north of the station. Here Hendon New Sidings were laid out, 11 roads holding 578 wagons with trailing connections from the down fast and up goods. Hendon Old Sidings were on the up side at the north end of the goods yard. The Hendon sidings were the

St Albans City in the 1950s, looking north from the down fast platform. The footbridge was then on the far side of the road overbridge *Lens of Sutton.*

outermost group of the Midland's marshalling facilities in the London area. For the remainder of the Extension, with the exception of a small group of sidings at Leagrave, the yards were provided to meet local requirements only.

The flyover was situated at a dip in the main line at the foot of the climb, averaging 1 in 176, to Elstree. The dip enabled the slope of the approaches on the goods/slow lines to the flyover to be kept down to 1 in 200 in both directions. The steepest gradient involved was about quarter of a mile of 1 in 127 on the down local where it climbed to meet the goods line at the junction. Much of the embankment work required at Silk Stream was built up from chalk excavated from the cuttings between Leagrave and Harlington. When the widening was completed in 1895, the quadruple track ran northwards from Silk Stream Junction in unchanging format. The slow or goods lines were uniformly on the east side of the fast or passenger lines. The original stations had been built with foresight, their entrances and main buildings all on the west side of the line.

Before electrification, Mill Hill probably saw greater changes to its immediate surroundings than any other station on the Extension. Opened with the line as a simple two platform station, it was rebuilt in style to accommodate the widening in 1890. The ridge and furrow glass canopies, gable ended as at Hendon and Elstree, were extended in matching fashion to all platforms to establish a pleasant station in an area awaiting enterprising developers and builders. A photograph, taken in about 1910, looking north from the station, shows a pastoral scene of trees and fields that could have been anywhere on the railway south of the Trent. In the 1930s there was much building locally, although transport requirements were supplied more by road than by the LMS. Already, however, the district was one of the earliest sufferers from the blight of trunk road traffic. The Barnet and Watford by-passes joined forces at Apex Corner, only yards

from the railway. Nevertheless, Mill Hill retained the air of a suburban outpost. In the 1950s, John Betjeman set his *Elaine* to alight at Ruislip Gardens -

> *Out into the outskirts edges*
> *Where a few surviving hedges*
> *Keep alive our lost elysium -*
> *Rural Middlesex again.*

This could equally well have applied to Mill Hill. Later, however, the final extension southwards of the M1 dealt a cruel blow to both suburb and station. The up slow platform is now crushed tight against the northbound carriageway and the entrance is hidden in a dark corner of the bus station. The 1930s proposal for the Northern Line extension to Bushey Heath was to have incorporated the ex-GNR branch to Edgware. This would have provided a Northern Line station within a short distance of the Extension. The scheme was postponed in wartime and subsequently abandoned. Cessation of the work which had been in progress on the bridge carrying the Extension over the GNR resulted in a long standing speed restriction which was a serious handicap to the heavy down expresses of the war period. The tube trains terminate at Mill Hill East, over one and a half miles from the Extension station, which became Mill Hill Broadway on 25th September 1950.

Various lengths between 1050 and 1060 yards have been quoted for the Elstree tunnels. The 1960 Appendix to the WTT, which listed other tunnel lengths to the nearest yard, defined both slow and fast line tunnels as 1050. The 1914 inspection of new works at Elstree reported the lengths as 1058 yards, slow line, and 1050 fast line, and these figures were also given on the final issue of the Midland's Distance Diagrams. However, a hand written correction to the latter altered the length of the old, fast line tunnel, to 1058 yards also, and this appears to be the authoritative word on the subject. The climb from Hendon continues at 1 in 176 for a quarter mile after the tunnels to a summit 302 ft. above sea level.

The tunnels were bored under the boundary between Middlesex and Hertfordshire. Despite some blurring due to the development of Borehamwood, there still remains the impression here of a dividing line between suburban London and the country. Elstree's population in 1871 was only 825, so initial business at the station would not have been brisk. The village, a mile from the station, still displays evidence of its rural past. It has been completely overshadowed, however, by modern and busy Borehamwood, built in the mile and a half between the railway and the Barnet by-pass, now the A1. The industrial area of Borehamwood is situated near the main road, so commuting inwards entails a bus ride - nevertheless the station enjoys a good patronage. Opening with the line as plain Elstree, it became Elstree and

4-4-2 2601 PRINCESS OF WALES prepares to leave St Pancras on 2 September 1901 with the 1.30pm express to Glasgow (St Enoch) . *Ken Nunn Collection.*

Boreham Wood on 1st June 1869. It reverted to Elstree on 1st April 1904. The claims of Borehamwood, which by the 1950s was virtually a new town, could not be overlooked and the name was changed to Elstree and Borehamwood on 21st September 1953. Inexplicably it reverted once again to Elstree on 6th May 1974. If the name had to be simplified, then the nettle should have been grasped and Borehamwood substituted. The commuters from Metro-land look alike Elstree are surely outnumbered by travellers to and from Borehamwood.

The station at Elstree was established just to the south of the Shenley Road overbridge. Immediately to the north of the bridge on the up side, was the signal box, the goods yard behind it extending both south and north of the bridge. There was a loading dock on the down side and a brickworks on the top of the cutting to the south of the station. After utilising clay from the first tunnel, pits were dug in the surrounding fields and when the second tunnel was bored, clay was once again obtained from the excavations. The works were in production from 1870 to 1915. Elstree station, rebuilt for the widening, became for many years one of the most attractive on the Extension. There was extensive ridge and furrow roofing and a covered footbridge at the south end of the buildings on the platforms. A new footbridge at the north end was constructed in 1959, connecting with a somewhat cramped booking hall and high level entrance on the east

side. Although convenient, the changes certainly did not improve the appearance of the station. Prior to electrification, the then deteriorating roofing and platform buildings were demolished and replacements in modern style provided.

From Radlett onwards, the stations built with the Extension fell into two categories, the larger ones - Radlett, St Albans, Harpenden, Luton and Ampthill and the less important - Chiltern Green, Leagrave, Harlington and the slightly later Flitwick. The first type had a separate station master's house and the single storey building on the down platform was dignified by a pavilion at the south end. So, although only serving a small hamlet when the railway was built, Radlett's station conformed to the larger of the two basic designs for the northern contract. The goods station, opened four months before passengers were carried, was actually called 'Aldenham' initially. There was uncertainty over the choice of name, Aldenham then had a much larger population than Radlett; in 1868, the monthly issue of the WTT referred to Aldenham in March, Radlett in April, then reverted to Aldenham for May and June, only finally adopting Radlett in July. As was the case with Mill Hill and Elstree, the station at Radlett was extended to provide platforms for all four roads at the time of the widening. The present day Radlett owes its inception almost entirely to the coming of the railway. Now, as a dormitory town, and a very pleasant one at that, it is

largely dependent on the Thameslink commuter services.

North of Radlett the line runs parallel to Watling Street through Harper Lane cutting. It then curves away to the east to cross the River Colne. It is 236 ft. above sea level here, having descended 66 ft. from the summit at Elstree. A climb of more than four miles, averaging 1 in 180, through St Albans to Sandridge, now commences. On the down side, the works built by Handley Page Aircraft Ltd. have now found other uses. After the firm's unfortunate demise in 1969, the adjoining aerodrome has been disused, and is now cut off from the factories by the M25 which passes under the railway. The aerodrome obliterated part of the course of the "St Albans branch" - the connection from the Extension to the LNWR at Park Street. This line carried materials for building the Extension, as noted earlier, but was never opened for public traffic. The Midland distance diagram for 1920 still showed the length ("not laid") to the LNWR as 1 mile 14 chains from the end of a siding 12 chains long. The bridge over the A5 Watling Street remained until removed for widening in recent years. At the Midland end, the curved termination (i.e the 12 chain siding) opposite Napsbury station was used for carriage storage. A siding and dock was added on the east side at Park Street in late 1895. This was probably in connection with the nearby Middlesex County Asylum, later Napsbury Hospital, which was then

On 28th November 1959, in the last year of suburban steam operation, 2-6-4T 42134 awaits departure from St Pancras with the three coach 12.45pm to its home station, St Albans. *J.Osgood.*

Kirtley 2-4-0 No. 153A waits to leave Bedford with an up stopping train in 1903/4. *NRM.*

being built. Napsbury station opened on 19th June 1905, primarily intended for visitors to the hospital. It comprised an island platform between the slow lines, the up slow being slued to make room. A wooden building on the platform was surmounted by two ornamental brick chimneys. At the south end, a covered footbridge provided an exit to the east side of the line. The station was closed on 14th September 1959. The timing suggests that the decision was made so that it would not be an embarrassment to the forthcoming diesel service. Commuters had not been encouraged - in its final year, Napsbury's last down train of the day left St Pancras at 4.38 p.m! Proximity to the A405 North Orbital Road and the possibility of unlimited parking space on the eventually disused airfield would have made it an ideal candidate for development as a Parkway station, if it had survived for a few more years.

A fine view of St Albans Abbey is obtained on the down side and it appears that the railway is going to give the city a wide berth. Indeed, if the railway had followed a straight course from Napsbury to Sandridge, St Albans station would have been somewhat remotely situated. But some pronounced curvature brings the line to the west and, having regard to the hilltop location of the city, the station is on a reasonably convenient site. The deviation was also necessary to preserve a constant gradient. As it is, there are some heavy earthworks and a notable brick arch over the now lifted GNR branch from Hatfield. A permanent speed restriction to 75 m.p.h was imposed in 1939 between mileposts 181/2 and 20, due to the curves. The station entrance was on the south side of a road overbridge which spanned the platforms. A *porte cochere* was added to the building which otherwise was generally in the style of Radlett. The footbridge was narrow and awkward due to the skew angle of the adjoining road bridge. It was little changed in LMS days, though the name became St Albans City to distinguish it from the ex-LNWR and GNR stations which gained the names Abbey and London Road respectively. A long overdue rebuilding commenced in 1972, a new main building and entrance on the east side opening in 1973 - at last an adequate footbridge was put up. For many years St Albans possessed a "back platform line" on the up side, a Midland term for a bay which extended the full length of a platform. Platforms for all four roads were provided when the goods lines to Harpenden Junction were converted to slow lines in 1906.

The engine shed, to the south of the station on the up side, was sited in 1868 with sufficient space left between it and the main lines for the eventual quadrupling. It was a handsome building, with the side windows surrounded by large blind arches. It remained basically unaltered throughout its life although the covered accommodation, in two rows for a total of four engines, was hardly adequate for the numbers allocated. Actually, allocation as a term is not strictly correct, for throughout most of its existence it was a sub-shed, first of Kentish Town and then of Cricklewood. It was not until 1934 that it became a "garage" depot in its own right as 14C. The 42 ft. turntable was adequate for its own engines but was too small for a 4-4-0. In later years a prominent water softener was installed. The shed closed on 11th January 1960 when the DMUs were introduced. At the end, the layout of the shed yard was virtually unaltered from that shown on an Ordnance Survey map of 1883.

4. THE ROUTE: SANDRIDGE TO BEDFORD

The long climb from Radlett ends at Sandridge, between St Albans and Harpenden. It is followed by a series of undulations with the trend still against down trains until a height of 390 ft. above sea level is reached at Harpenden Junction. Harpenden vies with Radlett as the most desirable address for commuters on the Extension. A village grown into a town, with good schools, golf and a common, it has most advantages and house prices in keeping. The station is well situated between town centre and residential area - there is much surrounding evidence of Edwardian building for the well-to-do but, judging from the timetables of past years, commuting, at least on any scale, is a comparatively recent development. Nevertheless, the station was provided with a "back platform line" on the up side until 1906, when passenger traffic commenced on the slow lines, upgraded from goods lines at that time. Two through platforms on the slow lines were then added, that for the down slow being converted from the old back platform. A short bay at the north end of the down fast platform was used by the Hemel Hempsted (sic) branch train.

When it was opened on 16th July 1877, the line from Hemel Hempstead, built by The Hemel Hempstead and London and North Western Railway Company, turned north to join the Extension, the trains working to and from Luton. The line was absorbed by the Midland on 25th June 1886. The Midland adopted the spelling "Hempsted" which prevailed without local support until the 1950s. The original junction at

Condensing 0-4-4T No 1377 is uncoupled from its train at St Albans on 9 May 1931. This particular engine enjoyed a long life and was still in existence twenty years later, working from Sheffield (Millhouses) MPD. *H.C.Casserley.*

Harpenden was located some 800 yards north of the site established on 2nd July 1888, when its direction was changed to permit through running from the south. The minor summit here is in a deep cutting at the end of which traces of the original course of the branch are still visible. The gradients remain undulating from

Harpenden Junction northwards. There is an initial fall to East Hyde where the River Lea and the course of the GNR's Hatfield to Dunstable branch are both crossed. A climb through Chiltern Green follows and then there is another fall to Luton. On the descent to the crossing of the Lea, the line is on the west side of the valley with traces of the GNR below. The Lea viaducts are substantial structures, brick for the original (fast) lines and girder for the newer (slow) lines.

Chiltern Green station was situated in sparsely populated surroundings. The only justification for its existence was the nearby Luton Hoo estate which was also served by the GNR's New Mill End station (Luton Hoo for New Mill End from about 1899). Only the station house remains standing at Chiltern Green. It was built in the style which can still be seen in its entirety at the intermediate stations between Luton and Bedford. No major alterations were ever made - on the up platform a low brick wall remained standing, shutting off the down goods line. Patronage at Chiltern Green was the lowest of any station on the Extension. In 1913 the average number of passengers booked per day was less than 12 and the year's takings from fares amounted only to £149. Somehow it managed to survive throughout the whole LMS era but its closure on 7th April 1952 was not unexpected.

North of Chiltern Green the railway threads a course between higher ground to the

A lonely figure waits to be met outside Harpenden station. *GWG Collection.*

Although the various 0-6-0 tender engines based on the extension were primarily for goods traffic, motive power shortages - especially in the years immediately after the last war - saw them pressed into stopping passenger service as was the case on 28 July 1951 when, photographed near Harpenden, 4F 43909 of Kentish Town found itself at the head of the 14.58 St Pancras - Bedford: a service which took no less than 126 minutes to cover the 50-mile distance. The 16.05 Luton - St Pancras passes on the opposite line. *E.D. Bruton.*

east and the Luton Hoo estate, which was already bounded by the GNR, to the west. The views from the Midland of the sharp curves and heavy gradients of the GNR served to emphasise the superb engineering of the former. With long sweeping curves and gradients which do not, for any appreciable length, infringe the southbound 1 in 200 limit, the most difficult stretch of terrain encountered by the Extension is traversed. The curvature, with a minimum radius of 51 chains at MP 283/4 caused a permanent speed restriction of 75 m.p.h between MPs 28 and 301/4 to be imposed in 1939. The Luton Hoo estate, landscaped by Capability Brown, provides fine views on the down side. In the winter, when the trees are unleaved, the full extent of the lake, formed by a dam on the River Lea, is revealed.

There is a dramatic change of scene at the northern boundary of Luton Hoo, now marked by a ring road overbridge. The works of the Vauxhall plant of General Motors come into view, together with a glimpse of the approach lighting

for Luton Airport. The railway now enters industrial and urban Luton. The final left handed curve past Crescent Road goods yard takes the line round to a westerly direction at Luton station. In mid-winter, London bound commuters see the rising sun through the down side windows.

Luton had a traditional trade of straw-plaiting. In pre-railway days it relied on local supplies of straw; better communications brought in material from further afield but the products of foreign competition now became available. This led to a gradual change to hat finishing, felt as well as straw. But traffic from the hat trade was soon to be overshadowed by the carriage of heavier goods. Luton Corporation offered cheap electricity as an encouragement to industry. At about the turn of the century and afterwards, many engineering firms moved their premises to the town. The GNR with a fine warehouse and nine years start on the Midland, had built up a large share of the hat traffic. Partly due to the siting of industrial premises and per-

haps also to a greater readiness to provide access, the GNR could eventually boast of a formidable list of private sidings. In 1912 these included:- Hayward Tyler & Co. (hydraulic machinery), T.Balmforth & Co. (boilermakers), Arnold's and Brown's timber yards, The Diamond Foundry, The English and Scottish Joint Co-operative Wholesale Society (chocolate and cocoa manufacture), Luton Corporation Electricity Works and the gasworks. The Midland, possibly reluctant to introduce a multitude of connections into their main line, had only a siding, potentially very important, to Vauxhall Motors Ltd. Later, there was also a connection from Crescent Road yard to the Co-operative Society bakery. Vauxhall Motors had been formed in 1907 as a branch of the Vauxhall and West Hydraulic Engineering Co. which had moved to Luton from Lambeth in 1905. The original business in hydraulic machinery and small marine engines was soon completely overshadowed by the expansion of motor car production. But once again, after World War 2, when the export trade in vehicles boomed, it was first the LNER and then the Eastern Region, with a staging depot at Oakleigh Park, which carried the traffic. The list of private sidings did not by any means complete that of Luton's immigrant industries. Laporte Chemicals (eventually with a siding from the GNR) came from Shipley, Yorkshire, in 1898. In 1907, the Davis Gas Stove Co. moved from Falkirk and, in the next year, George Kent & Co. makers of meters for liquids and gases, arrived from London. Finally, in 1910, the large Skefco plant for ball bearing manufacture was established as a subsidiary of a Swedish parent firm.

Eventually the large Midland goods yard at Crescent Road had to be supplemented by a new yard at Limbury Road, between Luton and Leagrave. Both Crescent Road and Limbury Road yards remained in commercial use into the 1980s. On the eve of electrification, Crescent Road, with end loading facilities, was still despatching a proportion of Luton's output of motors by rail and Limbury Road found use as the Coal Concentration Depot for the area.

The influx of factories led to a large increase in Luton's population and slowly it took on the aspect of a northern industrial town. From 1908 to 1932, trams were in operation and in the Edwardian era Luton overtook Bedford in the numbers of its passenger bookings. With shorter average journeys, however, receipts were less than those of Bedford until the final years of the Midland Railway. The station, an enlarged version of the Radlett, St Albans and Harpenden theme, remained unaltered with its back platform line on the up side. At last, increasing patronage drove the LMS, which was inclined to be sparing in expenditure in such matters, to embark in 1937 upon a major rebuilding. The platform plan was unaltered, but completely new buildings were erected including two refreshment rooms. That on the down side, regrettably

The 2-6-6-2 Beyer-Garratts were a regular sight on Midland line coal trains for twenty-five years until the mid-fifties when they were quickly replaced by BR 9F 2-10-0 locomotives. In this view 47995 of Toton is south of Chiltern Green with an up train for Cricklewood, on 28 July 1951. *E.D. Bruton.*

now closed, was particularly pleasant and spacious. A new booking hall and entrance was located over the platforms on the bridge leading to High Town from Bute Street, with alternative facilities at road level on the down side. New platform awnings were built throughout. The complete structure, with a restrained brick faced finish, has aged better than some contemporary Art Deco designs.

For the introduction of the DMU service in 1960, it was necessary to build an up slow platform. This was a narrow structure in the limited space between the line it served and the

through siding in front of the goods shed. The add-on footbridge was suitably restricted, in keeping with the cramped platform. The old back platform line was converted into a down through platform line, No.3, connected at each end with the down slow line. The latter did not itself have a platform face. This arrangement of the platforms lasted until 5th November 1977. The changes then made were planned with electrification in mind and are described under that heading.

From Luton the line heads north west through Leagrave, gently climbing to a summit at mile post 33 3/4. The line here, although only slightly higher than at some other points on the tableland from Sandridge, just tops the 400 ft. contour to reach 403 ft. above sea level, the highest point on the Extension. The long descent from the summit continues through Harlington to Flitwick. There are two versions of the detailed gradients, both of which have been used officially at various times. A late Midland version, repeated in *Gradients of British Main Line Railways* in 1947, shows a climb of 1 in 200 from just south of mile post 40 with an easing to 1 in 300 through Harlington. The alternative was used in a Midland gradient diagram of about 1903 and was repeated on the diagram which was displayed in Harlington signal box. It was reproduced in *The Railway Magazine* for October 1929 and also used in a BR diagram of 1948, revised in 1960. This shows the gradient as a constant 1 in 202, unbroken at Harlington and commencing at about MP 39 1/2. Leagrave is mis-named, it is the source and not the end of the River Lea. Luton has expanded to include it as a suburb, its station now busy with commuters at peak times and it has a brisk local traffic throughout the day. The renovated station buildings, together with those of Harlington and Flitwick, retain the style used for the smaller stations on the northern contract of the Exten-

Jubilee 5644 HOWE passes through Chiltern Green station with a northbound fitted goods on 12 July 1939. Although 5644 was not a regular sight on the Midland route - it later worked from Glasgow (Corkerhill) and Manchester (Longsight) - by the late 1930s other members of the class had taken over the principal services from St Pancras with most secondary expresses being handled by 5MT 4-6-0s. *H.C. Casserley.*

Luton Midland Road in 1960 after the addition of slow line platforms, to the left of the view, in preparation for multiple-unit operation and the running of local passenger trains on the former goods lines between Bedford and Harpenden Junction. *Lens of Sutton.*

sion. Including the 1870 additions there were five examples in all. Of the other two, nothing remains of Child's Hill at Cricklewood and the fragment at Chiltern Green has been separated from the railway for many years. Three out of the group of four sidings at the north end of the station were used in Midland days to adjust the loads of up coal trains, the gradients south of Leagrave being much easier than those to the north. An occasional up train was terminated and its wagons dispersed in the sidings to be taken on by following trains. The engine returned to Wellingborough propelling the van. The goods yard retained at least some work until a comparatively late date. In 1974, Yeoman's stone traffic arrived from the Mendips and wagon loads

of steel swarf were despatched by Skefco, by then removed from Luton to Sundon Park.

From the summit at mile post 33 3/4, the line starts its descent on a straight course through a deepening chalk cutting which is finally crowned by the tall arched bridge carrying the Chalton to Sundon road over the line. A long right handed curve then commences which takes the heading of the line to almost due north. At the end of the curve was the the large Sundon cement works on the up side. This had two separate siding connections. The gradient of the approach to the works at the southern siding was sufficiently steep for engines to be prohibited from going up tender first, due to the risk of uncovering the firebox crown. The pick-up goods

from Bedford had, therefore, to be worked tender first so that the engine could reverse chimney first up the incline. Some old Bedford goods engines were fitted with tender cabs for this duty. The Midland described the southern siding as Forder's Cement Works Siding and the northern as Forder's Sundon Lime Works Siding. From the latter, a siding for Inns & Co was provided in 1922. By 1978 the cement works had been demolished, all the connections lifted and the site had been landscaped. The rubbish dump adjacent to Inn's siding has developed into the Sundon landfill scheme. Here Luton's dustcarts bring their loads to be spread over the site, to the delight of the seagull population of Stewartby lake, who commute the nine miles in large numbers to scavenge during the day. At Sundon, the main line was crossed by a wide span footbridge and also, uniquely on the Extension, by an occupation crossing. This was the scene of two accidents in which agricultural tractors were destroyed, on 24th May 1963 and 9th July 1965. In both cases the driver jumped clear.

Harlington station, like the village it serves, has retained its charm. The addition in 1959 of an up slow platform and an extended footbridge seemed to make little difference to its attractiveness. This was in contrast to the more exposed Leagrave, which tended to look bleak when enlarged. Harlington is now the only village station on the Extension and proclaims the fact with a well kept garden. The village itself has sufficient new housing to provide its quota of commuters. There is also the larger Toddington, clearly visible on its hill to the west. Bradshaw used to have a note "station for Toddington, 2 miles". It is remarkable that several towns or villages built on hilltops had to be skirted by the course of the Extension - Ampthill, Toddington, St Albans and Elstree - all were necessarily some distance from the line which otherwise had each station commendably close to the centre of population which it served. On 1st November 1927, the LMS added (Beds) to the name of the station to distinguish it from a halt on the Dearne Valley line.

In 1893, B H Forder & Co., predecessors of the London Brick Co., built a brickworks north of Harlington, on the up side near MP 38. It was the first of any size in Bedfordshire, excepting Arlesey on the GNR. Difficulty in handling the local clay led to an early closure and bricks were only produced between 1894 and 1906. The remains of the kilns were visible until the 1930s and the overgrown site can still readily be identified from the train.

When the Extension was opened, Flitwick, then a village with a scattered population of some 800, was not even provided with a station. In contrast, Ampthill, a small market town with a population of over 2,000, was given one of the superior "Radlett" type stations with ample glass awnings. Now Flitwick station, opened on 2nd May 1870, thrives with commuter traffic while Ampthill, a mile and a half away, has been closed for 30 years and is forgotten. Such a change of fortune requires the two stations to be considered together. In 1868, Flitwick was small and comparatively dispersed. Although Ampthill was three quarters of a mile from its station this was not an undue separa-

Stanier 5MT 45221 of Leicester waits for the road at Luton with a down parcels train from London in December 1959. The fast lines, used by passenger trains, are to the left of the picture whilst the train is in the new down slow platform. *J. Osgood.*

A late Edwardian view of Leagrave station, looking south. Only the fast lines have platforms, the goods lines running behind the station to the right of the picture. *Lens of Sutton.*

tion at that time, given the position of the town on a hill and the absence of any effective competition. An omnibus drawn by two horses provided a link between station and town, eventually replaced by a motor bus.

The situation at Ampthill did not change but Flitwick station was convenient for new housing which was gradually built in its vicinity. From 1903 onwards, passenger bookings at Flitwick exceeded those at Ampthill. Even before 1914, a slight bias is detectable in the time-tables, with the odd train calling only at Flitwick between Luton and Bedford. The process very gradually accelerated with Vauxhall workers

commuting to Luton from Flitwick in the 1950s. Car owners now came into the picture and Flitwick's cross roads rather than Ampthill's cul de sac drew the early park and ride customers. Ironically, Ampthill's larger station, with its iron columns, glass awnings and covered footbridge, may have been its own worst enemy. When the last trains called, on 3rd May 1959, all was in an extreme state of dilapidation and the cost of refurbishment would have been high. Expenditure on a new up slow platform and an extension to the footbridge would also have been required for the forthcoming diesel services. In the next year the commercial success of the DMUs was demonstrated by the increased number of passengers using the other stations. There were rumours that the re-opening of Ampthill was being considered. But with the local patrons now accustomed to Flitwick it is doubtful if even the previous level of use could have been regained. Flitwick station, like Child's Hill, was modelled on Chiltern Green, Leagrave and Harlington. The waiting shelter on the up platform was of a more rudimentary type than the rather ornate structure at Harlington. The widening first reached Flitwick when an up goods line from Ampthill was opened on 15th October 1893. When the formation was widened opposite the station, the presence of the main road at the top of the cutting necessitated the provision of a retaining wall. Foresight at the time ensured that space was left for an up slow platform with an additional indent in the wall for a waiting shelter. 66 years later, the platform and shelter were built

5XP 5654 HOOD rushes through Harlington station with an up express on 7 June 1939. *H.C. Casserley.*

in their allotted positions without the long possession of the goods lines and the costly excavation and brickwork which would have been required if the development had not been foreseen - an object lesson in looking ahead, for today's planners to absorb.

The long 1 in 202 descent ends about a mile south of Flitwick. In general, the line still falls to Ampthill but there is a short adverse stretch north of the station. The line is 243 ft. above sea level at Flitwick, 160 ft. lower than the summit at MP 33 3/4. North of Ampthill the descent to the Ouse is resumed at 1 in 200. Ampthill possessed a long and spacious platform between the up passenger and down goods lines. Tradition has it that the intention was to provide for unusual traffic such as troop movements, but the necessary reliance on footbridge or sleeper crossing for access would have limited its usefulness in such cases. In World War 1, when a military hospital was established at Ampthill Park House, wounded soldiers were taken thence from ambulance trains which used the down passenger platform. In December 1914, a Weekly Notice authorised the use of the down goods line from Harlington to Bedford for passenger traffic when the passenger line was occupied in this way.

One of the major works of the widening in the 1890s was the boring of the second Ampthill tunnel. Logan & Hemingway, a firm well known at the time for the construction of railways, gained the contract; at 718 yards the new tunnel was 2 yards longer than the old. It is on the west side of the formation and the previous main lines were diverted to pass through it as passenger lines, leaving the old tunnel to be used by the new goods lines. The change in the alignment of what are now the fast lines is clearly evident at the northern approach to the tunnels. When the new bore was ready to accept the passenger lines the up goods was completed through the old tunnel. The down goods line through the tunnel was opened on 28th July 1895. This date marks the completion of the widening of the

Harlington in transition as platforms are added to the former goods lines in preparation for the dieselisation of the suburban service in 1960. In the background a Stanier 8F, 48625, shunts a ballast trains into the yard. *J. Osgood.*

Extension. From then four roads were available all the way from St Pancras Junction to Glendon North Junction. This continuous length of seventy-five and a quarter miles was unrivalled in Great Britain and is believed to have been bettered only by the New York Central..

The line falls from Ampthill for 5.75 miles to a point north of the site of Elstow box. Four and a half miles are at an average of 1 in 200, the remainder being easier for up trains. A short climb at 1 in 178 follows to Cow Bridge, where the Extension crosses over the ex-LNWR branch from Bletchley. Drivers of down trains stopping at Bedford would coast without steam up the gradient to Cow Bridge, taking the edge off the speed before braking for the junction at Bedford South.

From about a mile north of Ampthill tunnel the line is carried for over two miles on a long gently curving embankment. To early generations of Bedford railwaymen this was known as Wootton bank. Wootton stems from the signal box at one time located near the north end. Whether 'bank' was derived from the embankment or its 1 in 200 gradient is not clear. The embankment commenced at the site of Millbrook box, where the railway is rather exposed. Before their demolition in April 1989, the chimneys and cooling towers of Little Barford power station, nearly 15 miles away on the line from King's Cross, could be seen from the train. So the Midland provided Millbrook with an anemometer mounted on a telegraph pole. When the wind velocity exceeded a certain figure, the limits for unpiloted loads from Leicester to St. Pancras were reduced. It will come as no surprise to learn that Millbrook box was known in the district as Windmill Junction.

The clay vale between Ampthill and Bedford provides ideal material for brickmaking. Near the large works at Stewartby the line is flanked by claypits - to the brickmaker they are 'knot holes', whence the 'knots' of clay for the bricks are obtained. Most of the bricks that were transported by rail went onto the Bletchley to Bedford line, but two works had sidings connected to the Extension. These were Elstow, dating back to Midland days, and the Coronation works of the 1930s, served by sidings from Houghton Conquest box. The Coronation works possessed an electric industrial locomotive which took power from an overhead line. A very spacious signal box was provided at Houghton Conquest in 1935, a time when the brick industry was expanding. This gave rise to local rumours that a connection from Forder's Sidings box, less than a mile across country on the Bletchley line, was under consideration. But war came soon and the supposed spare capacity at Houghton Conquest was never utilised. Elstow brickworks had sidings with a single connection to the up slow

Flitwick occasionally did good business, at least in the early years of the century, as this circa 1912 view suggests, showing a well patronised stopping train leaving for Bedford. In the distance a coal train approaches on the up goods line. *Lens of Sutton.*

About to be consigned to history. Tickets are collected from passengers off the penultimate down train to call at Ampthill on 4 May 1959. Demolition of the station was so effective that it is now difficult to see exactly where the platforms had stood. *J. Osgood.*

line at Elstow box. There were no rounding facilities here so the daily trip of the 'Elstow Shunter' from Bedford had to return propelling the train with the van leading. The solemn procession along the down goods with guard and

shunter keeping watch from the verandah was a regular afternoon sight.

During World War II a major ordnance factory, 'Factory 16' was built alongside the line between Houghton Conquest and Elstow signal

boxes. A new signalbox and extensive sidings were installed. A terminal platform with two faces was used by special trains from Bedford, commencing on 18th August 1941. The box was named Wilshamstead, the official name of the village generally known as Wilstead. After the war the site has found various subtopian uses, only narrowly escaping a fate as dumping ground for nuclear waste. In 1874, the Royal Agricultural Show was held near the line at Elstow. The site was then known as the Racecourse - later it was part of Racemeadow Farm. A temporary station was erected at the bottom of the dip between Cow Bridge and the eventual location of Elstow Box. Up and down platforms were provided, together with a signal box on the former. The platforms were staggered, with the down side to the south. A crossover and trailing connection from the up main line gave access to a carriage dock on the down side opposite the up platform. The north end of the carriage dock had a short end loading bay and a trailing connection to the down main line. There was no footbridge, the down platform was adjacent to the road to Ampthill and the show site was just across the road. Passengers from the up platform could use the underbridge, known locally as Gaulty Arch, which later provided road access to Elstow brickworks. Home and distant signals were installed in each direction. Col. Hutchinson approved the arrangements on behalf of the Board of Trade on 26th June 1874.

From Cow Bridge to the Kempston Road overbridge at MP 49 1/4 the falling gradient is 1 in 184 for a full mile. This is the only instance where the rule of no gradient steeper than 1 in 200 against loaded coal trains was broken for any significant length. There were constraints at both ends, at Cow Bridge to clear the LNWR and at Kempston Road to pass under the highway. At the Kempston Road overbridge the line is at its lowest level locally and water has covered the rails at times when the Ouse has been in high flood, the last occasion being in the 1946/1947 winter. From Kempston Road bridge there is a slight rise to Bedford station. Here the line is 90 ft. above sea level, 18 ft. above the level at St Pancras. The fall in the last 16 miles is 313 ft., equivalent to an unbroken gradient of 1 in 270.

The extensive Ballast Pit Sidings, the "Ballast Hole" in the vernacular, were located on the up side to the south of Kempston Road Junction box. The low sided wagons of the Engineer, brick red and lettered "E D", were a familiar sight being propelled to the station and then drawn into the South Sidings to await weekend relayings. The Engineer also possessed sidings on the down side at Kempston Road. Sand and gravel had been excavated here until the boundary of railway land had been reached, close to the back gardens of the houses in Beatrice Street. The sidings appeared to be derelict in the 1930s and the excavated area is now the site of small factories.

Bedford was comparatively undeveloped in the 1860s and the vestiges of a past era still lingered. There was no piped water supply until 1866 and in the opening year of the Extension, a man was hanged in public, outside the County Gaol. Although the Britannia Ironworks were established in 1859, other industrial enterprises

Compound 4-4-0 41017 of Bedford attacks the climb to Sundon as it emerges from Ampthill tunnel with an up express in the early months of nationalisation. Although this particular engine was withdrawn within a couple of years of this photograph, survivors could be seen on occasional express work out of St Pancras until 1957; their last such duty being the 15.40 London - Leicester semi-fast. *L.N. Owen.*

were slow to follow. Grafton's had a private siding to their Vulcan works in 1886; then a major development came with the building of W H Allen's Queens Engineering Works to the west of the station in 1894. By 1900, Bedford had grown to a size which led the Corporation to obtain powers for tramways; powers which expired in 1907 with nothing built.

H P Saunderson produced wind pumps and agricultural machinery in a factory adjacent to the Midland at Cow Bridge. W H A Robertson came to the Ampthill Road in 1907 and then in 1913, the Igranic (electrical) and Meltis (confectionery) factories were established. The large building of Bedford County School was taken over by the Cosmic Crayon Company on a site now occupied by Granada TV Rentals. So the goods yard, expanded to the limits of its site, was kept busy, although Bedford, unlike Luton, was never dominated by industry. It remained a balanced town, with good schools and a pleasant riverside, much favoured in the days of the Empire by families with Army or Indian Civil Service connections.

The 1863 Powers for the Extension provided for a junction with the Hitchin line to the south of the LNWR crossing. Although there now appears to be obvious advantages in having the junction where it was finally located, it must be borne in mind that, as described in Chapter 1, there were still hopes at the time of building a joint Midland/LNWR station in the Ampthill Road area. The Act of 1864 which brought the Extension to its present course followed the final collapse of the plans for a joint station. The Britannia Works had a long river frontage which the Extension now had to pass on the west side, hence the sharp curve commencing at the junction. Ford End Road bridge was built literally over the site of the junction, to the south of the Cox Pit Lane level crossing which it superseded.

At Bedford station, two new platform faces were provided on the west side of the origi-

The southern approach to Bedford where Bedford Junction controlled the routes to London (left) and the branch (right) to Hitchin. The fast lines are out of sight to the left, by-passing the station. In steam days terminating trains remained on the down line; the engine having to shunt the stock upon arrival. After the start of multiple-unit operation in 1960, however, terminating services used the crossover in the left of the picture to arrive in the up platform. *A. Vaughan.*

nal pair, diverging slightly from them. The new platforms were sheltered by ridge and furrow glass awnings matching those of 1859. There appeared to be a curious constriction between the up and down lines in the new platforms. The clearances, measured in the 1950s, between 9 ft. stock were only 15 in. between the sides and 12 in. between the door handles. The original platforms were divided into two pairs of bays so that direct access from the booking office to the new up platform was possible. A narrow footbridge to the new down platform was erected -

originally open, it was later covered. The station led an uneventful existence after the changes of 1868. In the 1880s, at least, ticket platforms existed, both to the north and south. The 9.40 a.m all stations from St Albans was booked to stop at the south ticket platform daily in 1883 - Ampthill dep. 10.32, Bedford Ticket Platform arr. 10.43, Bedford station arr. 10.45. It was also used for three down stopping trains on Sundays. In 1883, the only train booked to use the north ticket platform was an up stopping train on Sundays.

Except through Bedford, the widening process from Kettering to Silk Stream Junction produced a pair of goods lines on the east side. At Bedford, the east side entrance to the station and the location of the Hitchin lines prevented this course. The chosen alternative was the "Bedford Curve", a pair of fast lines avoiding the station on the west side. The line of the curve diverged slightly from the old main lines after Kempston Road Junction to cross the Ouse by a new bridge. It then followed a long left handed curve to rejoin the old lines at Bedford North. The Bedford Curve permitted non-stopping trains to pass Bedford at speed. Previously they observed a 15 m.p.h speed restriction at Bedford Junction. The siting of the 1887 engine shed, which must have seemed rather remote when first built, indicates that the curve was then foreseen, although Powers for it were not obtained until 1890.

At about this time a remarkably prophetic scheme was produced showing the station rebuilt to take advantage of the new lines. Platforms would have been provided on the new fast lines and on a pair of slow tracks. The course of the lines from the 1978 station now follow that of these slow lines to an uncanny extent. The original through Hitchin platforms of 1859 were to be reinstated and the 1868 lines to the south

The south end of the platforms at Bedford as seen from the Ford End Road overbridge. Although the photograph was taken in 1914, very little change occurred during the ensuing half-century; even the withdrawn 'American' Brake-third vehicle staying in place as a stores office until (at least) the late 1950's. *L&GRP.*

The entrance to Bedford Midland Road station, which changed but little over the years - a month before closure in October 1978. The present station is located approximately a quarter of a mile to the north. *G.W. Goslin.*

were to be removed. This left a broad triangular space between the Hitchin and slow lines. Above this space a new, or alternative, entrance was to be provided from Ford End Road bridge. The scheme shows various bay platforms, not all of which would have been justified by traffic needs. They were probably included in the plan in order to show the full potential of the proposal. Even if the scheme had only partially been implemented it would have resulted in an immense improvement in the capacity of the station and its ease of working. As it was the place was left virtually unchanged by the widening, which had little effect on it except for the diversion of the non-stopping trains.

Bedford's first engine shed, the "old loco", was located opposite Bedford Junction box. In 1887, the "new loco" was opened on a site to the west of the alignment of the proposed "Bedford Curve". Although the Midland built many roundhouses, the new shed had four straight roads. It had what was termed a "northlight roof" with a saw toothed profile, but in this instance the roof lights did not face north for even lighting, but south east towards the shed entrance. This gave it a distinctly LNWR appearance although one may be sure that no Midland man would ever have admitted it. At first, the new shed was used only for housing engines, coaling facilities and the turntable remaining at the old shed.

In 1893, preparations were made for the new Bedford Curve. The new fast line bridge over the Ouse, with three 29 ft skew spans, was ready for use in September. On the 30th of that month all traffic was diverted over it so that the old bridge could be rebuilt. The new bridge was approached from Kempston Road Junction on a 1 in 189 rising gradient. When the work on the old bridge was completed, the new curve was opened to traffic, on 7th October 1894. At Bedford North the mid-point of the new double junction connecting the slow lines through the station with the fast lines was opposite the 50th

mile post. For those who delight in round figures, it may therefore be claimed that the Extension, as completed by the Bedford Curve, is exactly 50 miles in length. The new engine shed now became self contained and the scheme for its completion was approved by Samuel Johnson on 13th September 1893. Additional engine sidings and a coal stage on the west side were included. The loaded coal wagons for the stage had to be propelled up a gradient of 1 in 25. At the south end was a 50 ft. turntable.

The station and its surroundings now entered a long period with negligible changes. If the Bedford railwaymen of 1894 could have been brought back 65 years later they would readily

have recognised and understood the scene. Despite the growth of the town in the interim, the basic passenger facilities remained unaltered. The up and down platforms were supplemented by bays; at the south end adjacent to the parcels office was the Hitchin bay and at the north end bays to both up and down platforms, known as the Northampton bay and the Wellingborough bay respectively. All three were signalled for passenger train departures but arrivals were possible only at the Hitchin bay. Alongside the up goods line at the north end of the station were three carriage sidings where stock for the London trains was stabled.

Terminating down passenger trains was a lengthy procedure. Before the train arrived, the station shunter had to be despatched from its usual position at the north end to Bedford Junction in order to be attached in the rear while the train engine proceeded to the engine shed. When all the windows had been shut, a time consuming process in the summer, the shunter propelled the carriages forward on to the down goods line, brought them back again into the up platform or the Northampton bay and then propelled them again into the sidings. The alterations made for the DMU service of 1960 were simple but effective. A facing crossover was installed at Bedford Junction so that trains from St Pancras could terminate in the up platform. They could then depart for their return working without further movement and passengers did not have to use the footbridge.

There could be lengthy occupations of the down fast line at Bedford North by empty wagon trains stopping for water and examination. The examiner and his lad would emerge from their little hut near the down home signal, the former to tap each wheel and flip open the top of each grease box with his hammer, banging down those which were full, or, if they needed filling, leaving them open. His lad followed, struggling with the weight of a large can of grease from which

The Bedford main line platforms at Bedford in Edwardian days looking north towards Wellingborough. *Lens of Sutton.*

35

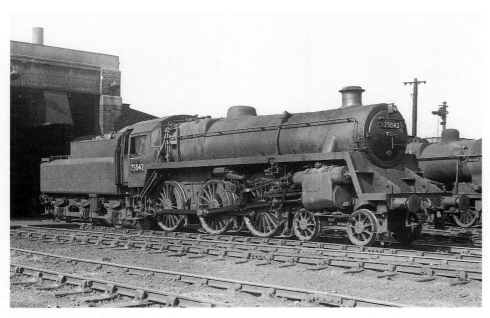

Considerable thought was given to the provision of motive power for the Bedford - St Pancras suburban services after the war with BR standard 4MT 2-6-4 tanks replacing Compounds on most trains from 1951. These engines, however, proved to have insufficient water capacity for the 50-mile trip and in 1955 they were replaced by standard 4MT 4-6-0's which remained in harness until dieselisation. 75042 is seen being prepared for a St Pancras working at Bedford MPD on 9 September 1958. *P.H. Groom.*

he ladled replenishments into the boxes left open. Gradually the introduction of oil axleboxes made the procedure obsolete - reducing the number of wagons removed from trains due to hot boxes.

The present enlightened treatment by Network SouthEast of its older buildings and structures may lead to the conjecture that Bedford Midland Road (so termed by the LMS from 2nd June 1924) was an attractive station in the 1920s and 1930s. Unfortunately, despite its wealth of Victorian ironwork, this was not true. A condi-

tion of the remission of the Railway Passenger Duty by the Government in 1929 was an undertaking by the railways to spend the capitalised value in improvements. The LMS had to spend £2.5 million of which £63,000 was devoted to improvements at passenger stations. Conditions at Bedford Midland Road accurately reflected this proportion. The waiting room on the up side, inconveniently situated in its pre-extension position, was dark and its furniture ancient. The bookstall and wooden refreshment room, both in the space once occupied by the Hitchin Main

lines, had a temporary appearance. Despite its lantern roof, the booking hall was also dark and unattractive. In it the LMS installed a Benn & Cronin Train Indicator of the type adopted by the Lancashire and Yorkshire Railway before grouping. Enamelled plates were used in mosaic fashion to make up a list of departure times to selected destinations. Its value to passengers was doubtful and the outlay might have been better spent on a coat of paint all round. It was this lack of fresh paint that is the most abiding image of the station. The LMS had to cope with declining revenues and the resultant economy measures meant that little or nothing was done to make the station attractive in answer to competitors such as Birch Brothers, who were building up a frequent and well patronised coach service to London. In the 1940s the old footbridge was unable to cope with workers returning from Wilshampstead and a second was installed, paid for by the firm who managed Factory 16 on behalf of the Government.

The LMS did, however, embark on a programme of improvements to motive power depots. In 1935, a vacuum operated 60 ft. turntable, able to accept the new 4-6-0s, was installed. By 1938 the shed had been equipped with new ash handling facilities and a mechanical coaling plant. Capstans were installed to move wagons at the coaling plant, they were similarly used by the Corporation Electricity Works to handle their 20 ton hoppers. The saw-toothed profile of the shed roof was lost in the 1950s when a flat roof of concrete was built, after some years during which the shed had been open to the sky. With its new roof, the locomotive depot faced its final years in good condition compared with that of many sheds in the rundown of steam traction. The same could not be said of Bedford Midland Road, always an uneasy compromise between its short-lived original purpose as a wayside station on the Leicester to Hitchin line and its much longer lasting adaptation to the needs of the Extension. The completely new station that was built for the electrification scheme was the only practical solution to the problem.

The Jubilee 4-6-0s gave some steaming problems when first introduced and, until being improved, were often relegated to Bedford slow trains rather than for the services for which they had been intended. Early in its career 5649 (later named HAWKINS) was photographed coming off shed at Bedford having been rostered for one of the St Pancras slows. The poor performance of the early Jubilees lead for a short time to such sights as the 10.23 non-stop leaving Bedford behind a Leicester 2P 4-4-0 whilst the following 10.38 stopping train was graced with a Kentish Town 5XP 4-6-0. After the modifications of 1937 matters changed considerably and the Jubilees settled down to a 25-year career which included the successful haulage of the principal Midland expresses from St Pancras. *GWG Collection.*

5: SIGNALLING AND TRACK
St PANCRAS TO St ALBANS

The track layouts of the Extension were drastically revised during the process of quadrupling north of Brent. The widening was carried out in stages over a period of 20 years from 1875 to 1895. It was followed by the costly provision of an extra pair of lines, making six in all, from Silk Stream Junction, north of Hendon, to St Paul's Road Passenger Junction, only excepting the section from Finchley Road to Carlton Road Junction which included the Belsize tunnels. The details which follow cover the development of the signalling and track layouts from the commencement of the widenings to the end of manual operation in 1981.

When the platforms at St Pancras were numbered in 1892, the two boxes then controlling the station were re-named West and East from Departure and Arrival respectively. Later, in 1900, both boxes were replaced by the back to back twin St Pancras Station box. The long St Pancras Junction box was sited in the fork of the divergence of the goods lines to Somers Town. It had a 48 lever goods frame facing west at the north end and an 84 lever passenger frame facing east at the south end. Block working, to Cambridge Street box on the passenger lines, commenced at St Pancras Junction box. Between the Station and Junction boxes, the working was covered by the enigmatic note - "No block or bell". St Pancras Station box was, therefore, effectively confined to setting the routes between the Arrival and Departure lines and the platforms. It might well have qualified for an entry

Nottingham-based Jubilee 45667 JELLICOE stands ready for the right-away from St Pancras with a northbound express during the mid-1950s. The view highlights the constriction of the layout due to the individual bridges over Pancras Road. *GWG Collection*

in the Guinness Book of Records as the world's largest ground frame.

The four roads between the Junction and Station boxes were known as East and West Ar-

rival and East and West Departure. In earlier years they were spanned by an impressive signal gantry, with 21 stop signals and 21 calling-on arms. On 28th June 1914 this gantry was replaced by a simplified one, using route indicators.

The St Pancras East Departure line led directly to the down passenger line. The West Departure line was extended to Cambridge Street on 6th May 1900. A down carriage line on the east side of the other running lines was provided between Cambridge Street and Dock Junction from 15th December 1907. There were special regulations for working down trains in the wrong direction on the up passenger line between St Pancras Junction and Cambridge Street in order to reach the carriage line. At Dock Junction, a single connection with slips extended across all four running roads and the down carriage line.

Manual signalling remained in force until 6th October 1957, when a new St Pancras signal box was commissioned. Situated on the west side near the platform ends, it replaced the old Station, Junction and Cambridge Street boxes. Power operated points were installed at St Pancras and at the same time colour light signals replaced the remaining semaphores as far as Haverstock Hill. Here, intermediate block signals had been brought into use previously, for

A reminder that Great Eastern services ran into St Pancras in the days before the Great War. GER 2-4-0 No. 703 backs out of platform 6 for Cambridge Street loco sidings to turn and prepare for a return trip to Cambridge. *GWG Collection*

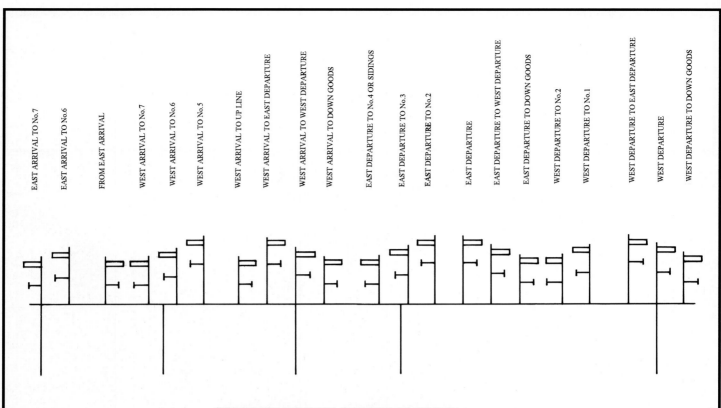

EAST ARRIVAL TO No.7
EAST ARRIVAL TO No.6
FROM EAST ARRIVAL
WEST ARRIVAL TO No.7
WEST ARRIVAL TO No.6
WEST ARRIVAL TO No.5
WEST ARRIVAL TO UP LINE
WEST ARRIVAL TO EAST DEPARTURE
WEST ARRIVAL TO WEST DEPARTURE
WEST ARRIVAL TO DOWN GOODS
EAST DEPARTURE TO No.4 OR SIDINGS
EAST DEPARTURE TO No.3
EAST DEPARTURE TO No.2
EAST DEPARTURE
EAST DEPARTURE TO WEST DEPARTURE
EAST DEPARTURE TO DOWN GOODS
WEST DEPARTURE TO No.2
WEST DEPARTURE TO No.1
WEST DEPARTURE TO EAST DEPARTURE
WEST DEPARTURE
WEST DEPARTURE TO DOWN GOODS

**ST PANCRAS SIGNAL GANTRY AS AT 1905
LOOKING SOUTH**

FIG.5

ST PANCRAS SIGNAL GANTRY LOOKING SOUTH, JUNE 1914

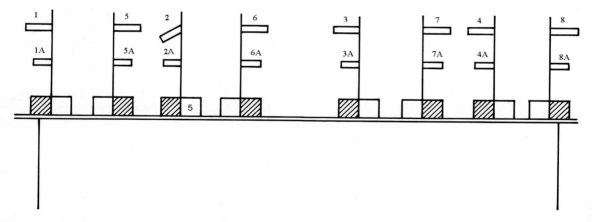

ST PANCRAS STATION SIGNALS
1 EAST ARRIVAL HOME
2 WEST ARRIVAL HOME
3 EAST DEPARTURE HOME
4 WEST DEPARTURE HOME
1A - 4A CORRESPONDING CALLING-ON ARMS
FIGURES 1 TO 7 DISPLAYED FOR ARRIVAL PLATFORM

ST PANCRAS JUNCTION SIGNALS
5 EAST ARRIVAL HOME
6 WEST ARRIVAL HOME
7 EAST DPARTURE HOME
8 WEST DEPARTURE HOME
5A - 8A CORRESPONDING SHUNTING SIGNALS

(TRAIN SIGNALLED FROM WEST ARRIVAL LINE TO PLATFORM 5)

LETTERS DISPLAYED:
G TO DOWN GOODS LINE
E TO WEST DEPARTURE LINE
U TO UP PASSENGER LINE

FIG.6

the passenger lines on 30th December 1945 and for the goods lines on 20th October 1946. Haverstock Hill box was closed on the latter date. At the south end of the St Pancras Goods station building, North London Incline signal box was fixed to the wall. It signalled the goods lines only, including the steeply graded single line to the NLR and the northern connections to Church-yard sidings. It was replaced by a ground frame on 31st December 1961. In Churchyard sidings, the "fourth line from the churchyard wall" was worked as an up goods line to provide access to Somers Town coal depot. The working of the North London incline was controlled by tablet (later by key token). The upper end of the token section was not the NLR St Pancras Junction signal box but a token box at the entrance to the exchange sidings. In this instance, "box" refers to a housing for the token apparatus. The northern approach lines to St Pancras Goods station left the goods lines at St Paul's Road Goods Junction, a narrow box sandwiched between the goods and passenger lines but with signals only for the former. It was closed on 21st December 1975.

Before the widening of 1898, the City branch diverged by a simple double junction at St Paul's Road Passenger Junction box. An accident at this junction is described in Chapter 9. An outcome of the accident was that the recommendations of the Inspecting Officer led to the provision of Lomond Street box, a block post for the City and passenger lines, situated only 7 chains south of St Paul's Road Passenger Junction box. Lomond Street was opened in about 1885 and protected the junction from conflicting movements in the down direction. This was long before the development of track circuits made outer home signals a practical proposition in such locations. The boundary between Midland and Metropolitan ownership at the lower end of the City branch was located just before the junction with the Hotel Curve of the GNR. Midland Junction signal box, situated in the fork was, therefore, staffed by Metropolitan signalmen. The cost of its provision was borne, however, by the Midland as the newcomer. In 1877, Airey's *Handbook of Railway Stations* defined the junction of the Midland with the Metropolitan as King's Cross Junction and the GNR to Metropolitan junction as King's Cross Medium Junction. The better known, but unofficial, title of Midland Junction received recognition in the GNR's 1912 Appendix to the WTT. Therein, the catch points in Hotel Curve tunnel were defined as being 43 yards north of the Metropolitan Company's Hole in the Wall box. A description of the box appeared in *The Railway Magazine* for May 1907.

The use of fouling bars and a treadle enabled the junctions to be controlled safely in visibility which, at the best, was severely restricted and often was practically nil. By 1926, more sophisticated equipment was available and the Metropolitan's King's Cross "C" box took over complete control on 6th March of that year and Midland Junction box was closed.

Similar considerations to those which led to the provision of Lomond Street applied to the installation of St Pancras Tunnel box, literally a "hole in the wall", which was brought into use on 21st July 1889. It was in the tunnel, 340 yards

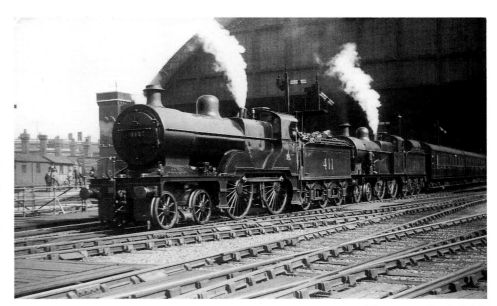

The 16.25 Manchester and Liverpool express gets ready to pull out of St Pancras behind 4-4-0's 411 and 768 on 30 July 1921. The post-war increase in trains loads combined with a small-engine policy had by this time resulted in many Midland mainline services running with two locomotives; a situation that was to conclude with Staniers standard large-engine regime fifteen years later. *GWG Collection.*

from Midland Junction and 1400 yards from Lomond Street, its 4 levers controlling disc home and distant signals in each direction. The main function of the box was to protect the junctions with the GNR. St Pancras Tunnel box survived until 2nd February 1958. An eight hour shift there must have been even more lonely than at Midland Junction. The signalman there at least set eyes on a fellow human being when the unfortunate wretch, whose duty it was to sand the rails of Hotel Curve tunnel after the passage of each train, reached the bottom end of his beat. Some idea of the conditions can be gained from

the instructions to guards of up freight trains to blow their whistles when passing St Pancras Tunnel box to indicate that their trains were complete.

On 13th November 1898, the layout at St Paul's Road Passenger Junction became a double running junction from up fast to up branch and down branch to down fast, the City lines continuing northwards to Kentish Town as the new slow lines. The number of conflicting movements at the junction was greatly reduced by the changes. With St Pancras Tunnel box breaking the section from Midland Junction, Lomond

Pancras Road coal drops. Wagons were winched onto the traverser from turntables on the reception road and distributed to the unloading bays which had a capacity of 90 wagons. The coal was fed by gravity into bunkers for bagging or for direct loading into road vehicles. *Irwell Collection.*

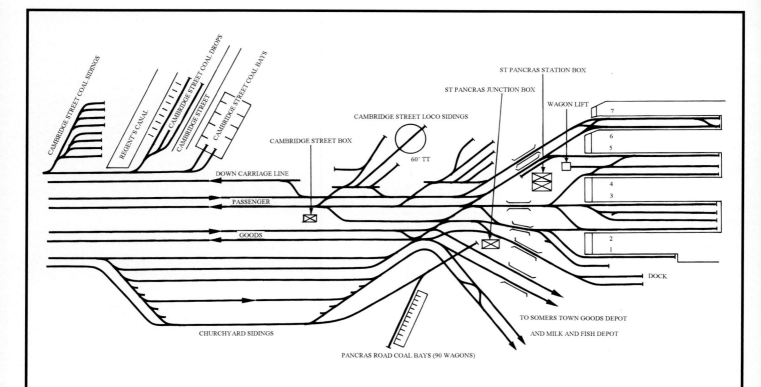

CAMBRIDGE STREET COAL SIDINGS

REGENT'S CANAL

CAMBRIDGE STREET COAL DROPS

CAMBRIDGE STREET

CAMBRIDGE STREET COAL BAYS

CAMBRIDGE STREET LOCO SIDINGS

60' TT

CAMBRIDGE STREET BOX

ST PANCRAS JUNCTION BOX

ST PANCRAS STATION BOX

WAGON LIFT

DOWN CARRIAGE LINE

PASSENGER

GOODS

7

6

5

4

3

2

1

DOCK

CHURCHYARD SIDINGS

PANCRAS ROAD COAL BAYS (90 WAGONS)

TO SOMERS TOWN GOODS DEPOT

AND MILK AND FISH DEPOT

FIG.7   **CAMBRIDGE STREET TO ST PANCRAS 1938**

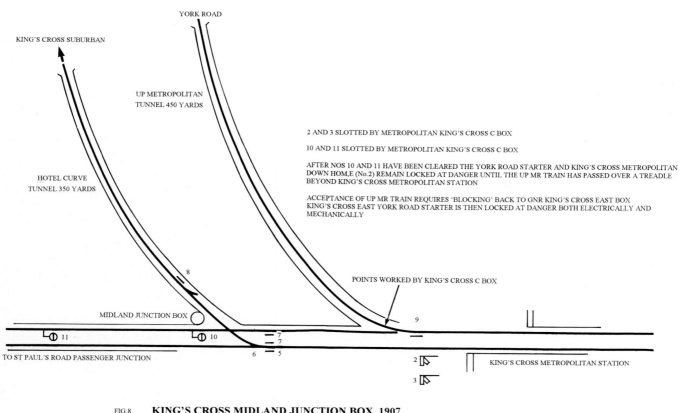

YORK ROAD

KING'S CROSS SUBURBAN

UP METROPOLITAN
TUNNEL 450 YARDS

2 AND 3 SLOTTED BY METROPOLITAN KING'S CROSS C BOX

10 AND 11 SLOTTED BY METROPOLITAN KING'S CROSS C BOX

AFTER NOS 10 AND 11 HAVE BEEN CLEARED THE YORK ROAD STARTER AND KING'S CROSS METROPOLITAN
DOWN HOM,E (No.2) REMAIN LOCKED AT DANGER UNTIL THE UP MR TRAIN HAS PASSED OVER A TREADLE
BEYOND KING'S CROSS METROPOLITAN STATION

ACCEPTANCE OF UP MR TRAIN REQUIRES 'BLOCKING' BACK TO GNR KING'S CROSS EAST BOX
KING'S CROSS EAST YORK ROAD STARTER IS THEN LOCKED AT DANGER BOTH ELECTRICALLY AND
MECHANICALLY

HOTEL CURVE
TUNNEL 350 YARDS

8

MIDLAND JUNCTION BOX

POINTS WORKED BY KING'S CROSS C BOX

9

11

10

7
7

TO ST PAUL'S ROAD PASSENGER JUNCTION

6   5

2

3

KING'S CROSS METROPOLITAN STATION

FIG.8   **KING'S CROSS MIDLAND JUNCTION BOX, 1907**

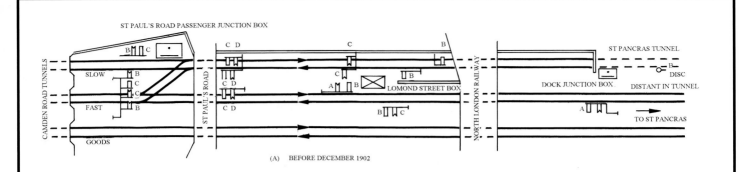

St Paul's Road Passenger Junction Box

(A)   BEFORE DECEMBER 1902

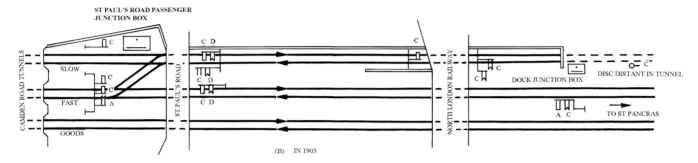

St Paul's Road Passenger Junction Box

(B)   IN 1903

A SIGNALS CONTROLLED BY DOCK JUNCTION
B SIGNALS CONTROLLED BY LOMOND STREET
C SIGNALS CONTROLLED BY ST PAUL'S ROAD PASSENGER JUNCTION
D SIGNALS CONTROLLED BY CAMDEN ROAD

FIG.9   **SIGNALLING ALTERATIONS DUE TO CLOSURE
OF LOMOND STREET BOX**

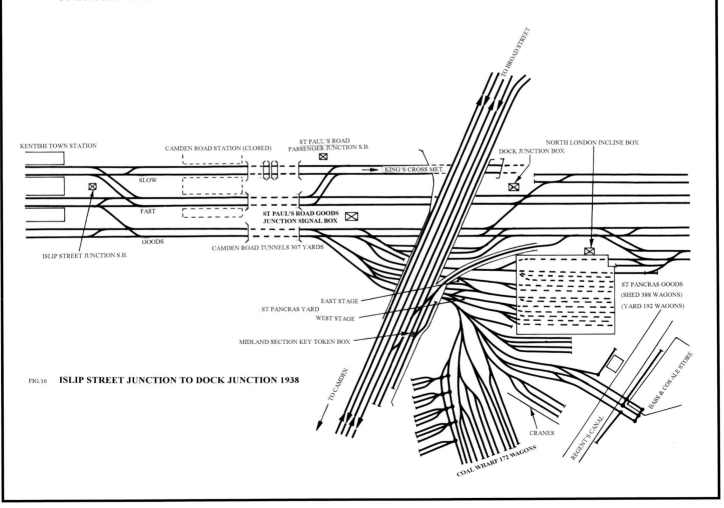

FIG.10   **ISLIP STREET JUNCTION TO DOCK JUNCTION 1938**

The curiously named North London Incline Box was built on the side of St Pancras goods depot - about half a mile north of the passenger terminus and not to be confused with Somers Town - and controlled the goods lines together with the inclined connection to the North London Railway. *NRM*

Kentish Town Curve went out of use and therefore survived longer than any of the other manual signal boxes replaced by the West Hampstead power box. Finally it was closed on 6th December 1981 and, with the exception of the listed shell of St Albans South, the Midland signal box was extinct on the main line of the Extension. There was, however, a remarkable survivor nearby on the T&HJ at Junction Road Junction, where the original box of 1883 remained in use until 10th November 1985. After 102 years it was the oldest Midland box still in service, finally acting as a fringe box to West Hampstead, a conjunction of the oldest and most modern boxes on the line. Its functions were taken over by a new panel box at Upper Holloway.

The local lines between Finchley Road and Watling Street Junction were opened on 3rd December 1905. From then the four track section from Carlton Road Junction through Haverstock Hill and the Belsize tunnels to Finchley Road formed a comparative bottleneck in an area where six running roads were otherwise available. Northwards from Finchley Road box the three pairs of lines were designated Local, Fast and Goods. The convergence of Fast and Local lines at Finchley Road was for long accompanied by an unusually severe speed restriction for trains using the latter lines. As defined in the 1937 Appendix to the WTT the limits were 15 m.p.h down and 10 m.p.h up. These limits were relaxed to 40 m.p.h down and 50 m.p.h up for the DMU service in 1960.

North of West Hampstead, the first Watling Street box was opened on 6th November 1892, together with a second down goods line to Child's Hill. Initially there were signals for the goods lines only. It evolved into the important Watling Street Junction which controlled double junctions from up local to up fast, down fast to down local, up fast to up goods and down goods to down fast. The two double junctions were side by side to minimise conflicting movements. A second up goods line was opened from Cricklewood to West Hampstead on 25th June 1899. This was on the east side of the other running lines to the north of Watling Street Junction and between the local and fast lines to the south. The local lines from Cricklewood were opened on 2nd October 1904 (up) and 24th September 1905 (down). From the latter date, there were no less than eight running lines between Watling Street Junction and Cricklewood.

Child's Hill South box was opened on 25th June 1899. After a short life it closed, as Cricklewood South, on 2nd October 1904 when temporary up goods lines to Watling Street Junction became the new up and down local lines. The 1875 spur from Dudding Hill Junction on the Acton branch joined the fast lines at Child's Hill Passenger Junction, eventually to become Cricklewood Junction. The lines from Dudding Hill crossed the goods lines without making connection with them. This rather unusual layout persisted long after regular passenger services ceased, although access to the spur was possible eventually from the second down goods line.

In 1876, Brent South Junction box, the point of divergence of the Acton branch, was situated on the west side of the railway without signals for the passenger lines. In October 1881, connections to the passenger lines were brought

Street was redundant. The Board of Trade, who had recommended its opening, had to give permission for its closure which took place on 14th December 1902. On 23rd January 1903, Major Pringle retrospectively approved the changes.

There was a block post at Camden Road station and a new box was opened with the slow lines on 13th November 1898. Situated at the north end of the platform between the fast and slow lines, it outlived the station by nearly four years, closing on 2nd November 1919. To the north of Camden Road was Islip Street Junction, a box which met a violent end in 1966 in an accident also described in Chapter 9. Before the 1898 alterations it was plain Islip Street.

The 1898 widening brought the new slow lines through Kentish Town station to Kentish Town Sidings box. Here were connections to the City Carriage sidings, Kentish Town Locomotive Depot and Read's sidings. The up slow was extended to commence at Carlton Road Junction on 23rd April 1899. The down slow reached there on 28th October 1900, from which date there were six running lines between Carlton

Road and St Paul's Road Passenger junctions. A new box had been provided at Carlton Road Junction on 5th June 1898. On 25th September 1898, Kentish Town Junction box - which did not signal the new slow lines - was also replaced. The Kentish Town to Mortimer Street Junction curve commenced at Engine Shed Junction. The completed widening and curves required four boxes in the short distance between Kentish Town station and Carlton Road Junction. On the up side, signalling only the slow lines of the Extension, were Kentish Town Sidings and Engine Shed Junction. On the down side were Kentish Town Junction, with signals for fast and goods lines, and Cattle Docks Junction with signals only for the goods lines.

Contraction of the facilities in the area led to the closure in 1969 of Kentish Town Junction and Kentish Town Sidings boxes, on 16th March and 7th September respectively. Engine Shed Junction took over the functions of Carlton Road Junction and Mortimer Street Junction boxes, both of which were closed on 22nd October 1978. Engine Shed Junction was retained until the

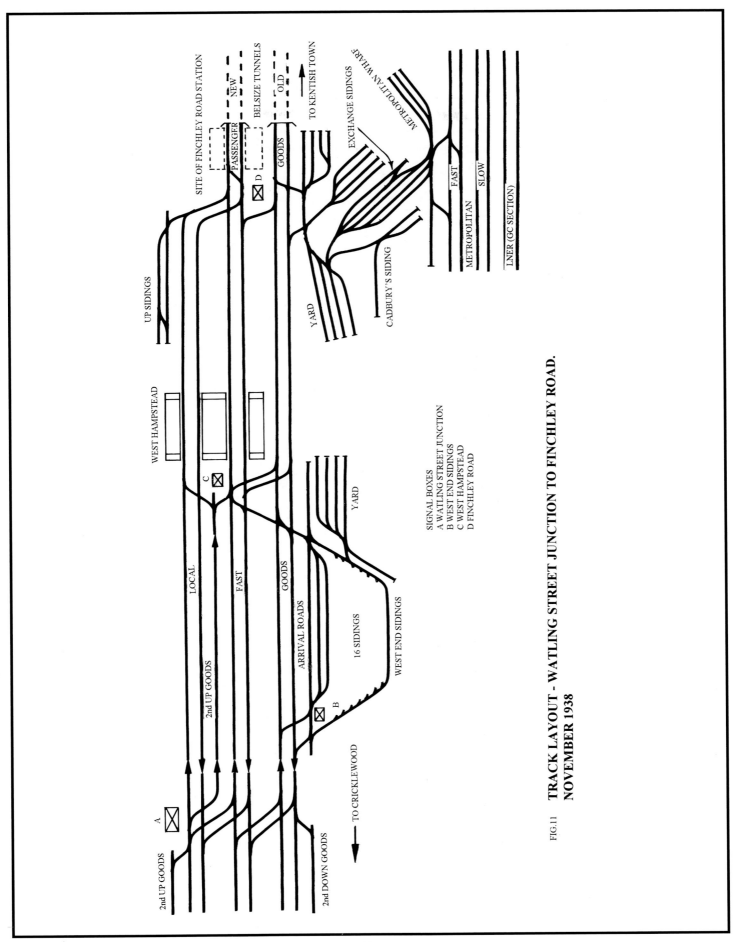

FIG.11   **TRACK LAYOUT - WATLING STREET JUNCTION TO FINCHLEY ROAD. NOVEMBER 1938**

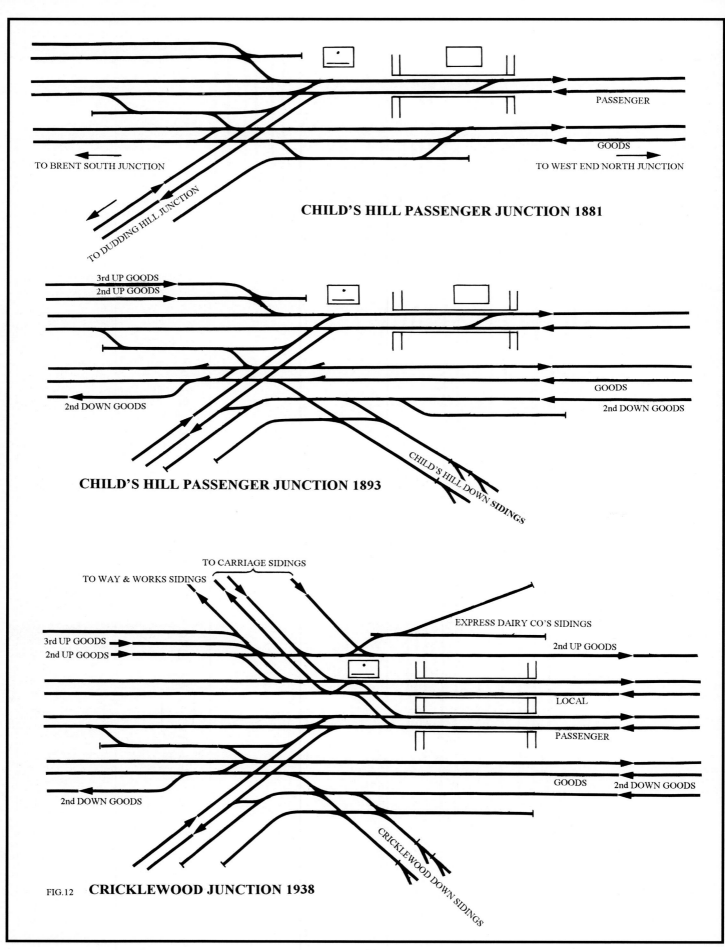

CHILD'S HILL PASSENGER JUNCTION 1881

TO BRENT SOUTH JUNCTION

PASSENGER

GOODS

TO WEST END NORTH JUNCTION

TO DUDDING HILL JUNCTION

3rd UP GOODS
2nd UP GOODS

2nd DOWN GOODS

GOODS

2nd DOWN GOODS

CHILD'S HILL PASSENGER JUNCTION 1893

CHILD'S HILL DOWN SIDINGS

TO CARRIAGE SIDINGS

TO WAY & WORKS SIDINGS

EXPRESS DAIRY CO'S SIDINGS

3rd UP GOODS
2nd UP GOODS

2nd UP GOODS

LOCAL

PASSENGER

GOODS
2nd DOWN GOODS

2nd DOWN GOODS

CRICKLEWOOD DOWN SIDINGS

FIG.12 **CRICKLEWOOD JUNCTION 1938**

Narrowly sandwiched between the running lines, St Paul's Road Goods Junction signalled the junction between the main goods lines and the connections to St Pancras goods station. *A. Vaughan.*

into use and a new Brent South Junction was opened on the east side with signals for all lines. The opening of the local lines from Welsh Harp Junction to Cricklewood Junction on 15th November 1903 resulted in a division of control between two boxes, Brent Junction No.1 for the fast and local lines and Brent Junction No.2 for the slow/goods and Acton lines. During the contraction of facilities prior to electrification, the 1881 situation was largely restored for a short period. Brent Junction No.1 was closed and complete control passed to Brent Junction No.2, which was then known as plain Brent Junction until its closure on 26th April 1981, when the West Hampstead scheme was extended to cover the area.

New up and down local lines were opened between Welsh Harp Junction and Hendon on 29th June 1890 (up) and 13th July 1890 (down). Welsh Harp Junction box had replaced Brent North Junction on the same site on 1st June 1890.

Hendon signal box was located to the north of the station between the fast and goods lines at the commencement of the latter's climb to the flyover where they crossed the fast lines to join the extended local lines at Silk Stream Junction. When the new works were completed in 1891, the box had an east frame of 36 levers (32 working) for the local and fast lines and a west frame of 12 levers (11 working) for the goods lines. A chord line, connecting the fast and goods lines diagonally across the site of Hendon New Sidings, was opened in April 1977. Initially bi-directional, it was signalled for movements in the up direction only when West Hampstead power box took over control in April 1981. In World War 1, a connection just north of the flyover was provided for an aircraft factory at Hendon aerodrome, controlled by Hendon Factory Siding signal box. The connection, facing from the down fast, led to a branch which went part of the way round the aerodrome in an anti-clockwise direction. A simple train staff was

used and speed was limited to 10 m.p.h. The branch was not opened until the last year of the war, on 19th May 1918, so its working life was short. It was officially closed on 29th January 1921.

The goods and local lines were opened to the north of Hendon on 12th October 1890, converging at Silk Stream Junction and continuing to Mill Hill. Silk Stream Junction box had been waiting in readiness since 14th September. Al-

though they were signalled to passenger standards, these lines were confined to freight traffic at first. They were not opened for passenger traffic until 2nd May 1892 (up) and 23rd June 1895 (down).

The original signal box at Mill Hill was on the up side of the line to the north of the station. On the down side, a loading dock and a refuge siding - the latter added in 1881 - survived into the 1960s. The box was replaced on 24th February 1890 on approximately the same site, eventually between the fast and slow lines. Separate frames were installed, at the southwest and northeast corners for the fast and slow lines respectively. Closure came at a comparatively early date, on 22nd December 1968, with intermediate block signals substituted. In the down direction, those for the fast lines were controlled by Hendon and those for the slow lines by Silk Stream Junction.

Scratch Wood Junction was the most southerly example of the temporary signal boxes installed during the widening process. It was first brought into use on 22nd September 1889 with a frame of 24 levers. The new lines of 1890 originally terminated here, to the south of the first Elstree tunnel. During the five years which elapsed before they were extended through the second tunnel on 23rd June 1895, Scratch Wood Junction controlled their connections to the main lines. They had been brought into use from Mill Hill as goods lines on 18th May 1890. On 12th October 1890 they were joined at Mill Hill to the new lines from Hendon and re-designated Slow Passenger Lines. Despite a terminology which specifically included passenger traffic, facing catch points were provided at the end of the new down line at Scratch Wood. However,

Class 3 4-4-0 No. 746 passes Watling Street Junction, a short distance south of Cricklewood, with an up express for St Pancras on 30 July 1913. The up and down goods lines lie to the left of the picture whilst the local lines are situated to the right of the train. *NRM*

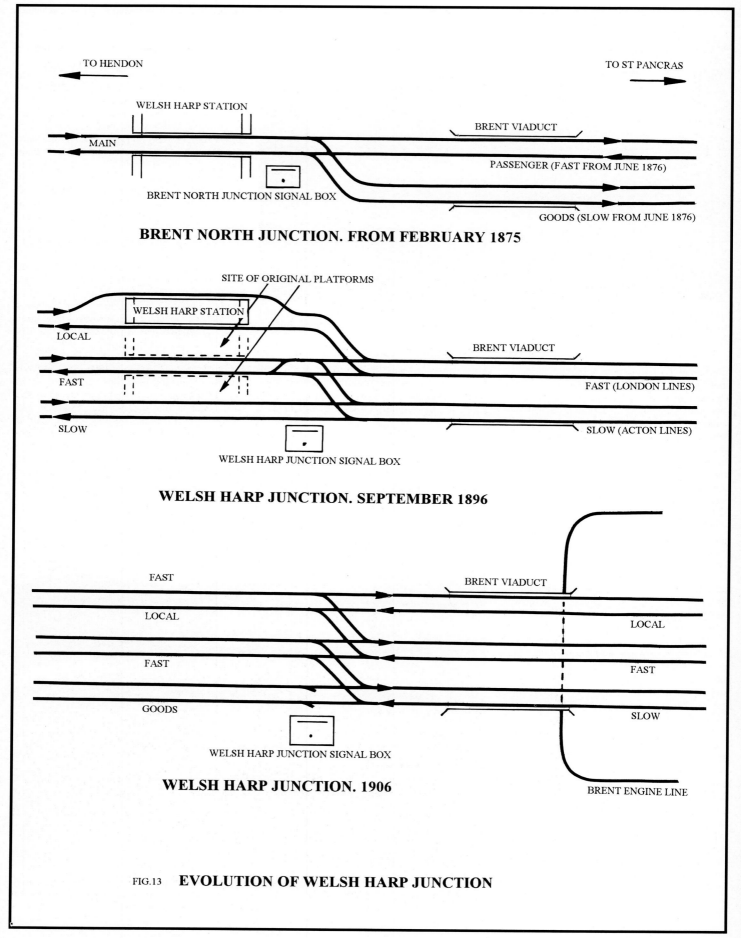

TO HENDON

TO ST PANCRAS

WELSH HARP STATION

BRENT VIADUCT

MAIN

PASSENGER (FAST FROM JUNE 1876)

BRENT NORTH JUNCTION SIGNAL BOX

GOODS (SLOW FROM JUNE 1876)

BRENT NORTH JUNCTION. FROM FEBRUARY 1875

SITE OF ORIGINAL PLATFORMS

WELSH HARP STATION

LOCAL

BRENT VIADUCT

FAST

FAST (LONDON LINES)

SLOW

SLOW (ACTON LINES)

WELSH HARP JUNCTION SIGNAL BOX

WELSH HARP JUNCTION. SEPTEMBER 1896

FAST

BRENT VIADUCT

LOCAL

LOCAL

FAST

FAST

GOODS

SLOW

WELSH HARP JUNCTION SIGNAL BOX

BRENT ENGINE LINE

WELSH HARP JUNCTION. 1906

FIG.13 **EVOLUTION OF WELSH HARP JUNCTION**

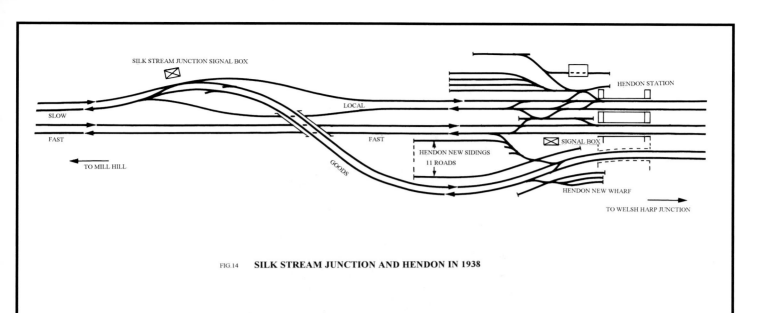

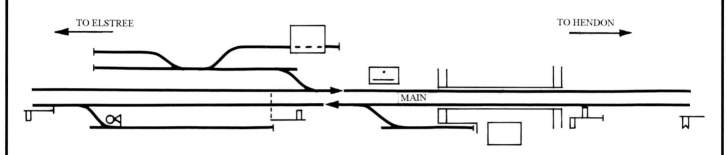

FIG.14   **SILK STREAM JUNCTION AND HENDON IN 1938**

SLOW

FAST

TO MILL HILL

LOCAL

FAST

GOODS

SILK STREAM JUNCTION SIGNAL BOX

HENDON STATION

HENDON NEW SIDINGS
11 ROADS

SIGNAL BOX

HENDON NEW WHARF

TO WELSH HARP JUNCTION

MILL HILL FROM OCTOBER 1881

TO ELSTREE

TO HENDON

MAIN

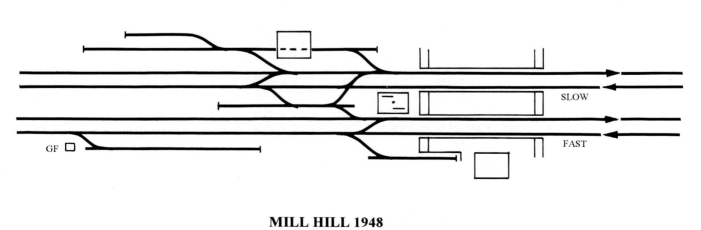

SLOW

FAST

GF

MILL HILL 1948

FIG.15

this line was confined to freight until the second tunnel was opened with the resulting closure of Scratch Wood Junction. The up fast and up fast to up slow splitting distant signals for Scratch Wood Junction were mounted at equal heights on either side of the slightly higher up main starter for Elstree South. This curious configuration, which gave no indication of which was the restricted route, was repeated at about this time at other locations including Harpenden Junction's down fast distants.

Disposal of spoil from the Kentish Town widening was the first function of the sidings at Scratch Wood, at first known as Cloke's Sidings. Later, they became in effect the Extension's rubbish dump. After the closure of the junction box, access from the up slow was controlled by a ground frame. This was replaced in 1897 by Scratchwood Sidings box with additional connections. (Note: Scratchwood was now one word).

An up goods line was opened from Aldenham Junction to Elstree on 1st September 1889, passing between yard and station to join the up main line at the newly opened Elstree South box. The original Elstree box was closed and replaced by Elstree North box at the north end of the yard. A corresponding down goods line was opened between the same two points on 23rd April 1893. As was the case in other instances where the gradient was adverse for loaded coal trains, the first line of the widening to be completed, next to the up main line, tem-

A double-headed express for St Pancras passes Radlett at speed during the early years of the century.

porarily became the up goods. When the second, easternmost, new line was ready, it became the permanent up goods and the first new line was re-opened as the down goods.

When quadrupling in the area was completed, with the opening of the second Elstree tunnel, the new lines were re-designated slow lines and became available for passenger traf-

One of Bedfords compound 4-4-0's, No 41038, passes Napsbury with an up special on 21 July 1950. At the time Bedford had an allocation of eight compounds which, with two inside cylinder 4-4-0's, handled the bulk of the stopping services to St Pancras.

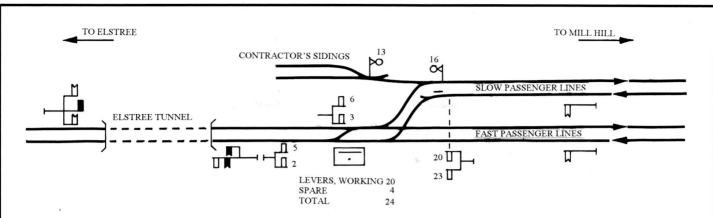

TO ELSTREE

TO MILL HILL

CONTRACTOR'S SIDINGS

13

16

SLOW PASSENGER LINES

6
3

ELSTREE TUNNEL

FAST PASSENGER LINES

5
2

LEVERS, WORKING 20
SPARE   4
TOTAL   24

20
23

SCRATCH WOOD JUNCTION FROM NOVEMBER 1893

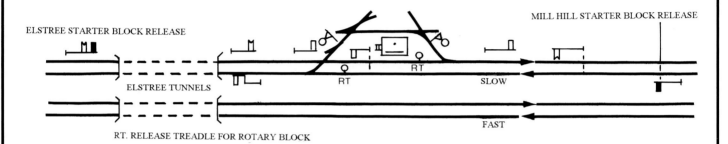

ELSTREE STARTER BLOCK RELEASE

MILL HILL STARTER BLOCK RELEASE

ELSTREE TUNNELS

RT

RT

SLOW

FAST

RT. RELEASE TREADLE FOR ROTARY BLOCK

FIG.16   **SCRATCHWOOD SIDINGS FROM JUNE 1918**

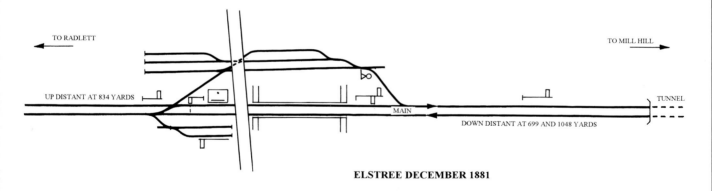

TO RADLETT

TO MILL HILL

UP DISTANT AT 834 YARDS

TUNNEL

MAIN

DOWN DISTANT AT 699 AND 1048 YARDS

ELSTREE DECEMBER 1881

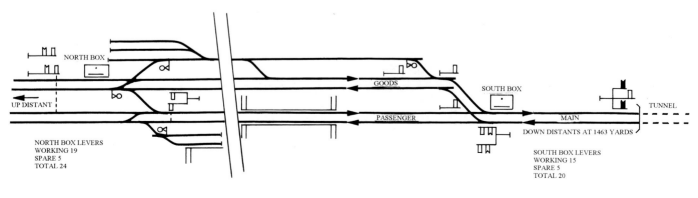

NORTH BOX

GOODS

SOUTH BOX

UP DISTANT

PASSENGER

MAIN

TUNNEL

DOWN DISTANTS AT 1463 YARDS

NORTH BOX LEVERS
WORKING 19
SPARE 5
TOTAL 24

SOUTH BOX LEVERS
WORKING 15
SPARE 5
TOTAL 20

FIG.17   **ELSTREE APRIL 1893**

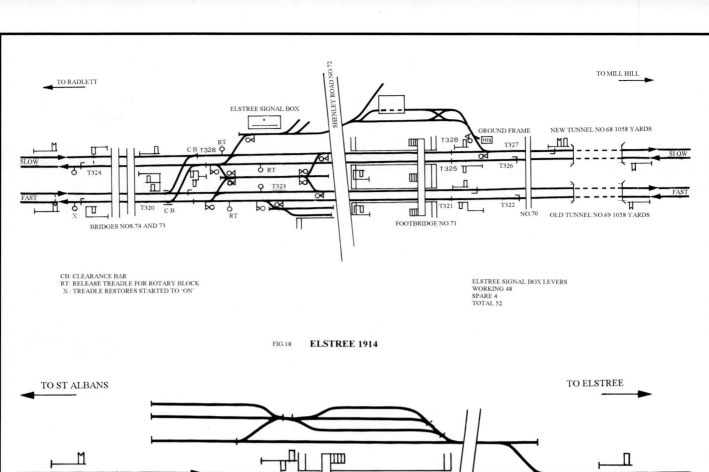

CB: CLEARANCE BAR
RT: RELEASE TREADLE FOR ROTARY BLOCK
X : TREADLE RESTORES STARTED TO 'ON'

ELSTREE SIGNAL BOX LEVERS
WORKING 48
SPARE 4
TOTAL 52

FIG.18   **ELSTREE 1914**

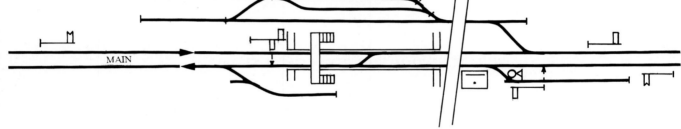

RADLETT OCTOBER 1881

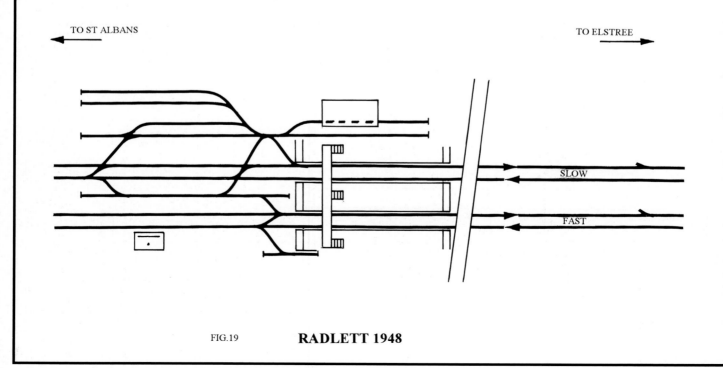

FIG.19   **RADLETT 1948**

Neck and neck. Kentish Town compound 4-4-0 41050 on a down evening semi-fast overhauls Bedford classmate 41009 with a Bedford slow at Napsbury on 4 August 1950. This was the last years in which the Ccompounds could be seen in such large numbers on the Midland, since 1951 saw many of their duties taken over by newly built standard locomotives. *E.D. Bruton.*

fic. Elstree South box was retained after the widening with trailing connections between all four running lines. It also controlled the connection to the south end of the yard. On 2nd November 1913, a double junction was brought into use at the far north end. The South box was then closed and the North box became plain Elstree, extended with a new frame of 52 levers. A ground frame was provided for the southern yard connection.

Final closure of Elstree box came on 2nd December 1979 under Stage 2 of the West Hampstead scheme. This stage also included the closure on the same date of all the remaining boxes northwards from Elstree to St Albans. Aldenham box, a block post about mid-way between Elstree and Radlett, was in existence before 1880. Its 8 lever frame was fully utilised when sidings were laid in 1889 for the widening works. On 1st September 1889, when the new lines to Elstree were opened, Aldenham was replaced by Aldenham Junction, about half a mile north and 79 chains south of Radlett box. The layout of Aldenham Junction resembled that of Scratch Wood Junction but the frame had only 20 levers. Up and down goods lines were opened in one length from St Albans to Aldenham Junction on 3rd June 1894. With four roads now available from St Albans to Elstree, longer sections were practical and Aldenham Junction was closed.

The epitome of the Midland during the last decade or so of steam. 45554 ONTARIO (Nottingham) speeds the twelve coach 06.43 express from Nottingham to St Pancras passed Colney Street, south of St Albans on 18 August 1951. A distinctive feature of the trackwork south of Bedford was the way in which the goods lines were slewed to the right in order to clear the supports of the numerous overbridges. *E.D.Bruton.*

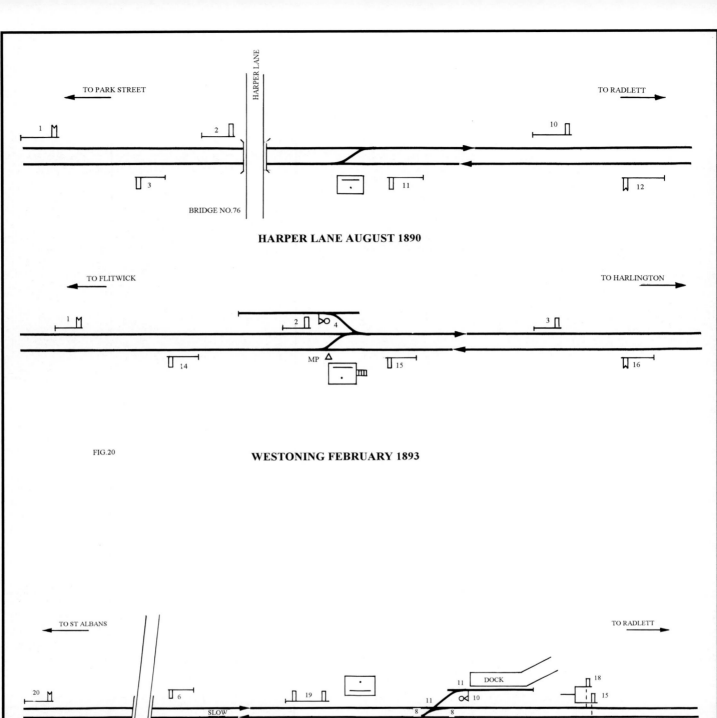

TO PARK STREET

HARPER LANE

TO RADLETT

1

2

3

10

11

12

BRIDGE NO.76

HARPER LANE AUGUST 1890

TO FLITWICK

TO HARLINGTON

1

2

4

3

14

MP

15

16

FIG.20

WESTONING FEBRUARY 1893

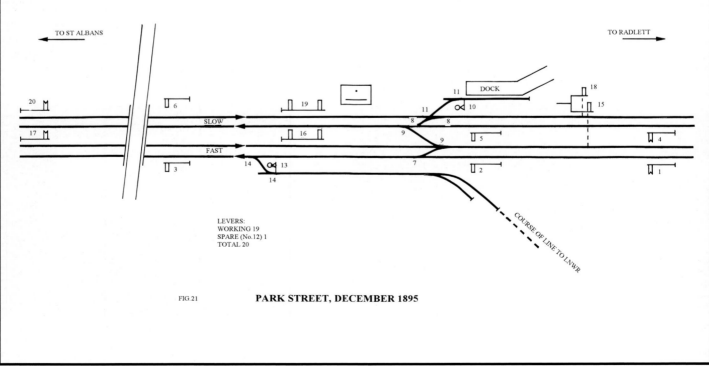

TO ST ALBANS

TO RADLETT

DOCK

20

6

19

11

18

17

11

10

15

8

8

SLOW

16

9

9

5

4

FAST

14

13

7

2

1

3

14

COURSE OF LINE TO LNWR

LEVERS:
WORKING 19
SPARE (No.12) 1
TOTAL 20

FIG.21

PARK STREET, DECEMBER 1895

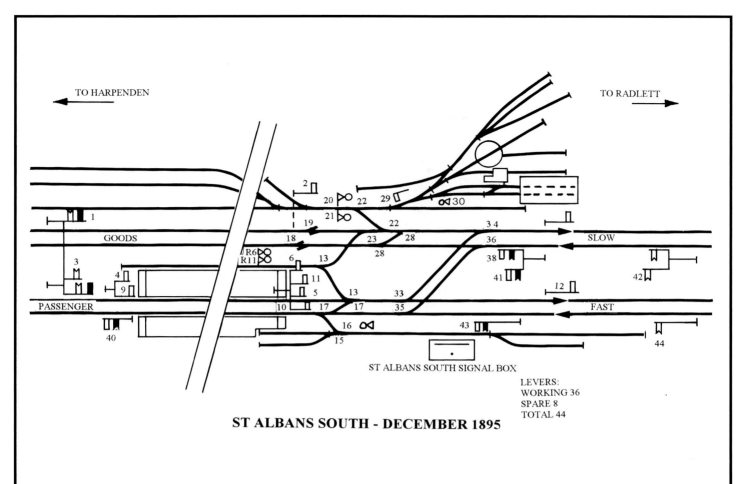

TO HARPENDEN

TO RADLETT

GOODS

PASSENGER

ST ALBANS SOUTH SIGNAL BOX

SLOW

FAST

LEVERS:
WORKING 36
SPARE 8
TOTAL 44

ST ALBANS SOUTH - DECEMBER 1895

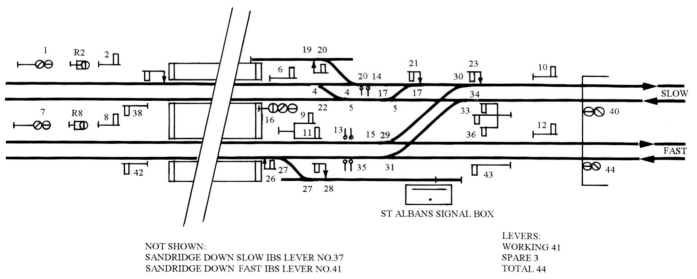

SLOW

FAST

ST ALBANS SIGNAL BOX

NOT SHOWN:
SANDRIDGE DOWN SLOW IBS LEVER NO.37
SANDRIDGE DOWN FAST IBS LEVER NO.41

LEVERS:
WORKING 41
SPARE 3
TOTAL 44

FIG.22   **ST ALBANS - SEPTEMBER 1976**

The only engine shed between the London area and Bedford was the one at St Albans (14C) which had an allocation of about twenty locomotives for working the inner-suburban duties and some local trip workings. Located on the up side to the south of the station it is seen here in 1949 with a freshly coaled 3F 0-6-0 ready for a northbound goods service. *L&GRP.*

The opening of the new lines throughout from St Albans to Aldenham Junction meant that Radlett was never a terminating point for the widening. It therefore saw only one change of layout. Despite this, the signal box, which in 1881 was on the down side to the south of the station, was replaced twice, on 9th November 1890 and 3rd June 1894. The second replacement established the box, still on the down side, well to the north of the station. Drivers of down expresses made best use of the falling gradient from Elstree, the longest stretch in the engine's favour for the first 34 miles. The signalman at Radlett would have had little chance of spotting smoking hot boxes or doors not properly closed as trains passed within a few feet of him at 70 m.p.h. Unusually, in April 1913, a calling-on arm was added below the up slow home signal to permit trains to draw forward to the starter. The home was not lowered unless the starter could be cleared.

A slight hump in the otherwise flat bottom of the Radlett dip takes the line through Harper Lane cutting. Here, about a mile north of Radlett, Harper Lane box was opened on 8th July 1890. Its brick retaining wall, built into the cutting on the down side, still exists. The 12 lever frame controlled distant, home and starter in each direction and a trailing crossover between the main lines, leaving 5 levers spare. The box was closed on 3rd June 1894 when the goods lines were opened.

Parkbury Siding, on the up side near MP 16 3/4, opened in 1894. A trailing connection from the up goods was worked from a stage and protected by home and distant signals. Park Street box was referred to as St Albans Junction during the building of the Extension when the branch from Park Street, LNWR, was in use. A new and larger box was opened here in 1894 to provide for the widened lines. The 20 lever frame controlled trailing connections between all four running lines and the sidings on the down side, including the truncated branch to the LNWR.

Park Street became Napsbury when the station of that name was opened at its site in 1905. The box was moved forward to a new location between the slow lines at the north end of the island platform. A private siding, over quarter of a mile in length, was laid to take coal to Napsbury hospital. Facing connections were brought into use from down fast to down slow, on 14th September 1913, and from up slow to up fast on 8th March 1914. Unusually for that period, splitting distants were not provided.

The first line of the widening to be opened to St Albans was the up goods from Sandridge to the North box on 27th December 1891. Up and down goods lines avoided the station from 12th June 1892. They were extended northwards to Harpenden Junction on 9th October of the same year, incorporating the up goods from Sandridge. On 10th June 1894, a week after the new lines were opened to Aldenham Junction, the double junction at St Albans South, from up passenger to up goods and from down goods to down passenger was brought into use. The down goods home signals had a higher doll for the turn-out to the passenger line than for the straight ahead line; convention was not finally established in these matters. Indications with higher dolls for the turn-outs remained until 1921 at Bedford South (up slow) and Kempston Road Junction (down goods). The goods lines to the south of St Albans were re-designated slow lines from 23rd June 1895. This led to the development of the connections to the back platform line to enable terminating down trains to run straight in. An engine release to the down goods line was controlled from the North box. Eventually the passenger traffic grew sufficiently for the goods lines to Harpenden Junction to be regraded as slow lines on 1st July 1906. Platforms were now provided for all lines at St Albans and an up slow to up fast crossover was added at St Albans South. There was then little further change to the layout until the advent of the DMUs in 1960.

The turn round of terminating DMUs was simplified by the provision of a facing point lock

A study of the down main (No.1) platform at St Albans (City) as passengers join and alight from a St Pancras - Bedford service on 24 May 1947. It is understood that some items from the Ampthill awnings were used to maintain those at St Albans in good condition. *E.D. Bruton.*

A view of the wooden buildings and awning of No.4 platform (up slow line) at St Albans City on 4 April 1954. *E.D. Bruton.*

on the down slow to up slow crossover at St Albans South. This enabled departures to St Pancras to commence from the down slow platform. A three aspect colour light signal was installed to cover this move. The up slow to up fast crossover was removed on 3rd October 1969. Sufficient levers in the 44 lever frame of the South box were thereby freed so that it could take over some of the functions of the North box, the latter closing on 19th December 1970. On 6th May 1973, a facing crossover from down slow to up slow was installed to allow terminating down trains to arrive at the up platform. Their running freedom at the north end was limited by a fixed stop signal, a provision repeated in similar circumstances at Luton and Bedford. St Albans South was plain St Albans from 19th December 1970 but the nameboard was not changed. After closure it became a Grade 2 listed building, although it seems doomed to deteriorate as it presents an obvious target for vandals and graffiti artists. Hopefully, it might yet be removed to receive special care on a preservation site, following the precedents established with Harlington and other Midland boxes.

With steam to spare Garratt 7988 passes Elstree in the late 1940s with an up coal train for Cricklewood. Although the trains hauled were of exceptional length, speed was slow and minutes would elapse before the brake-van passed the photographer. *C.R.L. Coles*

6. SIGNALLING AND TRACK SANDRIDGE TO BEDFORD

Sandridge, the first signal box north of St Albans, had been opened before 1880 to break the otherwise long section to Harpenden. Situated between posts 22 and 22 1/4 it was renewed on the up side of the line on 20th December 1891 to accommodate a 20 lever frame controlling the turn-out to a new up goods line to St Albans which was opened a week later. Within a year, on 9th October 1892, the quadrupling was completed between St Albans and Harpenden Junction with Sandridge acting as a block post for all four lines. Then, on 29th October 1893, the box was moved to a site near MP 21 1/4, still on the up side of the line. There were connections to a "manure siding", although industrial premises, at one time occupied by the Deep Well Boring Co., were served later. From 2nd December 1900, a single facing crossover from up slow to up fast was provided. The box was closed on 14th January 1962 and replaced by intermediate block signals.

A temporary signal box, Wheathampstead, "midway between Harpenden Station and Sandridge", was opened on 26th October 1891. The reference, taken from the Weekly Notice, would have been to the old location of Sandridge, so Wheathampstead was somewhere near MP 23 1/4. Distant, home and starting signals were provided in each direction. There was a co-acting arm for the up home signal. A likely position for Wheathampstead, therefore, was just south of the second overbridge south of Harpenden station. The box was closed on 9th October 1892, after a life of less than a year when the goods lines past its site were opened.

The original Harpenden signal box was situated at the south end of the station. In 1892, it was renewed for the widening with a frame of 32 levers, of which 27 were working. The addi-

Jubilee 5696 ARETHUSA of Derby burns through a layer or two of coal on 14 August 1948 as it storms the 17.32 St Pancras - Nottingham express up Sandridge bank on its 60-minute non-stop run to Bedford. *E.D. Bruton.*

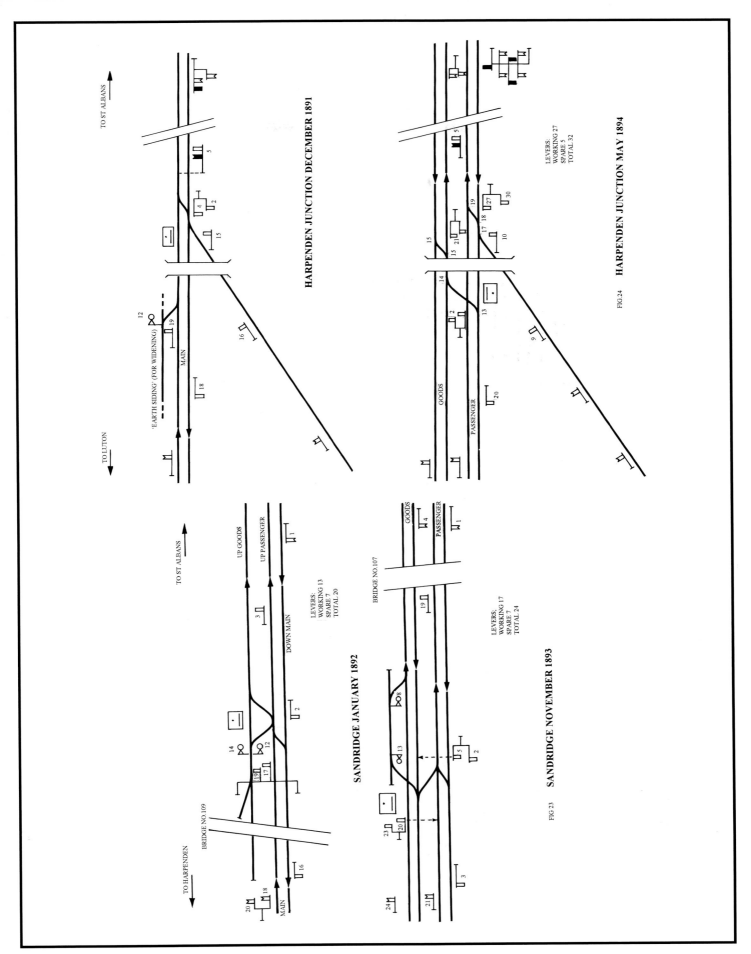

TO ST ALBANS

HARPENDEN JUNCTION DECEMBER 1891

12

'EARTH SIDING' (FOR WIDENING)

MAIN

19

5

4

2

15

16

18

TO LUTON

TO ST ALBANS

HARPENDEN JUNCTION MAY 1894

LEVERS:
WORKING 27
SPARE 5
TOTAL 32

FIG.24

15

15 21

17 18

19

27

30

10

14

2

13

GOODS

PASSENGER

9

20

TO ST ALBANS

UP GOODS

UP PASSENGER

1

3

DOWN MAIN

2

LEVERS:
WORKING 13
SPARE 7
TOTAL 20

SANDRIDGE JANUARY 1892

14

12

19

17

BRIDGE NO.109

TO HARPENDEN

20

18

MAIN

16

BRIDGE NO.107

GOODS

PASSENGER

4

1

19

8

13

5

2

LEVERS:
WORKING 17
SPARE 7
TOTAL 24

SANDRIDGE NOVEMBER 1893

FIG 23

23

20

24

21

3

57

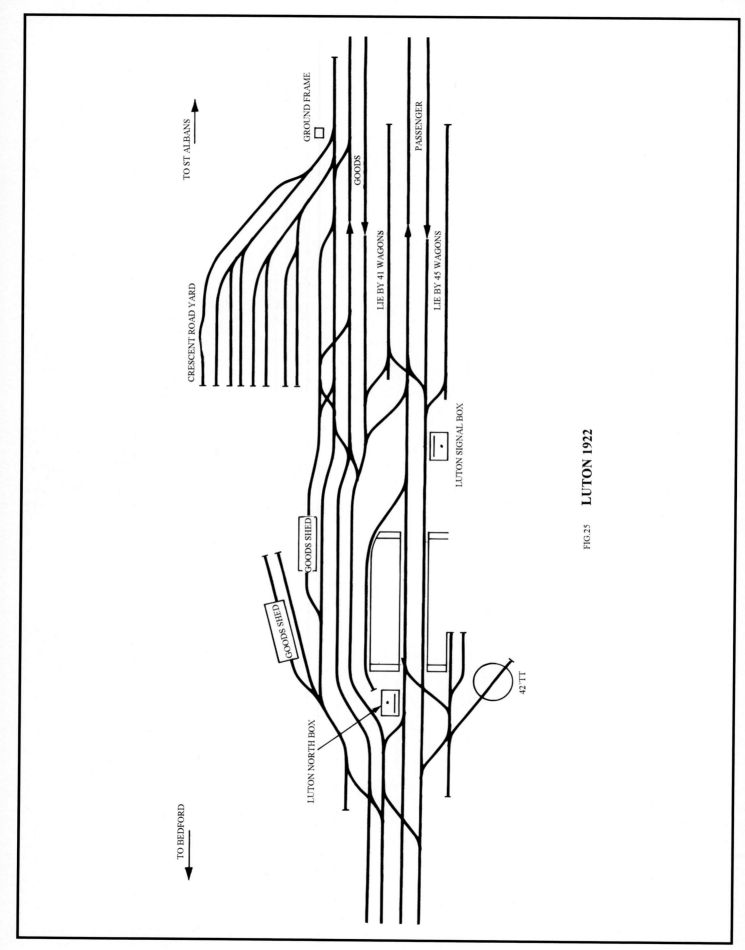

TO ST ALBANS

GROUND FRAME

GOODS

PASSENGER

CRESCENT ROAD YARD

LIE BY 41 WAGONS

LIE BY 45 WAGONS

LUTON SIGNAL BOX

GOODS SHED

GOODS SHED

LUTON NORTH BOX

42'TT

TO BEDFORD

FIG.25   **LUTON 1922**

A rather grimy LMS Compound - 41117 of Kentish Town - hurries a Bedford - St Pancras service through Chiltern Green and over the GNR Hatfield - Luton branch on 28 July 1951. *E.D. Bruton*

tion of a bay on the down side for the Hemel Hempsted train led to the provision of a North box in 1906, the 1892 box then being designated South. On 2nd April 1933, the bay was taken out of use and the North box closed. Harpenden South was replaced by a new structure, Harpenden Station, on the down side in a position which must have been very close to that of the original box of 1868. The down fast to down slow crossover which was previously at the north end, was moved to the south end to be under the control of the new box. West Hampstead took over the duties of all the boxes from Harpenden Station to Luton North inclusive on 21st October 1979.

The 1888 box at Harpenden Junction was situated on the up side of the line. The junction was difficult to protect, the branch from Hemel Hempsted approaching on a steeply falling gradient. Catch points to protect the main line were not acceptable with passenger traffic using the branch, so an early example of an outer home signal was provided at the top of the incline. The Midland nomenclature at that time was home and starter for what later would be known as outer home and home respectively. A new box,

situated in the fork of the junction, was brought into use on 13th March 1892. This had a 32 lever frame to allow for the additional functions required when the goods lines were opened southwards on 9th October 1892. On 22nd April 1894, when the goods lines were extended to Chiltern Green Junction, a new frame, still with 32 levers, was installed. The connection from down goods to down passenger was retained but the corresponding connection from up passenger to up goods was removed. When, in 1906, Harpenden Junction became the northern extremity of passenger working on the slow lines, this junction was reinstated and was afterwards an important feature of day to day traffic working. It was the first location south of Bedford where an up stopping passenger train could be diverted over facing points to allow a following express to overtake.

The comparatively late date of the completion of the goods lines between Harpenden Junction and Chiltern Green Junction reflects the scale of the work necessary on the viaduct at East Hyde. At Chiltern Green Junction, 30 chains south of Chiltern Green Station box, the new lines joined earlier widenings. The up goods had

been extended southwards from Luton on 10th August 1884. As usual, the down goods came later, from Chiltern Green Junction to Luton North by November 1885 and on to Leagrave on 10th November 1889. From 9th October 1892 to 22nd April 1894, there was a bottleneck of two lines only between Harpenden Junction and Chiltern Green Junction, with goods lines open to both north and south. The section was broken by a temporary box, Hyde Mill, during that period. When the gap in the goods lines was eliminated, Chiltern Green Junction and Hyde Mill boxes were closed, on 22nd April 1894, and the final block section became Harpenden Junction to Chiltern Green (the former Station box). Finally, Chiltern Green box was replaced by intermediate block signals on 15th March 1959.

At one time there was an intermediate signal box between Chiltern Green and Luton South. This was Dumhills, on the up side of the line to the south of the present ring road overbridge. It was shown on the Ordnance Survey map of 1879 and was listed in the 1880 Appendix to the WTT. It was probably closed when the up goods was extended past its site in 1884.

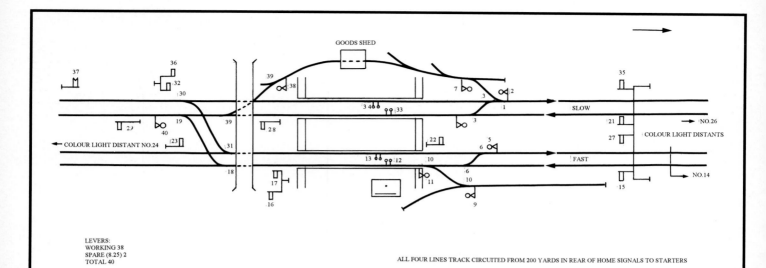

LEVERS:
WORKING 38
SPARE (8.25) 2
TOTAL 40

ALL FOUR LINES TRACK CIRCUITED FROM 200 YARDS IN REAR OF HOME SIGNALS TO STARTERS

FIG.26   **HARLINGTON 1959**

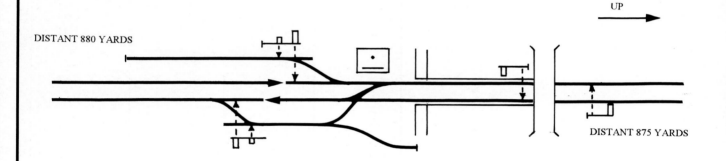

FLITWICK 1873

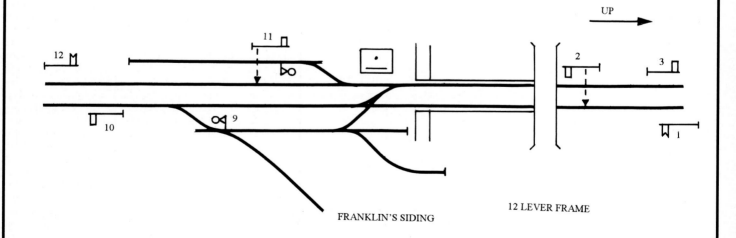

FIG.27   **FLITWICK 1885**

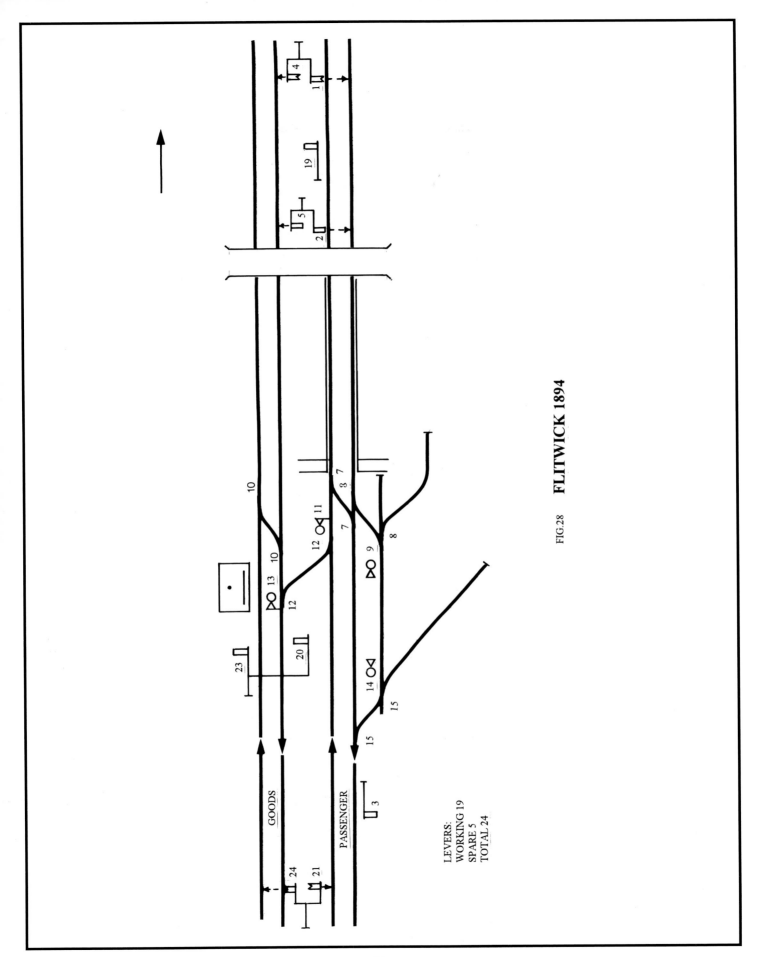

FIG.28   **FLITWICK 1894**

For over twenty years the largest express passenger locomotives to be seen on the Midland were the Stanier 5XP Jubilee 4-6-0's but in 1958 a redistribution of LMR power saw a number of 7P Royal Scot and Britannia engines being drafted to a number of important depots on the line. One of the former, 46142 THE YORK AND LANCASHIRE REGIMENT, passes Luton in March 1961 with a St Pancras - Manchester (Central) express. *Photomatic*

What might be termed the traditional Luton layout remained largely unaltered from the widening to the changes made for the DMUs. Before 1884, however, the Luton boxes were on opposite sides of the line to their later locations. The Ordnance Survey of 1879 shows the North box on the down side and the South box on the up. The 42 ft. 'table could turn the 2-4-0s, long used on terminating trains from St Pancras. It is instructive to consider the complexity of the moves required in order to terminate a down train, turn its engine and have the train with the engine at the London end, in the back platform road ready for its return journey, without over-long occupation of the down platform. Further use was made of the back platform line by up trains from Bedford, some of which terminated in the up main platform to be drawn forward empty and set back into the back platform. There they could be overtaken by an up express before setting out afresh for St Pancras.

Changes were necessary for the DMU service introduced in 1960. The old back platform line became No.3 down through platform line. Terminating down trains could leave again in the up direction and proceed either to the up fast or up slow. Permissive block working was instituted so that DMU sets could arrive independently and be coupled to leave as one train. This fell into disuse due to difficulties with the couplings. In order to permit the closure, on 2nd January 1966, of the Hatfield line between Luton and Blackbridge Sidings, a connection was provided in December 1965 from the Extension at Luton South to the branch at Luton East. This was facing from the up fast line at Luton South with a trailing slip into the down fast. The Eastern Region Luton East box was closed later and Luton South then took control of both ends of the connection. Access, with a necessary reversal, was thereby maintained to the remaining Luton to Dunstable section of the ex-GNR.

The developments of the 1960s involved considerable changes for both the Luton boxes. The South box gained a new frame of 55 levers facing the back of the box. The new No.3 Platform line, the connection to the Dunstable line and control of the intermediate block signals at Chiltern Green fully utilised the frame and there were no spare levers. The North box had a smaller frame of 32 levers and after some ingenuity was exercised in providing all the required functions, one lever remained spare. Lever No.27 released the Limbury Road ground frame, replacing the small Limbury Road box which, from

1915, controlled the entrance at the north end of Limbury Road yard. The points at the south end of the yard from the up goods/slow line were always worked from a ground frame. The latter was released by Limbury Road until its closure and subsequently by Leagrave. Release of the Limbury North ground frame from Luton North involved the co-operation of the Leagrave signalman, to whom Luton North "blocked back" on the up slow line, which had to be crossed by movements to or from the yard.

The first additional running line on the Extension north of Brent was the up goods from Leagrave to Luton, opened on 13th October 1875. Its early provision has had recent repercussions. The chalk subsoil here is so hard that blasting was necessary in the cuttings when the original line was built. After electrification, a section of the down slow line, now on the formation of the 1875 up goods, was plagued by the phenomenon of "roaring rails" to a very marked degree. In situ railgrinding was a temporary palliative, but trial excavations were noted between the sleepers. These appeared to disclose chalk only just below sleeper level, showing that the 1875 line was built on a shallow roadbed. It is probable that the line was then regarded as a goods loop. Combined with difficult subsoil, the result was a formation which is now proving troublesome when called upon to do duty for trains undreamed of 115 years ago.

In 1875, the Leagrave signal box was situated to the south of the up platform. It had a frame of 16 levers. On 6th October 1889, a new box was opened in the more familiar position, south of the station on the down side. On that day, the up goods from Chalton Junction was brought into use, soon to be followed by the down goods from Luton North on 10th November. The latter was extended to Harlington on 3rd August 1890. The first frame in the new Leagrave box had 24 levers. When the quadrupling was complete, a single facing connection was in-

In spite of Stanier standardisation and an influx of BR-designed classes, the old order could be seen at work until the arrival of diesels and as late in the day as March 1958 Johnson 3F 0-6-0 was captured on film as it arrived in Luton with a local goods from the north. 43531 was a Bedford engine. *Photomatic*

stalled from down goods to down passenger. After the further addition of an up goods to up passenger junction, the final refinement of the layout came on 3rd August 1913, when an up passenger to up goods junction was brought into use. A 36 lever frame was then installed, with only one lever spare.

Leagrave gained its new ladder junctions at the end of 1974, a considerable time before the introduction of Stage 3 of the West Hampstead scheme led to the closure of the box, together with all those northwards to Millbrook, on 1st June 1980. Leagrave controlled a partly modernised system in the intervening period. The up homes and starters, re-designated homes 2 and homes 3 respectively, remained as semaphores but all the other signals were colour lights. The new junctions were located some distance north of the station. In the absence of continuous track circuiting, "Guard's tail lamp" telephones were installed on the up platforms so that the signalman could be assured that the sections in rear of the junctions were clear.

By 1880 there were two signal boxes between Leagrave and Harlington. These were Toddington, between mile posts 33 3/4 and 34, and Chorlton. The brick retaining wall for Toddington still exists in the shallow cutting on the down side. Chorlton box was also on the down side, just north of MP 35 1/4. On 20th August 1883, an up goods was opened between Harlington and Chorlton, the latter being promoted to Chorlton Junction. By 1889 it was being referred to as Chalton Junction, in keeping with the present day spelling of the name of the nearby village. Toddington, however, was a mis-

The life-blood of the Midland was the very heavy volume of coal trains which ran to Cricklewood from Wellingborough and Toton and for which the 2-6-6-2 Garretts were designed. New power for these trains arrived in 1955 in the shape of the BR 9F 2-10-0s which, until the end of steam, were a familiar sight, sharing the coal workings with the equally ubiquitous Stanier 8F 2-8-0's. In this view 92109 of Leicester eases its train through Luton en route to Cricklewood. *Photomatic.*

leading choice - the village of that name being over 3 miles distant and north of Chalton - so that the two boxes were in the reverse order of their namesakes in relation to the line. Toddington box had only eight levers. A crossover and siding were added in 1888 in connec-

tion with the widening works. All the levers were then used, in fact there was no down starter at this time - possibly it had been removed to free a lever for the additions. When the siding was incorporated into the new up goods on 6th October 1889, Toddington was no longer required and closed. In the last three months of 1889, a series of possessions of the new line were given to the Engineer. These enabled chalk to be removed from the cuttings for use in forming the new embankments at Silk Stream. The removal of the material also helped to provide space for the fourth line on the eastern side of the formation.

On 17th June 1889, an intermediate siding between Harlington and Chalton Junction was opened. This was Forder's Siding, on the up side between mile posts 35 1/2 and 35 3/4, controlled by a stage released by Harlington. From 5th November 1893 it was known as Forder's Siding South, as there was also from that date a Forder's Siding North, between Harlington and Flitwick. With the quadrupling completed locally, Chalton Junction was demoted to plain Chalton for the last phase of its life as a block post controlling all four roads. It was closed when the stage at Forder's Siding South was replaced by Sundon signal box in 1897. A second siding, to Forder's Sundon Cement Works, was located further south near the site of Chalton box. This siding was controlled by a ground frame released by Sundon. Sundon lost its up fast to up slow junction on 15th June 1969. A week later it ceased to signal the fast lines, final closure coming on 21st July 1974. The connection to the adjoining siding - latterly "Inns Siding" - was severed. From then until the final closure of the Cement Works, the southern ground frame was released by Harlington.

The turn-out at Harlington for the new up goods line to Chorlton Junction in 1883 was con-

With steam to spare the 11.00 Bedford - St Pancras stopping train approaches the summit at Sundon at about 40 mph behind Compound 41048 of Bedford on 19 April 1952. The 11.00 ex Bedford took 119 minutes to reach St Pancras, calling at every intermediate station except Napsbury. It continued to run until dieselisation in 1960, being worked after the retirement of the Compounds by 2-6-4Ts from Bedford MPD. *E.D. Bruton*

A stranger in the camp as Black Five 45067 of Wakefield shed storms past Sundon on an up rugby special from Knottingley on 19 April 1952.
E.D. Bruton

trolled from a signal box at the south end of the up platform. There were 20 levers in the frame, 3 of which were spare. On 3rd August 1890, the down goods from Leagrave was opened on the alignment of the 1883 up goods which now took up its permanent position alongside. The box had been renewed with 32 levers on 20th April 1890 on approximately the same site. The up goods from Flitwick was not opened until 28th October 1894 and the use of the down goods to the north had to await the completion of the changeover at Ampthill tunnel on 28th July 1895. The whole stretch from Harlington to Elstow was then opened. Harlington then lost all its facing points. A replacement 32 lever frame was installed together with a ground frame, released by Annett's key, for the connection at the north end between yard and down goods.

Harlington was one of the chosen locations for the new junctions installed on the Extension in 1913. The connections, down passenger to down goods and up goods to up passenger, were laid on the far side of the road overbridge at the north end of the station and it was therefore necessary to change the site of the signal box. The new structure, with a 40 lever frame facing the back of the box, was built on the down platform. The new arrangements were brought into use on 31st August 1913. Rotary block was installed on the down passenger line from Sundon and the up passenger line from Flitwick. The installation lasted with only detail changes until the end of manual signalling.

North of Harlington, at MP 38, a new brickworks gave rise to a siding from the up main line and a 12 lever signal box, Forder's Siding North, was opened on 5th February 1893. Despite its name, the box should be regarded as a temporary installation pending completion of the widening work. On 28th July 1895, with both goods lines in operation, it was replaced by a ground frame released by Flitwick. An interme-

A study of Ampthill station taken during the Edwardian years, looking north and showing the up and down platforms together with a rather large complement of staff.
J. Parker Collection.

diate signal box, Westoning, had long been established on the down side near MP 38 3/4. When Forder's Siding North was opened it was moved to a new site at MP 39 1/4, still on the down side. The Weekly Notice's "near mile post 39" is rather misleading in this instance. Westoning had a 16 lever frame which still had 7 spare levers after a crossover and siding had been put in for the Engineer. It was closed after less than two years in its new position when the up goods from Flitwick was brought into use on 28th October 1894.

Two early layout diagrams are available for Flitwick. In 1873, the exit signals from the sidings were mounted as subsidiary arms on the same posts as the signals for the adjacent main lines. By 1885, when Franklin's sand siding was added, the down home signal had been re-positioned to the south of the overbridge for better sighting, the down starter was now in advance of the points and the subsidiary arms had been replaced by ground discs. So far as can be ascertained from the diagram, there was nothing to distinguish the signalling from many installations that still existed at country stations a century later. It is possible, however, that in 1885, the distant signals were still of the disc type and had not yet been replaced by semaphores.

Little change would have been incurred when the up goods from Ampthill was brought into use. At Flitwick it was effectively a rearwards extension of the up refuge siding. A new signal box was, however, commissioned in 1894 for the extension of the same line forward to Harlington. A frame of 24 levers (19 working) was installed in the new box, the correct levers (Nos.22 and 6) left spare in the frame for up and down starters to be provided when conversion from goods to slow lines took place 65 years later.

The first Ampthill Station signal box was on the down side. On 20th August 1893, a new box was brought into use on the up side to the south of the station, eventually to be between the passenger and goods lines. When the goods lines through the tunnel were completed, a replacement frame was required. It had 28 levers,

The Cricklewood - Carlisle milk empties north of Ampthill tunnel behind Nottingham Compound 4-4-0 41082. *G.W. Goslin.*

23 of which were working. A 3 lever ground frame, released by Annett's key, controlled the connection to the yard from the down goods at the north end. An unusual feature of Ampthill Station box was the skylight in the hipped roof at the north end. This enabled the signalman to see the arm and backlight of the up passenger home signal which was very close to the box. Without the skylight, arm and light repeaters would have been required.

Ampthill Goods Junction box was situated close to the northern mouth of the tunnel on the up side. The up goods line from Cow Bridge, opened on 25th September 1876, ended here. The down main line distant for Ampthill Goods Junction survived to become a very late example of a disc signal. It was not replaced by a semaphore until 8th August 1889. The new signal shared a post with Ampthill Station's up

main line distant. An unusual arrangement of signals was provided for the up goods line from August 1893, possibly due to sighting difficulties caused by the construction work for the new tunnel. The upper arm was described as applying to trains not stopped and the lower arm, on a short bracket from the main post, applied to trains which had been stopped. The description implied that separate levers were provided for the two arms. Ampthill Goods Junction was closed when the up goods was extended through the old tunnel on 16th June 1895.

Provision of an up goods line was completed as early as 1876 over the whole length of the climb from Bedford to Ampthill tunnel, a forerunner of the present day crawler lanes on motorways. The first section to be opened was from Bedford South to Cow Bridge on 29th May 1876. This was followed by the remainder from Cow Bridge to Ampthill Goods Junction on 25th September 1876, as already noted. For a period after the completion of the new line, the intermediate block posts were Cow Bridge and Wootton. Cow Bridge box was on the down side, immediately north of the underbridge for the LNWR. Until 1891 it had an up passenger to up goods junction. Wootton box was also on the down side, between mile posts $45_{1/2}$ and $45_{3/4}$. It was opposite a small brickworks, the site of which is partially obscured by dumped spoil from the second Ampthill tunnel. It had an up goods to up passenger junction.

A new box, Elstow Junction, between Cow Bridge and Wootton, was opened on 13th August 1893. It controlled the junction to a down goods line which was opened to Kempston Road Junction on that date. Millbrook box was opened on 8th October 1893, at MP $43_{3/4}$ near the end of the long embankment from Wootton. Just over three weeks later, on 30th October it gained an up goods to up passenger junction. The completion of the down goods line resulted in the closure of Cow Bridge and Wootton boxes on 28th July 1895. The block posts between Bedford

Kempston Road Junction looking towards Luton. Its junctions enabled freight trains to avoid Bedford station, using the fast lines. *G.W. Goslin Collection.*

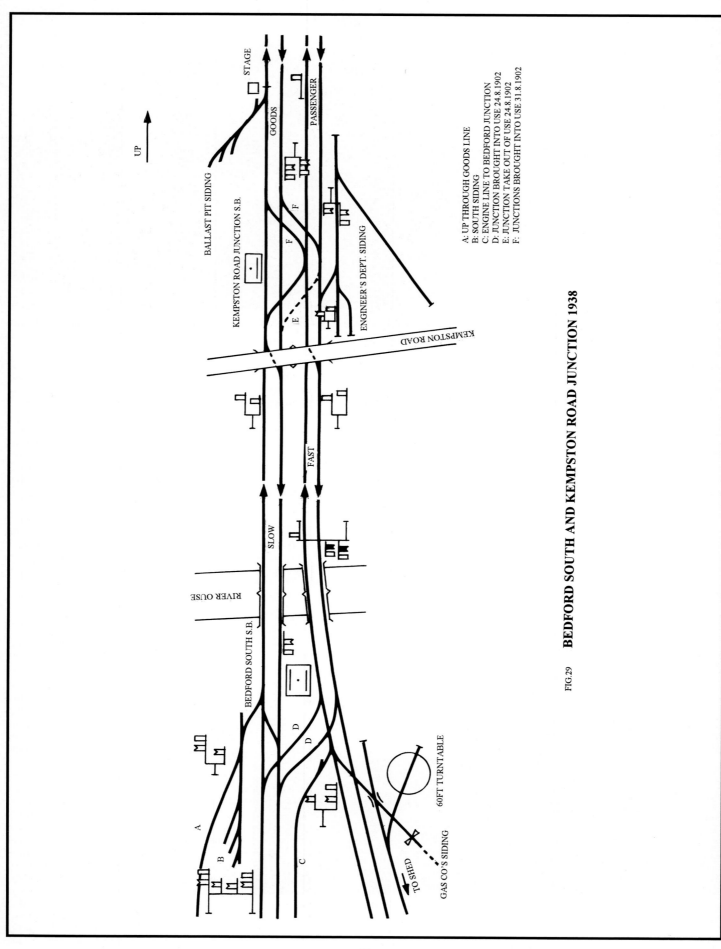

FIG.29   BEDFORD SOUTH AND KEMPSTON ROAD JUNCTION 1938

A: UP THROUGH GOODS LINE
B: SOUTH SIDING
C: ENGINE LINE TO BEDFORD JUNCTION
D: JUNCTION BROUGHT INTO USE 24.8.1902
E: JUNCTION TAKE OUT OF USE 24.8.1902
F: JUNCTIONS BROUGHT INTO USE 31.8.1902

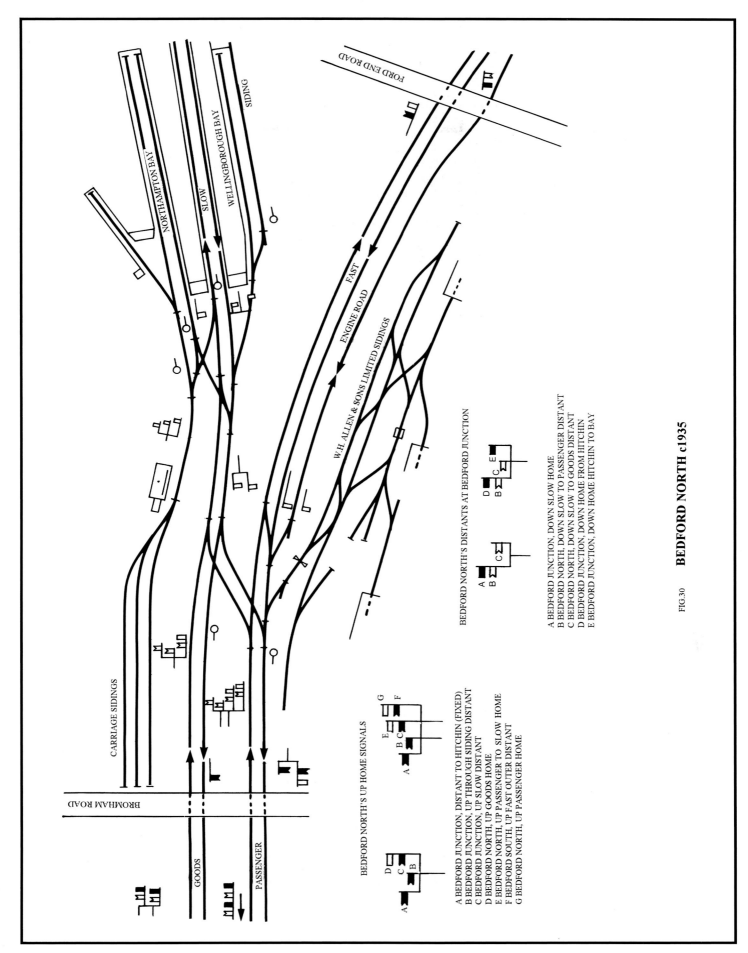

BEDFORD NORTH'S DISTANTS AT BEDFORD JUNCTION

A BEDFORD JUNCTION, DOWN SLOW HOME
B BEDFORD NORTH, DOWN SLOW TO PASSENGER DISTANT
C BEDFORD NORTH, DOWN SLOW TO GOODS DISTANT
D BEDFORD JUNCTION, DOWN HOME FROM HITCHIN
E BEDFORD JUNCTION, DOWN HOME HITCHIN TO BAY

BEDFORD NORTH'S UP HOME SIGNALS

A BEDFORD JUNCTION, DISTANT TO HITCHIN (FIXED)
B BEDFORD JUNCTION, UP THROUGH SIDING DISTANT
C BEDFORD JUNCTION, UP SLOW DISTANT
D BEDFORD NORTH, UP GOODS HOME
E BEDFORD NORTH, UP PASSENGER TO SLOW HOME
F BEDFORD SOUTH, UP FAST OUTER DISTANT
G BEDFORD NORTH, UP PASSENGER HOME

FIG.30   **BEDFORD NORTH c1935**

Stanier 3MT 2-6-2T 40165 sits in the Northampton bay at Bedford during station pilot duties on 3 August 1957. *S. Summerston.*

Inspecting Officer of the B.O.T questioned the necessity of the latter set. They were taken out but the additional space which they had occupied between the junctions remained. This made the layout look somewhat untidy for the rest of the existence of the box. On 30th June 1935, the up goods line from Kempston Road Junction to Millbrook became the up slow line, thereby providing an alternative routing for passenger trains from Bedford when up expresses were running late.

The Millbrook/Elstow section was broken in 1935 when Houghton Conquest box opened, controlling the connection to the Coronation brickworks. Houghton Conquest was on the up side, nearly opposite the site of the old Wootton box. It had a long trailing connection from the up slow line to the sidings on the down side. At the north end, an outlet to the down passenger was controlled by a ground frame. Wilshampstead box, also on the up side, was opened in World War 2 between Houghton Conquest and Elstow. The sorting sidings and passenger station for "Factory 16" were entered from the up slow line at Wilshampstead. Elstow box, which latterly had been reduced to signalling the slow lines only, was closed on 5th November 1961. Wilshampstead followed on 9th September 1968 but Houghton Conquest soldiered on until 16th April 1973. For the next seven years, the block section was Kempston Road Junction to Millbrook, a length of nearly 5 1/2 miles, illustrative of the low ebb then reached by the line.

South and Ampthill then became Kempston Road Junction, Elstow Junction and Millbrook. On 4th October 1896 the facing connection from the down passenger at Elstow Junction was taken out of use and the box lost the title of "junction". It remained a useful block post, in fact the section southwards to Millbrook was rather long at just over 3 1/2 miles. Millbrook was provided with a down passenger to down goods junction on 17th August 1913, the frame being extended to 30 levers with 28 working. In addition to catch points in the down goods which protected both junctions, an additional set was installed between the up and down junctions. The

A 4-4-2 brings an up stopping train round the sinuous northern approach to Bedford around 1900. In the foreground the exit from the Northampton bay is still laid with inside keyed permanent way. The lifting bar for the facing point lock is perforce fitted on the outside of the rails. *NRM.*

2-4-0 No.1481 (231 post-1907) in the Wellingborough bay at Bedford. The site on which the engine stands is now about the centre of the present No.3 platform. *NRM*

Kempston Road Junction box was opened on 9th July 1893. When the Bedford Curve was opened, Kempston Road Junction was provided with a double junction, down fast to down slow and up slow to up fast, at that time the only connections between Bedford station and the passenger lines to the south. On 24th August 1902, similar connections were brought into use at Bedford South. Kempston Road Junction lost its down fast to down slow junction on the same day. The new connection at Bedford South was about quarter of a mile nearer the station and braking could be later. The actual junction was rather inelegant, the right handed turn-out being situated on what had become a pronounced left handed curve for the fast line. Nevertheless, careful laying out of the junction and good maintenance enabled the speed restriction for trains stopping at Bedford to be 20 m.p.h. The retained up slow to up fast junction at Kempston Road was sometimes used by up passenger trains from Bedford station. The preferred junction for turning them out on to the up fast was at Bedford South. This was close enough to the station to avoid a slackening of effort, at least until the advent of the Stanier 4-6-0s. Their accelerative capabilities required an easing even at Bedford South, but the more dignified acceleration of Midland engines only needed steam shutting off momentarily if they were turned out at Kempston Road. The deciding factor for which junction was used was whether Bedford South had accepted a freight on the up fast line. If so, the passenger was kept on the slow line to Kempston Road to preserve the freight's 440 yards overrun. On 31st August 1902, one week after the opening of the connections at Bedford South, Kempston Road Junction was provided with down goods to down passenger and up passenger to up goods junctions. These were much used by freight trains using the Bedford Curve to avoid the station.

Immediately behind Kempston Road Junction box was the Firtree firelighter factory. Here scrap timber was sawn up and then impregnated with grease. A tall thin chimney belched black smoke intermittently. All the ingredients for a spectacular conflagration were present and inevitably it occurred. The fire brigade attended and Kempston Road bridge made a fine grand-

stand for onlookers. The local press made much of the heroic signalman who stuck to his post and prevented disaster etc., etc. The truth was slightly different - the bobby was only too keen to bale out. But this was not in accordance with the wishes of the inspector who was watching the situation from a safe distance and each time he tried to leave the box the firemen drove him back with a spray on the door from the hose.

In the 1880s, the up goods loop from Bedford Junction to Bedford South was extended into the up goods line which continued southwards. With only one double line bridge available across the Ouse, the solution originally adopted at Belsize tunnel was repeated. The up goods was interlaced with the up main line to cross the river. This arrangement lasted until the rebuilding of the bridge in 1893. After the completion of the Bedford Curve and the accompanying changes in the next year, the goods loop from Bedford Junction became known as the up through siding and saw little use for through traffic.

Bedford Junction box was situated in the fork between the Hitchin and Extension lines. At the height of the fashion for splitting distants, they were duly provided for Bedford Junction's up through siding home signal, despite the 6 m.p.h restriction on that line. They were on low dolls on the brackets of Bedford North's up goods and passenger home signals. To their immediate left, on slightly higher dolls, were fixed splitting distants for the Hitchin branch. Bedford seemed to sprout splitting distants. Many of them saw little or no use but much complexity in wire runs and slotting was involved. A typical example, added in 1913, was Kempston Road Junction's distant on Bedford South's up slow home gantry, applicable to a train turned out from up slow to up fast at Bedford South and turned in again a few hundred yards later to the up goods at Kempston Road Junction! By the late 1930s the cost of maintaining such signals was being counted and in many locations the distants were rationalised to one arm, cleared only for the least restricted route.

Bedford South box was renewed when the new bridge over the Ouse was opened on 30th July 1893. The old box had been situated close

to the river on the up side of the line. Its replacement was on a site opposite, between fast and slow lines. It was an unusual structure, two standard boxes back to back, with a frame in each. A spacing section was interposed to bring the frontages close to the lines concerned. A single large roof covered the whole assembly. The connection from the new engine shed of 1887 was a single line about 250 yards long which trailed into the up main line at Bedford South. Another line of the same length trailed from the down main line at Bedford Junction to the gas works siding. At its far end, a wagon turntable gave the necessary change of direction through a right angle to reach the works. The shed and gas works lines crossed at about one third of their respective lengths from the main lines.

When the Bedford Curve was opened, a new exit road from the now completed locomotive depot and a direct connection to the gas works siding were both provided at Bedford South. A second connection to the shed was available at the new Bedford Central box, midway along the curve. A replacement box at Bedford North was opened on the same day, 7th October 1894, as Bedford Central box and the new curve. It controlled the north end of the station, including the double junction formed by the new fast lines and the previous divergence of passenger and slow lines from the pair through the station. On 2nd June 1930, Bedford Central box was closed. The connection to the shed was maintained by the provision of a long engine line from Bedford North.

In 1978, a temporary flat roofed replacement took over at Bedford North. It had a miniature lever frame with electric locking which could cope with the alterations and additional functions which were required during the changeover to the new station and layout.

The advancing boundary of the West Hampstead scheme led to the closure of Kempston Road Junction and the other two remaining local boxes, Bedford Junction and Bedford North, on 2nd November 1980.

7: PRE-ELECTRIFICATION TRAIN SERVICES

The appearance of Stanier 5MT 45253 (Kentish Town) on the 09.15 St Pancras - Edinburgh 'Waverley' suggests a power shortage since Jubilee 4-6-0's were the usual choice for the principal expresses on the Midland. *G.W.G. Collection*

In pre-railway days, the complex and well established system of coaches provided, at least in the context of the times, a comparatively good service for the towns later served by the Extension. Once a railway was built, however, the coaches were no match for even the earliest and most primitive of passenger train services. St Albans, at the confluence of Watling Street with the route from London to the north via Barnet, Luton, Bedford and Leicester was specially favoured by the road network. The 'Peahen' corner must have been a paradise for coach spotters, if such a genus existed, for in 1826 no less than 72 coaches passed each day.

Details in Alan Bates's *Directory of Stage Coach Services, 1836* show that Luton was the terminal for two coach services - A Bryan's 'The Times' left Luton at 8.0 a.m each day for London via St Albans and Barnet, returning from the 'Golden Lion' in St Johns Street at 5.0 p.m, the journey taking 4 hours. 'The Industry', owned by T Finch, left London from 'The Saracens Head' in Friday Street at 11.0 a.m on Mondays, Wednesdays and Fridays for Luton via Hatfield and Wheathampstead, returning from Luton at the same time on Tuesdays, Thursdays and Saturdays. The time on the journey was 6 hours.

The Ampthill coach, run by W Smith & Co., left at 9.0 a.m on Mondays, Wednesdays and Fridays for London via Silsoe, Luton, St Albans and Edgware, returning from 'The Three Cups' in Aldersgate Street on Tuesdays, Thursdays and Saturdays at 2.0 p.m with a 6 hour journey time.

Bedford's own coach, 'The Times', left 'The Swan Hotel' at 8.30 a.m for London via Shefford, Hitchin and Hatfield, returning from the 'George and Blue Boar' in Holborn at 2.0 p.m. The journey took 5 hours each way. Accommodation was provided for 4 inside and 11 outside passengers.

The first contact of Bedford with a railway service came in 1838 when the London & Birmingham was opened from Euston as far as Denbigh Hall bridge on Watling Street, just north of Bletchley. A daily coach service in connection was established between Bedford and Leighton (later Leighton Buzzard). When the London & Birmingham was opened throughout, the coach was diverted to Wolverton. The major breakthrough occurred on Tuesday 17th November 1846, with the opening of the Bedford & London & Birmingham Railway (The Bedford Railway) from Bletchley to Bedford. Connections at Bletchley provided four services per day in each direction. The best journey times between Bedford and Euston approximated to two and a half hours. 'The Times' coach could not offer effective competition and ceased operations, leaving Bedford for the last time on Saturday 21st November 1846.

On 8th August 1850, the Great Northern Railway was opened from King's Cross to Peterborough. At Sandy it was less than 9 miles from Bedford. The combined road and rail journey from Bedford to King's Cross was 9 miles shorter than the railway to Euston via Bletchley but the slower speed of the road portion made the overall journey time longer. Nevertheless,

Fairburn 4MT 2-6-4T 42237 of Kentish Town gives a helping hand to a down express as far as Cambridge Street on 19 May 1961. *R.A. Panting.*

Although the 3MT 2-6-2 tanks were generally considered rather poor tools, they were regularly seen at the London end of the extension and played a dominant role in the working of the Moorgate - St Albans stopping trains. In this view one of the condensing variety, 25 of Cricklewood, is seen approaching Elstree on 22 May 1948 a the head of a stopping train formed of early LMS non-corridor stock. *F.M. Gates.*

in 1855, an omnibus made two return journeys per day from the 'Red Lion' in Bedford High Street to connect with Great Northern trains at Sandy. When the Leicester to Hitchin section of the Midland was opened to passengers on 8th

May 1857, Bedford was provided with its shortest ever route to London, almost exactly 48 miles, nearly 2 miles shorter than the later Extension. Conditions were not ideal at first. The GNR did not agree to through bookings and it was neces-

sary to re-book at Hitchin when changing trains. Use of the LNWR station at Bedford involved a reversal for all trains over the sharp connecting curve. Overall times ranged from a best of 1 hour 47 minutes to a slowest of 2 hours 35 minutes. Four up and three down services were provided, the first Midland down train, at 6.0 a.m from Hitchin, lacking a connection from King's Cross.

Midland trains commenced to run through to King's Cross on 1st February 1858 and exactly one year later the Midland station at Bedford was opened. The GNR agreed to through running on condition that local traffic between Hitchin and King's Cross was not carried by the Midland trains. This was of benefit to Bedford travellers. Apart from the services which stopped at the intermediate stations north of Hitchin, all trains ran non-stop to Bedford. By January 1868, towards the end of the King's Cross workings, the number of passenger trains in each direction south of Bedford had risen to 10. Of these, 4 up trains stopped at stations between Bedford and Hitchin, continuing to King's Cross. There were 5 non-stop trains from Bedford to King's Cross taking between 65 and 73 minutes for the journey. The tenth train was the 6.15 p.m from Leicester, non-stop from Wellingborough at 7.0 p.m, passing Bedford at 7.21 p.m and arriving at King's Cross at 8.30 p.m. In the down direction, Bedford had 6 non-stops from King's Cross in times ranging from 62 to 65 minutes. At some later periods, Bedford passengers might well have looked wistfully at the last pre-Extension timetable.

The same engine two years later, renumbered 40025 but still displaying LMS insignia. The train concerned is the 19.00 St Pancras to St Albans which is seen passing Napsbury on 21 July 1951. *E.D. Bruton*

A very grimy 1P 0-4-4 tank poses at the south end of Bedford Midland Road. Renumbered 58039 by British Railways, 1272 was an early casualty of nationalisation, its duties being taken over by new Ivatt 2MT 2-6-2T's which not only monopolised the Hitchin and Northampton workings but also took over the Bedford (St Johns) - Bletchley motor trains. *J. Osgood.*

stations to Hendon, then Kentish Town and all stations to Moorgate Street, arr. 9.23 a.m.From Bedford to Moorgate Street: 8.45 a.m, 12.12 p.m, 3.7 p.m, 5.35 p.m and 7.05 p.m. Trains stopped at all stations except the 3.7 p.m which passed Chiltern Green, Radlett and Mill Hill.

DOWN
From Luton to Bedford: 7.35 a.m, all stations. From Moorgate Street to Bedford: 9.10 a.m, 1.22 p.m, 4.16 p.m and 7.10 p.m. Trains stopped at all stations except the 4.16 p.m which passed Mill Hill, Radlett and Chiltern Green.From Moorgate Street to Luton: 5.10 p.m and 8.33 p.m, stopping at all stations.

Trains took 140 minutes in each direction between Bedford and Moorgate Street, reduced to 129 minutes for the 3.7 p.m up and the 4.16 p.m down. The most interesting feature of this service is the commencement in the morning of two trains from Luton and their termination there in the evening. There is no evidence in the WTT of light engine or empty carriage workings. Although the "engine houses" were sited at St Albans and Bedford they were probably incomplete at this time. Certainly the turntables had not been installed two months previously when Lt. Col. Rich made his inspection and an estimate for the turntable foundation at Bedford was approved by the Way and Works Committee as late as 1st September 1868. Condensing tank engines had to work the trains between Kentish Town and Moorgate Street. However, no allowance appears to have been made in the WTT for any additional time required for engine changing at Kentish Town. It appears probable, therefore, that, despite their limited coal and water capacity, the condensing tanks worked the ini-

Luton had to wait longer than Bedford for a rail service. Although Dunstable was connected to Leighton as early as 1st June 1848, it was nearly ten years later that the short link to Luton was completed by the Luton Dunstable and Welwyn Junction Railway. The name of the line had been changed to the Hertford Luton and Dunstable by the time the eastern portion to join the GNR at Welwyn Junction was opened on 1st September 1860. In 1864 there were 6 up and 7 down trains between Luton and Hatfield. The single line and heavy gradients of the branch were operating disadvantages, but best Luton/King's Cross times of 71 minutes up and 80 minutes down were not outclassed by the initial stopping services of the Extension. Once the Midland had commenced to run fast trains to St Pancras, the GNR was left with London traffic only from Dunstable and the intermediate stations south of Luton. Through business trains ran from Dunstable for many years; in 1923, the first year of the LNER, the time to King's Cross was 85 minutes from Dunstable(LNE). St Albans was joined to the railway network when the LNWR branch from Watford was opened on 5th May 1858. A branch from the GNR at Hatfield was opened to a station at London Road on 16th October 1865. Passenger trains were extended to the LNWR station in the next year. After working the Hatfield to St Albans branch from the outset, the GNR absorbed it in 1883. A third GNR branch, that to Edgware, was crossed by the Extension at Mill Hill. As with the two St Albans branches, its effect on the passenger traffic ultimately obtained by the Extension was negligible. The timetable for the first Bedford/Moorgate Street passenger service which com-

menced on 13th July 1868 was arranged as follows:-

UP
From Luton to Moorgate Street: 8.05 a.m, all

Johnson 1P 0-4-4T 1377 pauses between pilot duties at St Pancras circa 1930. This engine was destined to travel far and spent most of its post-war years at distant Gloucester where, as 58071, it was a regular performer on the Tewkesbury branch. *C.R.L. Coles.*

tial service throughout from Bedford to Moorgate Street and that two were temporarily stabled overnight at Luton, possibly using a engine pit installed by the Contractor for his own locomotives.

The opening of St Pancras (without ceremony) on 1st October 1868 saw the final cessation of Midland passenger services to King's Cross. Initially the timings over the Extension did not compare favourably with those which had been current over the slightly shorter GNR route. All down trains from St Pancras stopped at Kentish Town, the best time to Bedford was made by the 9.0 a.m and the 3.0 p.m from St Pancras, 68 minutes overall and 62 minutes from Kentish Town. The Mail now left St Pancras at 8.35 p.m, compared with 8.48 p.m from King's Cross. With stops at St Albans and Luton, the Bedford arrival was at 9.51 p.m, one minute later than previously.

By 1883, the passenger services on the Extension had settled down to a pattern which persisted with little change for the remainder of the nineteenth century. The Settle and Carlisle line was by then well established. Bedford reaped an indirect benefit, two overnight trains from Scotland making stops and providing excellent morning services to London at 6.41 a.m, and 7.25 a.m(MX). The St Pancras arrivals were at 7.45 a.m and 8.30 a.m. There were two morning trains from north of Hendon. The 7.17 a.m from Luton, all stations to Hendon except Chiltern Green, then Kentish Town, arrived at St Pancras at 8.24 a.m. This was followed by the 7.0 a.m from Bedford, all stations to Mill Hill, then Kentish Town, arriving at St Pancras at 9.0 a.m. Three early trains to Moorgate Street commenced their journeys at Hendon at 6.50 a.m, 7.54 a.m and 8.29 a.m, stopping at all stations and taking 34 or 35 minutes.

Most of the morning trains to St Pancras or the City branch originated on the T&HJ. 8 trains from South Tottenham reached Kentish Town between 8.0 a.m and 9.0 a.m. and of these, two were destined for St Pancras, one for Victoria via Ludgate Hill and five for Moorgate Street. With two of the trains from Hendon and the 7.0 a.m from Bedford, Kentish Town had eleven up trains stopping in the peak hour from 8.0 a.m to

WEEKDAY MOVEMENTS(MORNINGS). BEDFORD (M.RD) 1957/8				
Train	Arrive	Depart	Destination	Route
21.20 Bradford F.Square	03.54	04.02	St Pancras (05.15)	Derby
00.05 Manchester Central	04.56	05.12	St Pancras (06.40)	Derby
04.20 St Pancras	05.36	05.42	Manchester Central (09.46)	Derby
		05.45	St Pancras (07.13)	
		06.12	Hitchin (06.59)	
		06.25	St Pancras (07.59)	
		06.38	Northampton (07.22)	
		07.00	Luton (07.41)	
		07.23	St Pancras (08.38)	
		07.32	Northampton (08.22)	
		07.35	St Pancras (09.05)	
05.55 St Pancras	07.49			
07.05 Kettering	07.50	07.55	St Pancras (09.11)	
07.30 Hitchin	08.05			
		08.09	St Pancras (09.42)	
21.45 Edinburgh Waverley	08/15		St Pancras (09.20)	Nottingham
06.20 St Pancras	08.15	08.18	Wellingborough	
07.51 Northampton	08.37			
07.00 St Pancras	08.38			
06.18 Derby		08/40	St pancras (09.30)	Nottingham
		08.43	Hitchin (09.20)	
07.55 St Pancras		08/50	Manchester Central (11.45)	
07.42 Leicester	08.48	08.51	St Pancras (09.50)	
08.26 Leicester		09/15	St Pancras (10.05)	
07.05 Sheffield		09/28	St Pancras (10.18)	Derby
08.15 Nottingham		09/35	St Pancras (10.25)	Melton
08.00 St Pancras	09.52			
08.15 St Pancras	09.21	09.23	Nottingham (11.09)	Leicester
09.15 St Pancras		10/04	Edinburgh Waverley (18.52)	Nottingham
09.35 Hitchin	10.11			
08.20 Nottingham	10.12	10.15	St Pancras (11.07)	Melton
07.25 Manchester Central		10/25	St Pancras (11.15)	Derby
09.20 St Pancras	10.32	10.36	Leicester (11.43)	
08.34 Sheffield		10/50	St Pancras (11.42)	Trent
		11.00	St Pancras (12.55)	
10.15 St Pancras		11/04	Glasgow St Enoch (19.46)	Trent
10.25 Northampton	11.05			
10.25 St Pancras		11/21	Manchester Central (14.31)	Derby
10.05 Leicester	11.25	11.28	St Pancras (12.40)	
09.55 St Pancras	11.46			
07.20 Bradford F.Square	11.49	11.51	St Pancras (12.50)	Nottingham

9.0 a.m. All these, and two non-stopping trains in addition, had to share one up passenger line from Kentish Town Junction through Kentish Town and Camden Road stations to St Paul's Road Passenger Junction.

The Victoria service was circuitous, but at the time, long before electric trams and motor buses offered competition, it was a useful facility for Londoners. The timing of the 12.10 p.m LCDR train from Finchley Road to Victoria with its 16 intermediate stops was typical - Finchley Road dep.12.10 p.m, Haverstock Hill 12.14, Kentish Town 12.19, Camden Road 12.21, King's Cross Metropolitan 12.26, Farringdon Street 12.30, Snow Hill 12.32, Ludgate Hill arr.12.35 dep.12.36, Elephant & Castle 12.40, Walworth Road 12.43, Camberwell New Road 12.46, Loughborough Junction 12.49, Brixton 12.52, Clapham 12.55, Wandsworth Road 12.57, Battersea Park 1.0, Grosvenor Road 1.4 Victoria arr.1.7 p.m. Stopping trains on the Extension north of Hendon were not frequent in 1883.

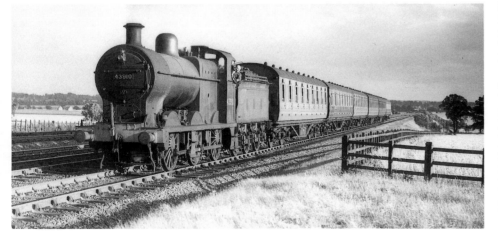

Whether the crew are looking at the photographer or watching out for hot axleboxes is not certain although a spell on a 50-mile passenger working for a 4F 0-6-0 involved higher speeds than the class was used to. 43910 passes Napsbury with a Bedford-bound stopping train on 21 July 1950. *E.D. Bruton.*

WEEKDAY MOVEMENTS (AFTERNOONS). BEDFORD (M.RD) 1957/8

Train	Arrive	Depart	Destination	Route
08.55 Manchester Central		12/10	St Pancras (13.00)	Derby
11.15 St Pancras	12.26	12.30	Leicester (13.48)	
08.55 Bradford F.Square		12/55	St Pancras (13.47)	Nottingham
12.15 St Pancras		13/04	Bradford F.Square (17.00)	Trent
12.25 St Pancras		13/14	Manchester Central (16.31)	Derby
10.25 Manchester Central		13/25	St Pancras (14.15)	Derby
		13.30	Northampton (14.15)	
		13.35	St Pancras (15.08)	
13.10 Luton	13.45			
		13.55	Hitchin (14.29)	
12.55 St Pancras	14.02	14.05	Leicester (15.23)	
12.00 Nottingham	14.14	14.16	St Pancras (15.18)	Trent
10.40 Bradford F.Square		14/53	St Pancras (15.43)	Nottingham
14.15 St Pancras		15/04	Bradford F.Square (19.17)	Nottingham
		15.05	St Pancras (16.30)	
14.25 St Pancras		15/14	Manchester Central (18.09)	
14.42 Kettering	15.28			
14.20 St Pancras	15.36	15.42	Leicester (17.18)	
15.08 Northampton	15.53			
12.00 Bradford F. Square	16.05	16.07	St Pancras (16.57)	Derby
15.15 St Pancras		16/11	Bradford F.Square (20.19)	Nottingham
		16.15	St Pancras (17.38)	
15.45 Hitchin	16.20			
15.20 St Pancras	16.32	16.36	Kettering (17.23)	
		16.44	Northampton (17.27)	
13.48 Sheffield	16.44	16.50	St Pancras (17.45)	Nottingham
14.55 St Pancras	16.58			
15.20 St Pancras	16.32			
16.15 St Pancras		17/04	Sheffield Midland (19.32)	Nottingham
16.25 St Pancras		17/14	Manchester Central (20.36)	Derby
14.25 Manchester Central		17/20	St Pancras (18.10)	Derby
		17.25	St Pancras (19.15)	
16.45 St Pancras	17.44		*(Fwd at 18.00)*	
		17.50	St Pancras (19.07)	
		17.53	Hitchin (18.30)	
17.05 St Pancras		17/54	Bradford F.Square	Derby
(16.45 St Pancras)		18.00	Nottingham (19.32)	Melton
09.20 Glasgow St Enoch		18/10	St pancras (19.00)	Trent
		18.12	Kettering (18.58)	
16.33 St Pancras	18.25			
16.38 Leicester	18.27	18.30	St Pancras (19.53)	
17.30 St Pancras	18.37	18.41	Leicester (19.57)	
10.05 Edinburgh Waverley		19/00	St Pancras (19.50)	Nottingham
17.38 St Pancras	19.08			
17.58 St Pancras	19.17			
16.25 Manchester Central		19/23	St Pancras (20.15)	Derby
		19.30	St Pancras (21.21)	
18.56 Northampton	19.42			
18.50 St Pancras	19.45	19.47	Manchester Central (23.00)	Derby
19.15 Hitchin	19.50			
19.25 Wellingborough	19.56			
18.55 St Pancras	20.12	20.20	Leicester (21.46)	
		20.24	Northampton (21.06)	
18.10 Nottingham	20.21	20.25	St Pancras (21.42)	Melton
19.05 St Pancras	20.40			
19.20 St Pancras	21.02			
19.55 St Pancras	21.13			
20.15 St Pancras	21.25	21.30	Derby (23.33)	Leicester
21.00 St Pancras		21/49	Edinburgh Waverley (07.50)	Nottingham
17.55 Manchester Central	21.46	21.50	St Pancras (22.55)	Derby
21.15 St Pancras		22/04	Glasgow St Enoch (08.30)	Derby
		22.10	St Pancras (22.55)	
21.32 Northampton	22.14			
21.20 St Pancras	22.55			
22.00 St Pancras	23.29			
23.50 St Pancras	01.04	01.08	Leeds City (06.07)	Derby

Only 10 trains daily were required:-
St Pancras dep.6.10 a.m, most stations to Bedford, arr. 8.15.
10.42 a.m, all stations to St Albans, arr.11.35. then forward at 1.15 p.m to Luton.
1.30 p.m, all stations to Bedford, arr. 3.32.
3.03 p.m, (SO), most stations to St Albans arr. 3.50.
4.20 p.m, Kentish Town, St Albans (4.52) and all stations to Bedford, arr. 5.55.
4.37 p.m, most stations to Bedford, arr. 7.00. (including 20 mins. at Luton).
6.30 p.m, most stations to Bedford, arr. 8.30.
7.20 p.m, most stations to St Albans, arr. 8.14.
10.20 p.m, most stations to Luton, arr.11.32.
Also 9.01 a.m, from Moorgate Street, all stations to Radlett.

The original cautious timings of fast trains on the Extension had disappeared by 1883. The 10.0 a.m from St Pancras to Leeds was booked to pass St Albans at 10.25, Luton at 10.37 and Bedford at 10.59 a.m.

The 1898 timetable, compared with that of fifteen years earlier, reveals refinements to the passenger services rather than radical changes. The volume of traffic had increased generally - no less than 89 engines whistled off Kentish Town loco each weekday. Although the two morning up trains of 1883, the 7.17 a.m from Luton and the 7.0 a.m from Bedford, were practically unchanged, they were now supplemented by a 7.50 a.m from Luton, stopping only at Harpenden and St Albans and arriving at St Pancras at 8.40 a.m. This was a sign of growth in regular business travel.

Slip carriages were first used by the Midland in 1886 and in 1898, the 5.15 a.m from St Pancras carried a slip for St Albans. The newspapers on the main part of the train had a fast ride to Bedford, then booked as first stop in 58 minutes. Luton had three daily slips in the down direction, off the 10.5 a.m, 3.0 p.m and 4.0 p.m from St Pancras. For the privileged, special arrangements even extended to slip carriages. The following notice was included in the November 1898 WTT:-

Hunting Arrangements
Special arrangements will be made for the conveyance of Hunting gentlemen when required. 9.1 a.m Moorgate Street to St Albans. Hunting traffic off the above train to be worked special to Harpenden when required. 10.5 a.m St Pancras to Manchester. Will convey a slip carriage from London to St Albans or Harpenden: also from Bedford to Sharnbrook or Irchester as may be required, of which notice will be given in each case.

The 10.5 a.m already carried a regular slip for Luton, and the provision of a second portion on the same train gives rise to thoughts about tail lamps. The problem was later addressed and solved by the GWR for their 10.30 a.m from Paddington - what St Pancras did for the special workings remains unknown. A slip carriage from Bedford to Sharnbrook or Irchester strains the imagination. It must not be forgotten, however, that, by 1903, Sharnbrook had a regular slip, at 6.3 p.m off the 5.0 p.m from St Pancras (first stop Kettering). The carriage went forward at

Stanier 5MT 4-6-0 4986 of Sheffield (Millhouses) passes Colney Street with an up express on 12 March 1948. The engine is paired with the LMS self-weighing tender whilst the train, at seven coaches, is three or four vehicles lighter than the norm for Midland workings at the time. *E.D. Bruton*

6.10 p.m to Irchester and Wellingborough.

In 1900, the Kentish Town curve and the widenings in that area had been completed. This enabled the inner suburban service to burst into a brief full flowering before tram, bus and tube competition began to take its toll in 1908. In 1903 there were two up and two down platforms available at Kentish Town with non-conflicting routes from the T&HJ to the City branch and from the Extension to St Pancras. In the busiest morning hour, from 8.10 to 9.10 a.m, 15 up trains called at Kentish Town as detailed in an accompanying table.

Compared with 1883, there was more variety in the originating stations as the South

Stanier Jubilee 45570 NEW ZEALAND (Derby) cruises through Elstree with the 07.55 Derby - St Pancras on 11 October 1952, three days after one of the class was destroyed in the Harrow disaster on the adjacent LNWR main line. *E.D. Bruton.*

Tottenham trains were reinforced by those from the T&FG line. The train from South Tottenham to St Pancras, calling at 8.38, used the Highgate Incline to gain the fast lines in order to keep clear of the closely following train from South Tottenham to Moorgate Street, which reached the slow line platform two minutes later via the Kentish Town curve.

The opening of the T&FG in 1894 brought LTSR trains into St Pancras to join the long standing GER workings from Cambridge. Midland trains could work to Southend, including excursions from the northern part of the Extension. The LTSR ran boat trains to Tilbury, not, as later, for an Orient or P&O liner, but for the day trips of the paddle ships of New Palace Steamers Ltd. In July 1903, the new lines at Kentish Town and the closely spaced signal boxes on the T&HJ enabled such seasonal trains to be fitted in with the regular services with remarkably close headways.

In the summer of 1905, through trains to the South Coast were instituted. Hendon was the point where the train from the north, (Nottingham with through carriages from Bradford),

Once the cost of the former small engine policy became apparent, the LMS drafted in a number of six-coupled engines to work the principal express turns on the Midland. Until the advent of the Black 5 and 5XP engines, a number of Claughton and Patriot locomotives relieved the indigenous 4-4-0 classes; 5522 (later named PRESTATYN) being seen at Cricklewood on 31 July 1934 with the 16.25 St Pancras - Manchester express. As with the LNW-based members of the class, as soon as the Stanier engines appeared in numbers, the Patriot 4-6-0's fell from favour and became only rare visitors to the Midland extension. 5522 was rebuilt with a taper boiler after nationalisation and spent the 1950's working from Camden MPD. *H.C..Doyle.*

was divided. One portion was taken on by an LSWR locomotive to Eastleigh via the Acton branch. From Eastleigh the Nottingham carriages went on to Southampton and the Bradford portion went to Portsmouth. The second portion from Hendon was taken by an SECR locomotive via Snow Hill to Folkestone, Dover and Deal, using the new loop between Bickley and Orpington.

In the January 1913 timetable, a trend towards catering for the longer distance season ticket holder is noticeable. There were fewer morning trains commencing from Hendon, the

		T&HJR timing margins (1903)	
		MR train	LTSR train
Moorgate St	dep	09.37	
St Pancras	dep		09.50
		Slow line	Fast line
Kentish Town	arr	09.55	09.56
	dep	09.57	09.57
		Kentish Town curve	Highbury incline
Highgate Rd	dep	10.00	-
Junction Rd	dep	10.02	10.00
		all stations	most stations
S.Tottenham	dep	10.15	10.11
		To East Ham	To Tilbury

four between 5.22 and 7.35 a.m were denoted "Workmen's Train" by Bradshaw. Luton had trains to St Pancras at 6.45 and 7.15 a.m, stopping at most stations, 7.48 a.m with stops at St Albans, Harpenden and Kentish Town, and 8.18 a.m, Chiltern Green, Harpenden and then Kentish Town. At 8.55 a.m there was a train to Moorgate, calling at Harpenden and St Albans only before King's Cross Metropolitan. The 7.15 and 8.18 trains originated at Bedford and served all the intermediate stations to Luton.

There were some smart timings for down trains. The 8.0 a.m from St Pancras picked up passengers at Luton at 8.35 and arrived at Bedford at 9.0 a.m. The 2.5 p.m from St Pancras to Leeds left Kentish Town at 2.11, arriving at Bedford at 3.5 p.m. The Kentish Town stop was made in order to connect with an all year round working from the SECR of carriages from the 10.25 a.m from Deal. After making numerous calls in Kent, this train finally got away from Paddock Wood at 12.9 p.m for Herne Hill, arr. 1.2 p.m and Victoria, arr. 1.11 p.m. At Herne

Far from home. Manchester (Belle Vue) 5MT 44845 passes Napsbury with a down express on 4 August 1950. *E.D. Bruton*

The final nail in the coffin of many Midland 4-4-0's came with the introduction of the BR standard engines, the useful 5MT variety appearing on the Midland early in the 1950's. They were not as highly regarded as the Stanier 5MT locomotives but those allocated to Leicester and Derby performed much useful work on the extension. In this view 73004 of Leicester works an up special past Harpers Lane Crossing, Radlett, in the mid-1950's. *E.D. Bruton*

ter London Road at 6.23 p.m. The portion for the Midland called at Ludgate Hill at 1.15 p.m and arrived at Kentish Town at 1.36. After dropping the Leeds passengers, the carriages were worked to St Pancras and attached to the 2.30 p.m to Manchester Central, reached at 6.25 p.m, two minutes after the LNWR portion had arrived at London Road. Those who consider the present Thameslink service to be a little leisurely in its traverse of London should spare a thought for the through travellers of 1913, whose train took 1 1/4 hours from leaving Ludgate Hill to leaving St Pancras.

The intermediate stations between Luton and Bedford were served by 9 up and 11 down weekday trains in 1913. The 11.10 a.m from Bedford (9.44 from Leicester) called at Flitwick, Luton and Kentish Town en route to St Pancras. There was a corresponding Sunday service. Flitwick also had an early Sunday morning set-down off the 12.15 a.m Manchester express. 13 up trains called at Kentish Town in the busiest morning hour, additionally the 8.30 a.m from St Albans to St Pancras passed without stopping. Of these trains, the number of those originating on the Extension (8) now exceeded those from the T&HJ (6).

The GER services from St Pancras comprised two express trains to Cambridge and Ely at 12.20 p.m and 5.5 p.m. At Ely the carriages were marshalled with trains from Liverpool Street to Hunstanton and Norwich. The 12.20 p.m reached Cambridge in the excellent time of 71 minutes. Three workings to Tottenham Hale made connections into down expresses from Liverpool Street and there was a through train from

Hill, portions for the GNR, MR and LNWR were detached. The portion for the GNR terminated at King's Cross at 1.25 p.m, connecting with the 1.40 and 2.20 p.m down expresses. The LNWR carriages were worked via Kensington, Addison

Road, to arrive at Willesden Junction at 1.36 p.m. There they were attached to a train from Eastbourne and Brighton which had followed from Addison Road. The combined train left Willesden at 2.20 p.m and arrived at Manches-

Fairburn 2-6-4T 42230 passes Cole Green Lane, near Radlett, on 14 August 1948 with the 16.04 St Pancras - St Albans stopping train. 42230 was a well travelled engine and moved in later years to Shoeburyness and Neasden. *E.D. Bruton*

New arrival on the Midland. Rebuilt Royal Scot 46116 IRISH GUARDSMAN makes a smoky start through Kentish Town with the 10.15 St Pancras - Manchester Central on 9 November 1957. *P.H.Groom.*

St Pancras at 5.55 p.m to Hertford, Railway Street, arriving at 6.46 p.m.

A special working of more than usual interest was the Royal Train conveying Their Majesties King George V and Queen Mary on a visit to Bedford on 27th June 1918. The train, of six carriages, left No.5 Platform at St Pancras at 9.55 in the morning and arrived at Bedford North Junction via the fast line at 10.58 a.m. It was then set back into the up platform to arrive at 11.0 a.m. In a rather hectic programme, the King and Queen visited the works of W H Allen, went on to Bedford High School and attended a Civic Reception at the Town Hall before arriving back at the station to leave on the Royal Train from the up platform again at 1.30 p.m. The train proceeded to Oakley Junction, to stand on the down Northampton line from 1.35 to 2.50 p.m. Sheltered from the common gaze in that rather isolated spot, Their Majesties lunched in solitary state. Meanwhile the Mayor was entertaining the press and other visitors at the Swan Hotel. Arrival at Bedford up platform again was at 2.55 p.m. "The train must be brought to a stand with the leading end of the vehicles two yards on the South side of the overbridge at the South end of the platform and as soon as the Royal Party has alighted the Train will be set back into the up sidings at Bedford North Junction". At Oakley Junction, the engine had run round through the down sidings, so that in one direction between Oakley Junction and Bedford it worked tender first! After visiting Bedford School in the afternoon, the King and Queen finally departed at 4.0 p.m for St Pancras, Stationmaster H Ward no doubt breathing a huge sigh of relief.

The end of the Midland came in December 1922 with recovery from the effects of wartime still incomplete. Unrest in the coalfields had resulted in the use of poor quality imported coal and timings still lagged behind those of 1913. The standard booking for down trains making a first stop at Luton was 41 minutes, departure to departure. The suburban service had

recovered well, 12 up trains passing through Kentish Town in one hour. The emphasis had shifted further to the Extension (8 trains) from the T&HJ (4 trains). Of the 12, 7 went to St Pancras and 5 to Moorgate Street. A curiosity was the 5.4 p.m from Moorgate Street, which ran through to Upminster, arriving at 6.27 p.m. There was no corresponding up service. Regular GER services had ceased but a Hunstanton express ran to and from St Pancras in the summer peak. It was reinstated in 1923, so, for 8 weeks, LNER trains actually used St Pancras.

The services of the 1932 WTT are typical of those of the first 14 years of the LMS. "Special Limit" down expresses passed Bedford in 54 minutes from St Pancras and "Limited Load" Bedford non-stops took 59 minutes up (10.25 a.m) and 62 minutes down (5.32 p.m). The prestigious 4.55 p.m from St Pancras to Bradford passed Bedford in 52 minutes to arrive at Leicester at 6.42 p.m. The suburban service was practically unchanged in volume from that of 1922. One of the trains from the T&HJ now terminated at Kentish Town; Moorgate, now without the 'Street', therefore had only 4 LMS arrivals in the peak hour.

The introduction of "XL Limit" timings on the Midland Division in 1937 revolutionised the express services using the Extension. Luton now had 60 m.p.h trains to London, the 30 minute booking leaving little margin for checks, however, over the short distance. Bedford had an "XL Limit" service to St Pancras, the excellent 5.35 p.m from Sheffield via Nottingham called at 8.1 to 8.3 p.m and then made St Pancras in 52 minutes. The Jubilee used to make itself heard when accelerating this train on the down grade from Cow Bridge to Elstow box. The terms Limited Load, Special Limit and XL Limit were used to classify the tonnage limit for unpiloted express trains in accordance with their timing and motive power. The limits in force in 1954, which by then included Class 7 engines, are given in the appendix.

The suburban service of 1938 showed a slight expansion compared with that of 1932. Kentish Town saw 14 up trains in the peak hour, 9 from the Extension and 5 from the T&HJ. 7 proceeded to St Pancras and 6 went into the tunnels to Moorgate, the remaining one having terminated. The 8.38 a.m "Limited Load" semifast from Manchester (2.12 p.m from Bedford and 2.41 p.m from Luton) stopped at Cricklewood at 3.8 p.m to detach a milk van for the Express Dairies depot. Arrival at St Pancras was at 3.22 p.m. The 1939 timetable contained two 19 minute start to stop bookings from Luton to Bedford. At 61.9 m.p.h, these were the fastest timings on the Midland Division.

The initial reaction to war in September 1939 resulted in a very sparse emergency service. This was short lived and, for the next six years, a decelerated and just adequate provision was made. If anything, although the timetable showed only small changes, the general wear and tear of wartime resulted in a steady deterioration of the service. Longer trains than ever before were worked in and out of St Pancras, some fouling of connections during platform occupation being acceptable with the reduced services. The most surprising feature of the 1945 timetable is that the "Mail" at 8.15 p.m was the last down train to Bedford on Mondays to Fridays. Bedford servicemen on leave arriving in London from the south and west in the late evening had to wait for the 4.25 a.m to complete their journey home. For intermediate stations between Luton and Bedford the service was even more restrictive. Their last down train was at 7.15 p.m from St Pancras on Mondays to Saturdays and 7.5 p.m on Sundays. Suburban services reached their lowest ebb. Moorgate services were suspended for the duration, Kentish Town's rush hour was five trains from the Extension to St Pancras and two terminating from the T&HJ.

Suburban services were slow to recover from the wartime cuts. In 1952, there were still only 6 trains from the Extension through Kentish Town in the peak hour; two trains to Moorgate had been restored, arriving at 9.15 and 9.58 a.m from St Albans and Harpenden respectively and non-productive mileage was incurred due to the lack of rounding and stabling facilities at Moorgate. A light engine had to precede the first train to deal with the stock, there were two down empty carriage workings from the two inbound trains and the engine of the second train finally returned light. The evening departures from Moorgate required a similar mileage.

Some classes of locomotives were particularly associated with the services described above. Ten 2-4-0Ts, Nos.230 - 239, were specially built by Beyer Peacock in 1867 for the Extension. They were fitted with condensing apparatus for working to Moorgate Street but were found unsuitable and converted to tender engines in 1870. Their replacements were the Kirtley 0-4-4 well tanks of the "690" class, which appeared in 1869. The last survivor, No.1219, was withdrawn from pilot duties at St Pancras in 1935. A few Beyer Peacock 4-4-0s of the type standard on the Metropolitan and Metropolitan District Railways supplemented the 0-4-4WTs. Some of the Johnson 0-4-4Ts, a class first introduced in 1875, were fitted for condensing. It was not until 1930 that the Fowler 3 2-6-2Ts appeared and those of the class with condensing gear could replace the Johnson tanks on the City branch trains. The 2-6-2Ts also had a long stint in the tunnels, giving way only to diesels.

For many years, 2-4-0 tender engines of both Kirtley and Johnson varieties shared the St Pancras to St Albans services with the 0-4-4Ts. In the 1920s and early 1930s, Whitelegg 4-6-4Ts displaced from the LTSR were sub-shedded at St Albans for the St Pancras services, a vivid contrast to the small 0-4-4Ts. In 1927, the first three Fowler 2-6-4Ts were sent to work on the suburban traffic. Lively engines with long travel valves, they were immediately popular with the men who ran and maintained them. Despite the large scale building of taper boiler 2-6-4Ts, the Fowler engines were always well represented on the suburban workings.

WEEKDAY MOVEMENTS(1). St PANCRAS:1957/8

Train	Arrive	Depart	Destination
		00.25	Barking
		02.35	Woodgrange Park
02.50 Wanstead Park	03.26		
		04.05	Barking
		04.20	**Manchester Central**
03.45 Wanstead Park	04.21		
		04.35	Luton
		05.00	East Ham
21.20 Bradford F. Square	**05.15**		
05.00 Barking		05.45	
05.05 St Albans		05.48	
		05.30	St Albans
		05.55	Bedford
		06.00	Barking
		06.20	Wellingborough
05.38 Barking		06.24	
05.50 St Albans		06.34	
00.05 Manchester Central	**06.40**		
		06.53	Barking
		07.00	Bedford
06.20 East Ham		07.06	
05.45 Bedford		07.13	
		07.15	Luton
21.05 Glasgow St Enoch	**07.20**		
06.47 St Albans		07.31	
		07.35	Harpenden
06.50 Luton		07.40	
		07.55	**Manchester Central**
07.13 St Albans		07.55	
06.25 Bedford		07.59	
		08.00	Bedford
		08.15	**Nottingham**
		08.20	St Albans
07.27 Luton		08.20	
07.52 St Albans		08.33	
07.23 Bedford		08.38	
08.20 St Albans		08.45	
08.05 Luton		08.54	
07.35 Bedford		09.05	
07.05 Kettering		09.11	
		09.15	**Edinburgh Waverley**
		09.20	**Leicester**
21.45 Edinburgh Waverley	**09.20**		
08.40 St Albans		09.24	
		09.25	Southend Central
06.40 Nottingham	**09.30**		
08.09 Bedford		09.42	
		09.45	Luton
07.42 Leicester	**09.50**		
		09.55	Bedford
09.25 Harpenden		9.58	

All early references to locomotives used on the Bedford to St Pancras services are to 2-4-0s. By 1892, two 4-2-2s were allocated to Bedford, a number which grew to nine in 1914, although it is difficult to visualise singles as ideal engines for the Bedford workings. Also in 1914, six "483" class superheated 4-4-0s were stationed at Bedford. In 1924/25, the Midland Division received 45 newly built Compounds. Many Class 3 4-4-0s were then taken off express work. Of these, eventually eleven were allocated to Bedford, primarily for the London trains. The first Compound to be shedded at Bedford was No.1038 in 1934. Gradually the London workings became the preserve of Compounds, nine being allocated in 1950. Some BR Standard 2-6-4Ts were tried as replacements but their tank capacity was barely adequate for the 50 mile run. So Standard 4MT 4-6-0s were substituted - with success on the whole but some trains, such as the 7.20am up, loading regularly to ten coaches, were not easy to time. There were criticisms in the local press and calls from enginemen for Class 5 power to be provided. When, at long last, 5MT 4-6-0s were sent to Bedford in 1955, the remaining Compounds were ousted from the London workings. The final Bedford stud of passenger tender engines that handed over to DMU sets comprised five each of BR Standard Class 4 and Stanier Class 5 4-6-0s.

The replacement of steam trains by DMUs on the suburban services in January 1960 was a revolutionary change. The introduction of an interval service was probably as great an advantage as the improvement in timings. The basic service was arranged with hourly trains Bedford/ St Pancras stopping at all stations between Bedford and Elstree, and hourly trains Luton/St Pancras stopping at all stations. Incredibly, the DMU sets specially built for the Extension were out of gauge for the Widened Lines. Overall times were 70 minutes from St Pancras to Bedford and 54 1/2 minutes from St Pancras to Luton. In each case 3 minutes recovery time was included. Comparable 1958/9 steam hauled timings for the same duties were 95 and 71 minutes respectively.

Diesel haulage for the express services had been codified by 1963 into timings for 350 and 400 ton loads. The 350 ton timings from St Pancras were 29 1/2 minutes to stop at Luton or 43 minutes to pass Bedford. The "Midland Pullman" had been running from Manchester to St Pancras from July 1960 to relieve the line from Euston, then in the throes of electrification; its timings were the fastest yet on the Extension, 39 1/2 minutes to pass Bedford on its 190 minute evening run to Manchester or its mid-day fill in with a first stop at Leicester in 82 minutes. Truly, the Blue Pullmans were the direct predecessors of today's HSTs.

In January 1868, with the unfinished Extension available at night, three freight trains still ran up to St Pancras goods via the GNR. They left Bedford at 8.50 a.m, 1.26 p.m and 5.10 p.m, with goods, cattle and coal respectively. 11 up and 9 down goods trains used the Extension. Departures from Bedford ranged from 8.4 p.m to 7.40am and from St Pancras Goods from 7.50 p.m to 3.0 a.m. Two trains in each direction called at Ampthill, Harlington, Leagrave, Luton,

Chiltern Green and Harpenden. The goods yards south of Harpenden were evidently not ready for traffic at this date. The workings via the GNR reappeared in the February 1868 WTT but were absent from March onwards. In April 1868, the stopping goods trains were booked to call additionally at St Albans, Radlett, Elstree, Mill Hill and Hendon. There was still a daytime gap in the traffic but gradually there was encroachment, both early and late, into the period for the Contractor's occupation.

WEEKDAY MOVEMENTS(3). St PANCRAS:1957/8

Train	Arrive	Depart	Destination
17.20 St Albans	18.04		
		18.05	St Albans
14.25 Manchester Central	**18.10**		
		18.17	Harpenden
17.48 Luton	18.26		
		18.33	**Derby**
		18.42	**Sheffield Midland**
17.58 St Albans	18.43		
		18.50	**Manchester Central**
		18.55	**Leicester**
09.20 Glasgow St Enoch	**19.00**		
		19.05	Bedford
17.50 Bedford	19.07		
		19.10	St Albans
17.25 Bedford	19.15		
		19.20	Bedford
10.05 Edinburgh Waverley	**19.50**		
16.38 Leicester	**19.53**		
		19.55	Bedford
18.00 Southend Central	20.02		
		20.15	**Derby**
16.25 Manchester Central	**20.15**		
		20.20	Harpenden
		20.33	Barking
19.25 Luton	20.40		
		21.00	**Edinburgh Waverley**
		21.15	**Glasgow St Enoch**
		21.20	Bedford
19.30 Bedford	21.21		
20.46 Barking	21.33		
18.10 Nottingham	**21.42**		
20.45 Luton	21.51		
		22.00	Bedford
		22.15	Barking
		22.30	Luton
21.48 Barking	22.34		
17.55 Manchester Central	**22.55**		
22.09 Harpenden	23.04		
		23.10	Barking
		23.15	Luton
		23.30	St Albans
		23.50	**Leeds City**
22.10 Bedford	23.55		
		00.25	Barking

By 1883, goods traffic on the Extension had grown to a remarkable extent, both in bulk and in destinations served. The growth is well illustrated by the marshalling instructions for down express freight trains from St Pancras goods of which a precis is given in the accompanying table.

Prominent among the destinations for wagons from up express goods trains were Victoria Docks and the Midland's goods station for the City at Whitecross Street. All up goods trains had to stop at Leagrave or Luton for examina-

WEEKDAY MOVEMENTS(2). St PANCRAS:1957/8

Train	Arrive	Depart	Destination
08.26 Leicester	**10.05**		
09.25 St Albans	10.12		
		10.15	**Glasgow St Enoch**
07.05 Sheffield	**10.18**		
		10.25	**Manchester Central**
08.15 Nottingham	**10.25**		
10.10 St Albans		10.54	
		10.30	St Albans
08.20 Nottingham	**11.07**		
07.25 Manchester Central	**11.15**		
		11.15	**Leicester**
10.28 Luton	11.20		
		11.20	Luton
08.34 Sheffield	**11.42**		
11.20 Luton		12.10	
		12.15	**Bradford F.Square**
		12.20	Southend Central
		12.25	**Manchester Central**
		12.30	Harpenden
10.05 Leicester	**12.40**		
07.20 Bradford F.Square	**12.50**		
		12.55	**Leicester**
11.00 Bedford		12.55	
08.55 Manchester Central	**13.00**		
		13.20	Harpenden
12.42 St Albans	13.30		
11.40 Southend Central	13.37		
08.55 Bradford F.Square	**13.47**		
		14.15	**Bradford F.Square**
10.25 Manchester Central	**14.15**		
		14.20	**Leicester**
13.25 Harpenden		14.22	
		14.25	**Manchester Central**
		14.30	Southend Central
		14.34	St Albans
		14.55	Bedford
13.25 Bedford		15.08	
		15.15	**Bradford F.Square**
12.00 Nottingham	**15.18**		
		15.20	Kettering
		15.30	East Ham
10.40 Bradford F.Square	**15.43**		
		15.55	Harpenden
14.52 Luton		15.58	
		16.15	**Sheffield Midland**
		16.25	**Manchester Central**
15.05 Bedford		16.30	
		16.33	Bedford
		16.38	St Albans
		16.45	**Nottingham**
12.00 Bradford F.Square	**16.57**		
		16.58	Luton
		17.05	**Bradford F.Square**
16.34 Luton		17.07	
		17.10	St Albans
		17.18	Harpenden
16.10 Luton		17.21	
		17.30	**Leicester**
		17.38	Bedford
16.15 Bedford		17.38	
		17.45	Harpenden
13.48 Sheffield	**17.45**		
		17.58	Bedford

tion and greasing, down trains similarly stopping at Luton only. In 1898, instructions for marshalling up coal trains included details which show the areas served by the various London yards:-

Brent Extension Sidings [i.e down side]:- Traffic via Acton Wells inc. LSWR and LBSCR except that taken to Child's Hill New Sidings.
Child's Hill New Sidings [i.e up side]:- Traffic for SER Stewarts Lane, LCDR, LBSCR Epsom, Wimbledon to Tooting Bec line, Leatherhead, Havant and Portsmouth area.
West End:-
Finchley Road, T&HJ, Bow, Poplar, Victoria Docks, Tilbury line.
Hendon New Sidings:-
Midland Railway in London.

A further instruction ensured that trains arrived in London with full loads:- "All coal and coke trains, Wellingborough and stations north thereof to London, must stop at Leagrave to make up to 35 [wagons] with double framed and 42 with single framed engines."

The goods traffic of the late 1890s had the benefit of the completed widening of the route. Change for many years later was mainly con-

UP GOODS WORKINGS (1934)

Train	Bedford	Destination	Traffic
09.40 Toton	00/12 FL	Brent (Down) 02.29	Mineral (Garrett-hauled)
20.27 Leeds (Stourton)	00/23 FL	Dock Junction 01.35	Goods
20.50 Derby (Chaddesden)	00/43 SL	West End 02.47	Goods
21.45 Nottingham	00/51 FL	St Pancras Goods 02.40	Goods
20.35 Birmingham (Lawley St)	01/00 FL	St Pancras Goods 03.15	Goods
00.45 Wellingborough (Finedon Rd)	01/33 SL	Brent (Down) 03.39	Mineral (Garrett-hauled)
22.15 Sheffield (Wicker)	01/46 FL	Dock Junction 03.07	Goods
21.25 Toton	01/51 SL	Brent (Down) 03.59	Mineral (Garrett-hauled)
01.25 Olney	02/25 SL	Brent (Up) 04.18	Goods
22.15 Rowsley	02/47 SL	Brent (Up) 04.35	Goods
22.15 Nottingham	03/00 SL	Dock Junction 05.15	Goods
20.37 Leeds (Stourton)	03/15 SL	St Pancras Goods 05.45	Goods
23.20 Burton	03/16 FL	Dock Junction 05.02	Goods
22.45 Manchester (Ancoats)	03/59 FL	West End 05.18	Goods
23.35 Burton	04/12 SL	Brent (Down) 05.50	Goods
03.45 Wellingborough (Finedon Rd)	04/31 SL	West End 06.56	Mineral (Garrett-hauled)
22.35 Rotherham (Masborough)	04/46 FL	West End 06.35	Goods
22.10 Carlisle	04/57 FL	Dock Junction 06.14	Goods
00.16 Broom Junction	05/06 FL	West End 06.50	Goods
01.00 Birmingham (Lawley St)	05/30 FL	Brent (Up) 07.06	Goods
05.50 Wellingborough (Finedon Rd)	06/28 SL	St Albans 08.25	Mineral
02.30 Rowsley	07/20 SL	Brent (Up) 09.48	Goods
03.20 Toton	07/47 SL	West End 10.36	Mineral (Garrett-hauled)
07.15 Wellingborough (Finedon Rd)	08/02 SL	Brent (Down) 10.45	Mineral
08.40 Bedford	08.40 SL	West End 17.45	All
08.40 Wellingborough (Finedon Rd)	09/26 SL	Brent (Down) 11.59	Mineral
05.20 Toton	09.47 SL	Brent (Down) 12.15	Mineral (Garrett-hauled)
10.10 Bedford	10.10 SL	Luton 15.23	All
09.50 Wellingbrough (Finedon Rd)	10/47 SL	Brent (Down) 13.38	Mineral
11.10 Wellingbrough (Finedon Rd)	11/57 SL	Brent (Up) 14.15	Mineral (Garrett-hauled)
11.35 Wellingborough (Finedon Rd)	12/50 SL	Luton 14.13	Mineral
09.00 Toton	14/00 SL	Brent (Down) 16.29	Mineral (Garrett-hauled)
13.40 Wellingborough (Finedon Rd)	14/31 FL	West End 16.45	Mineral (Garrett-hauled)
14.40 Wellingborough (Finedon Rd)	15/36 SL	Brent (Down) 18.14	Mineral
11.30 Toton	16/53 SL	Brent (Up) 19.00	Mineral (Garrett-hauled)
14.30 Burton	19/09 SL	Brent (Down) 21.22	Goods
19.20 Bedford	19.20 SL	Brent (Up) 22.27	Mineral
19.50 Bedford	19.50 SL	Brent (Up) 01.10	All
20.00 Wellingborough (Finedon Rd)	20/46 SL	Brent (Up) 22.56	Mineral
21.15 Bedford	21.15 SL	Somers Town 00.03	Goods
15.47 Leeds (Stourton)	21.22 FL	St Pancras Goods 23.15	Goods
20.30 Wellingborough (Finedon Rd)	21/36 SL	Brent (Up) 23.53	Mineral (Garrett-hauled)
18.30 Leicester	22/23 FL	St Pancras Goods 00.15	Goods
17.55 Toton	22.23 SL	Brent (Down) 00.40	Mineral (Garrett-hauled)
20.00 Nottingham	22/48 FL	St Pancras Goods 00.35	Goods
22.10 Wellingborough (Finedon Rd)	23/05 SL	St Albans 01.22	Mineral
18.00 Burton	23/10 FL	Brent (Up) 00.48	Goods

NIGHT GOODS DEPARTURES 1883

St Pancras	Destination	Traffic
16.15	Derby	Perishables for Chesterfield & stations North
18.35	Barnsley	L&Y, NER, Leeds & stations beyond
20.30	Mansfield	Nottingham & Lincoln branches
21.15	Liverpool	Stockport, Guide Bridge and Manchester traffic
21.35	Barnsley	Leeds and stations beyond Leeds
21.45	Leeds.	NER, Carnsforth, Morecambe, stations beyond Leeds, Scotch, Bradford
22.00	Wakefield	LYR traffic
22.10	Swinton	Knottingly, Rotherham, Doncaster & Sheffield.
22.20	Kettering	Kettering - Cambridge branch, Peterborough and Lynn, Manton, Oakham and Melton
22.30	Derby	Liverpool, CLC, Manchester
22.45	Rugby	Ullesthorpe, Midland Counties, Chesterfield, Sheffield, Oakenshaw, Normanton.
23.10*	Coventry	Nuneaton, Stafford, Birmingham, Redditch, Ashchurch, Cheltenham, Gloucester, Nailsworth branch, Bath and Bristol
23.20	Rotherham	NE Leeds and beyond, Scotch.
23.35	Ilkeston	Erewash Valley, Mansfield branch, Lincoln branch, Nottingham
00.05	Whitacre	Birmingham, Redditch, Worcester, Hereford, Ashchuch, Malvern branch, Cheltenham, Gloucester, Nailsworth branch, Bath branch, Bristol.
00.20	Bedford	Northampton, Hitchin branch, stations Bedford to Leicester.
00.25*	Leicester	Midland Counties
01.20	Luton	Hemel Hempsted branch, Bedford branches, stations to Leicester.
03.00	Bedford	Leagrave, Harlington and Flitwick
03.35	Luton	St Albans, Harpenden.

Horwich 2-6-0 No.13134 at Kentish Town in pre-war days. Although never allocated in significant numbers to the extension, the 'Crabs' were familiar visitors on fast goods services and excursions. *GWG Collection.*

fined to a steady growth in volume of traffic. Even with the quadrupled line, there were limitations to capacity, so individual trains had to be longer. Double heading became general, with a variety of locomotive types for the inflated traffic of the 1914-1918 war. After the war years, the haulage of mineral trains reverted solely to the traditional 0-6-0s, in pairs if required. The pattern was broken by the Garratts, dealing singlehandedly with 87 loaded wagons. In 1934, despite the lingering effects of economic depression, the volume of traffic was still impressive. Tabulated in this chapter is a summary of all booked goods trains proceeding south from Bedford in 24 hours.

Conditional and suspended workings and trains which ran on less than four days per week have been excluded from the table, the 47 trains listed represent, therefore, the minimum service of that time. The 1.25 a.m from Olney carried traffic from the Stratford-upon-Avon and Midland Junction line and the 12.16 a.m from Broom Junction ran through to London via that route. Three conditional paths for trains carrying bananas from Avonmouth Docks to Somers Town via Broom Junction and Olney were provided: Avonmouth dep.12.30, 1.55 and 4.15 p.m,

Bedford dep.7.45, 9.32 and 11.58 p.m, Somers Town arr.9.51, 11.0 p.m and 1.45 a.m.

An unusual working of long standing was the coupling of an evening freight from Hendon to Mill Hill behind a Cricklewood to Derby train. In the 1937 Appendix to the WTT under the heading of "Assisting Trains in Rear" was the entry "Hendon New Sidings to Mill Hill, goods and slow lines, freight with 7.30 p.m Cricklewood to Derby only. Assisting engine coupled". The Derby train was booked to call at Hendon from 7.50 to 7.58 p.m and at Mill Hill from 8.8 to 8.11 p.m, the assistance was given by what was termed a stopping freight, with the same Hendon to Mill Hill times as the main train. The practice went back at least as far as 1931 and the entry still remained in the 1961 Appendix with the timings brought up to date.

Midland goods engines were standardised to the extent that it is difficult to associate any particular class with the Extension. An exception was a series of 0-6-0Ts built around the turn of the century. Some of these were fitted for condensing and spent their lives on transfer goods workings, including those using the City branch and the Widened Lines. Mention must also be made of Bedford's first large post-Fowler locomotive, Stanier 2-8-0 No.48177, which had a regular working with a brick train to West End Sidings, returning with a long train of empty wagons.

By April 1966, the number of up goods trains entering the Extension at Bedford, counted on the same basis as the 47 of 1934, had declined to 25. Coal still formed an important part of the traffic, for nearly half the trains were Class

7 mineral, staged from Wellingborough to Brent. Notable among efforts to retain freight traffic was the 'Condor', a container service from Glasgow to Hendon taking only 9 hours 10 minutes for the journey. Traditional routes were still operative in 1966. There were 6 daily exchange trips from Camden to Churchyard Sidings via the North London Incline and 5 workings from the Extension used the Snow Hill link. The latter comprised 2 trains from Brent to Walworth Road Coal Depot, a through Brent to Three Bridges working and 2 trains from Temple Mills via the T&HJ to Hither Green.

The 25 trains of 1966 had been reduced to 14 by 1974. The 'Condor' had been replaced by the 'Tartan Arrow', a freightliner now terminating at a depot on the site of Cattle Dock Sidings. The freight WTT of 1982/3, the last before the electrification of passenger services, shows the number of daily up trains unchanged at 14. It is probable that the average load carried per train had now increased as all workings now involved specialised traffic with Company trains prominent. The remaining coal trains were either Merry-go-round trips or through workings from Toton, staging at Wellingborough having ceased.

8: CONTROL OF TRAINS

Diesel traction was a novelty until 1960 and the sight of 10000 heading the 07.15 Manchester - St Pancras on 24 April 1948 was an event to speak of. Apart from occasional visits throughout the fifties none of the early diesels, other than the Fell diesel-mechanical, remained on the Midland; most of their time being spent on the LNWR and LSWR mainlines. *E.D. Bruton*

Three particularly individual institutions of the Midland Railway were eventually involved in the regulation of traffic on the Extension. These were the train control system, the signalling of the goods lines by telegraph bells and the rotary interlocking block instrument.

The train control system was first developed as a result of the increase in mineral traffic in the South Yorkshire and Nottinghamshire districts in the early 1900s. This had made for severe congestion which in turn led to high movement costs and excessive hours for trainmen. The General Superintendent, Cecil Paget, together with his ultimate successor, J H Follows, devised a system of control which was introduced in 1909 for freight traffic in the area between Cudworth and Toton. This was the first instance of train control in Great Britain and was inaugurated by a historic circular from W Guy Granet, the General Manager, dated 14th December 1908:- "Commencing January 4th 1909, the movements of all goods and mineral trains be-

tween Cudworth and Toton will be under the control of district controllers situated at Cudworth, Masboro', Staveley, Westhouses and Toton, from whom signalmen are liable to have orders affecting their own work and instructions to transmit to other members of the staff affecting theirs".

There had been previous indications that a scheme for train control was in the offing. In 1905, the locomotive stock had been classified in terms of power rating. That, and the general renumbering of engines in 1907 into logical series with the numbers prominently displayed, were both necessary adjuncts of the control scheme. The success of the Cudworth to Toton experiment led to its general introduction on all lines. Overall, it extended beyond the local supervision of traffic movements to centralised planning of train timings and loadings, trainman's workings, engine workings and rolling stock distribution. Following the establishment of freight train control, the scheme was

expanded on 1st January 1917 to encompass passenger traffic. Organisational changes were necessary for its full scale implementation - the major innovation was that responsibility for locomotive running was transferred from the Locomotive Superintendent to a Superintendent of Motive Power who reported to the General Superintendent. The District Locomotive Superintendents, who had charge of the enginemen and shed staffs, reported to the Superintendent of Motive Power, hence the position of Locomotive Superintendent was re-designated "Chief Mechanical Engineer". Reporting also to the General Superintendent was a Superintendent of Operation to whom, via Superintendents of Freight Trains and Passenger Train Services, reported the District Controllers. The latter were in charge of the 25 District Control Offices (DCOs) and were responsible for train movements in their area.

Reporting "stations", i.e marshalling yards, large goods stations and selected signal

82

boxes, notified recorders in the DCOs of train movements. In the case of the yards and goods stations, a telephone conference at 8.0 a.m daily kept the DCO informed of the rolling stock situation. The 8.0 a.m conferences were followed at 9.0 a.m by a series of discussions between the DCOs and the Superintendent of Freight Trains at the Central Control Office, Derby. In this way, a complete daily picture of the overall freight situation was maintained, and this in days when telecommunications technology was in its infancy. It was claimed that the Control System had reduced the weekly average delay to freight trains from 21,869 hours in 1907 to 7,749 hours in 1913. Control of passenger train loading reduced the proportion of piloted mileage from 5 per cent in 1916 to 1.9 per cent in 1920. Over the same period, punctuality of passenger trains improved, with the percentage of expresses arriving at their destinations not more than five minutes late increasing from 47.9 to 87.0.

The original DCOs associated with the Extension were Luton, with a control area covering Oakley Junction to Elstree together with the Hemel Hempsted, Hitchin and Bedford to Northampton branches, and Kentish Town, responsible for lines south of Mill Hill, handing over to Plaistow DCO for the Tilbury section. Luton DCO was situated between Luton North signal box and the up platform whilst at Kentish Town the DCO was on the up slow platform. In 1929, Luton DCO was closed as an economy measure and responsibility for its area was apportioned between Kentish Town and Wellingborough. Regulation of trains, because of the generous allocation of goods lines, was in BR days of secondary interest to the control organisation, although the section controllers

The only one of the early diesel locomotives to be closely identified with the Midland was the Fell diesel-mechanical 10100 which worked regularly between Manchester and St Pancras during the 1950's until, late in the decade, it caught fire in Manchester Central and was withdrawn for scrap. This view shows the engine shunted out of sight in Derby works on 15 March 1959 after the fire. *A.R. Goult.*

would give instructions to signalboxes when conditions required, whose main function was to ensure that trains were loaded efficiently and run economically. However, the extent to which a large number of signalmen could reasonably co-ordinate was of necessity limited - especially at times of difficulty - and the Midland line took the almost unique step of locating a number of its section controllers in Key signalboxes; one

each being positioned at St Pancras and Bedford North (others being located at Leicester and Trent). Diplomatically - since signalmen and their representatives were often on their guard against the possibility of salaried staff eroding what they regarded as their traditional duties - they were referred to as controller (regulators).

The outward and visible signs of this inward orderliness were few, apart from the large numerals on tenders and the lanterns - "reporting lamps" - beamed across the lines at chosen signal boxes, both of which aided identification of trains by signalmen. For a time, freight trains were also identified by a letter code displayed on the brake van. The code was arranged on two lines, the top line representing the departure time with the second line denoting the origin and destination of the train. On the top line, the first letter stood for hours, A to M being 1 to 12 (I was excluded). The second letter, similarly selected, represented minutes in 5 minute steps from 5 to 60. On the second line the first and last letters of the origin and destination were displayed. As an example, the 10.20 London to Rowsley would carry the letters: KD

          LN RY.

The metal symbols were issued to the goods guard when he booked on and this proved a stumbling block, which led to the eventual disuse of the system. The guard already had to carry between the time office and the train his kit of flags, detonators and timetables etc. The addition of the symbols made the weight to be carried, often over a considerable distance, unacceptable. Such was the priority accorded to the control system that a major change was made to the method of handling the kit. Instead of being issued at the timekeeper's office, the flags, detonators and timetables were kept in a locker in the van as part of its equipment. The guard was issued with a locker key, and a complex system of certificates was instituted to ensure the in-

The first sign of the production diesels came late in 1958 when the curious Co-Bo 1200hp Metropolitan-Vickers locomotives took over a number of Manchester - St Pancras services; the diesels working in pairs. They were also used on the Condor night goods between Cricklewood and Glasgow but enjoyed only a short reign on the Midland due to their poor reliability. As soon as sufficient class 45 locomotives became available in 1962 the Metrovicks were banished to Barrow where they plagued the Furness area with their questionable availability untl being withdrawn only ten years after their first appearance. This view depicts D5707 at Derby MPD on 15 March 1959, shortly after their introduction to the Midland. *A.R.Goult.*

The Midland Pullman was introduced in 1960 to compensate for electrification works on the LNWR and maintained a daily return working between Manchester (Central) and St Pancras with an intermediate trip from London to Leicester or Nottingham as a filling-in working. Whilst it was successful in allowing BR to retain much of the Manchester traffic, it suffered the disadvantage of carrying only first-class passengers which made it very difficult to utilise fully. The six coach set was also reputed to be very rough-riding due to rapid deterioration of the bogies and the service was withdrawn in 1966 upon completion of the west coast electrification. It is seen here passing St Albans on 14 March 1960. *A.R. Goult.*

tegrity of the kit. Even so, the weight of the symbols was still considerable. It was, therefore, halved by the adoption of a single letter to represent a particular pair of originating and terminating stations. The code had now lost its universal application and ease of deciphering and its use was eventually discontinued.

There is no doubt that the control system became an essential factor in the successful handling of the Midland's enormous mineral traffic. After grouping, with J H Follows appointed as Chief General Superintendent of the LMS, and later promoted to Vice President (Railway Traffic Operating and Commercial), its extension to the other constituents was inevitable. Some of its attendant requirements undoubtedly contributed to the friction between Crewe and Derby. This existed at all levels and was not confined to the well publicised differences in the locomotive department. An ex-Midland signalman, in a box newly equipped with a Permissive Block Instrument of LNWR origin, could only refer to it as "This thing off the Wessy", meanwhile banging his levers over until the box shook.

In addition to the pioneering of a train control system, the Midland was a large scale user of a permissive system for working its many miles of goods lines. On such lines, trains were controlled in accordance with "The Regulations for Train Signalling by Telegraph Bells". On the Extension, the goods lines between Kempston Road Junction and Harpenden Junction were covered by these regulations, except for the imposition of absolute block working through Ampthill tunnel and between Luton North and Luton South. Permissive block working was sub-

stituted in 1935 on the up road between Kempston Road Junction and Millbrook.

Generally known as the "Telegraph Bell System", the operating procedure was a drastically simplified version of absolute block working with, additionally, a provision for admitting

a train to an already occupied section. There were no block instruments and, normally, no "Call Attention" bell signal was used. Trains were not offered forward for acceptance by the box in advance as was the case with absolute block. Instead they were merely "belled on" as they passed, using the bell codes defined for "is line clear?" on the absolute system. When a train entered the advance section, the regulations required "a metal link or clip" to be placed on the lever of the signal controlling the entrance to the section until "Train out of section" had been received.

When a train arrived at a box with the section in advance already occupied, the regulations provided for the train to be brought to a stand at the home signal, the signal taken off, the train brought to a stand again at the box by a red hand signal, the driver warned verbally that the section ahead was occupied and, finally, a green hand signal given for the train to proceed. The driver of a Garratt with 87 loaded wagons would not have been amused. The practice was to keep the home signal "on", the train approached slowly and when close to the home signal the driver popped, the signal was pulled off and the signalman showed first a red and then a green flag (or lamps at night), the driver popped again in acknowledgement and set off cautiously, all without stopping. The signalman would say "I gave him a flag (or, a lamp)", the driver would say "I was warned in".

The signalman in advance gave "Train out of Section" when the last of the trains which had been belled to him arrived within the home signal (there was no 440yds clearance). However, he only had the entries in his block register as a reminder. Failure to enter a bell signal received for an approaching train could result in a premature "Train out of Section" being sent.

Suburban services south of Bedford were taken over by 4-car Rolls-Royce multiple-units in 1960; a step that banished much of the interest of the system. Noisy with exhaust arrangements that filled the coaches with diesel fumes their sole improvement over steam was a marginally better rate of acceleration. Their reputation was not enhanced during the early days of their career when they had to be withdrawn from traffic because of a propensity for bursting into flames. In this photograph one of the sets pauses at Flitwick shortly after its introduction with a St Pancras - Bedford stopping train, neither indicator nor destination board - as was usual - serving much useful purpose. *J. Osgood.*

Aesthetically a poor replacement for a compound and six non-corridors and not much better to ride in. A 4-car Rolls-Royce DMU passes Kentish Town with a St Pancras - Bedford working in 1960. *Lens of Sutton.*

by a commutator which could only be turned in the clockwise direction. The traditional indications, "Line Blocked", "Line Clear" and "Train on Line" could, therefore, only be displayed in their correct sequence. The safeguards associated with other lock and block systems could be applied. In general, the home signal lever was proved to be in the normal position, i.e back in the frame, before "Line Clear" could be sent.

Initially the commutator handle was locked unless the lever was normal. An amendment to the regulations in 1941 indicated that the instruments were being modified so that the handle could be moved but the indication would remain at "Line Blocked" unless the lever was normal. The lever for the starter at the box in rear was locked normal until "Line Clear" was received, whereupon it was released for one pull only. In many cases, sequential locking was added to ensure that the order of pulling off was home before starter. Once the commutator handle had been turned to "Train on Line" it was locked until the train had arrived and passed over a release treadle near the home signal. In some cases the release was only operative with the home signal lever reversed. As with all lock and block sys-

There was no blocking back signal, the only means the advance signalman had of preventing the entry of a train into the section was by verbally "blocking back" on the telephone or by sending "Obstruction Danger".

In many cases only one block bell was provided for both passenger and goods lines, the signals being distinguished by the presence or otherwise of an introductory "Call Attention". Even where separate bells were provided, it was in some instances the practice to use only one, the goods road bell being reserved for an illicit call to the omnibus telephone for the exchange of local news without alerting other users. The call was traditionally made by giving a "sloppy one", that is a single ring with the bell damped by holding down the ringing key. So by bell, book and, if not by candle, by oil lamp and flag, the goods lines were enabled over the years to carry the enormous tonnage of coal despatched to London and other destinations in the south. The ability to allow trains to queue at the entrance to absolute block sections was especially useful at such locations as Bedford North and Harpenden Junction on the up road. Considering its minimal safeguards, the Telegraph Bell System stood the test of time well. A sad accident at Oakley in 1949 resulted in the deaths of two enginemen and that effectively spelt its end. It was replaced for a time by Permissive Block, but with declining freight it would soon have outlived its usefulness in any case. That it survived for so long is a tribute to the professionalism of the generations of signalmen who were responsible for its operation.

The third special feature of Midland traffic control was the Rotary Interlocking Block Instrument, to give it the title by which it was known in the regulations. It was introduced in February 1909, coincidentally within one month of the train control system. Its basis was a simple and logical development of the conventional three position block instrument. The pegging handle on the accepting instrument was replaced

Perhaps the most curious engines to regularly work the Extension were the ten Crosti-boilered 9F 2-10-0's which appeared in 1955 and were all based at Wellingborough. Although this view of 92027, taken at Ampthill on 28 March 1959, shows the exhaust lifting clear of the engine, most of the time it drifted into the cab, making life very tiresome for the crew. After a short time in service smoke deflectors were added but the complaints continued and eventually the Crosti preheating arrangement was blanked off. *J. Osgood.*

Sharing the heavy mineral traffic with the 9Fs and Garretts were the Stanier 2-8-0s which for thirty years were a familiar sight on the extension. In this view 8269 of Wellingborough blasts its way out of London on 24 April 1948 with a northbound load of empties. *E.D. Bruton*

tems, the inherent simplicity of the concept had to be compromised in order to accommodate secondary functions. These included requirements for cancellation, blocking back, transmission of routing signals and switching out of signal boxes.

Cancellation of the "Line Clear" indication was the Achilles heel of some systems. The integrity of the Midland rotary block was safeguarded in this respect as it required the cooperation of the signalmen at both ends of the section to effect a cancellation. In addition to its safety function, the rotary block also gained a useful exemption from Rule 55 at home signals. On the Extension it was installed on both fast and slow lines between St Albans and Finchley Road and at some other selected locations. South of St Albans, the rotary block controlled a heavy traffic for some 70 years and functioned with

complete safety, a truly remarkable record. A collision involving two trains which had entered a single section did occur at Napsbury in 1977, only two years before the introduction of multiple aspect signals and track circuit block. As described in Chapter 9, however, the rotary block system itself was in no way responsible.

In 1874, James Allport, the General Manager, contributed to the discussion on a paper by Richard Rapier *On the Fixed Signals of Railways* given at the Institution of Civil Engineers. He "feared the tendency of the present day was so to increase the complications of these things [patents for working locking apparatus and signals] that it would be almost impractical to work the railways unless a stop was put to the introduction of many of these inventions. With regard to the block system, the Midland was, if not

the first, one of the first to introduce it nine or ten years since, on their main line. ...no doubt the locking apparatus was a great improvement on the old system; but it was a fallacy to suppose that it would altogether prevent accidents." He also spoke against the use of facing points for refuge sidings and the introduction of a third line for short distances, "because the additional junctions and facing points must necessarily increase the danger." His remarks reflect accurately the early policy of the Midland on signalling - enthusiasm for the block system, distrust of facing points and the eventual grudging acceptance of interlocking.

The principle of interlocking having been adopted, the Midland went ahead and produced their own locking frames. Like many other features of the railway, they were of quite distinctive design. The frames were notable for having all the locking apparatus above the level of the operating floor of the signal box. From the start, the locking was actuated by the catch handles of the levers.

From about 1908, the Midland fell into line with what was becoming universal practice and adopted tappet locking, still contained behind the frame above the operating floor. The frames now incorporated rockers to drive the locking. The rocker was similar to that introduced by the important Saxby and Farmer patent of 1871. The frames were, however, known as Tappet, rather than Rocker, Frames. There were only superficial differences in the external appearance of the two generations of Midland frames. The Midland tappet frame was adopted as standard by the LMS but with a 4 1/2 inch lever pitch instead of the 6 inch pitch used by the Midland.

A familiar feature of operations on the Extension were the whistle codes which enabled signalmen at junctions to have advance warning of the routes required by approaching traffic. These were officially known as "passing whistles" and were given at selected signal boxes in advance of junctions. The number of whistles given were repeated as "beats" or "ticks" on the block instruments from section to section. The normally non-pegging instruments at the boxes in the sections involved were provided with a spring loaded handle so that the signalman could transmit the code visually after sending "Train on Line" or "Is Line Clear?" on the block bell. During the LMS regime, the block instrument beats were replaced by the use of special bell codes.

In order to assist signalmen at the London end during the 1970s when the speed and frequency of trains was causing regulation problems through Belsize tunnels - of which one was used to the maximum whilst the other saw few if any trains - an 'overland bell' code was installed directly between Hendon and Finchley Road boxes so that the latter had advance information on approaching up traffic independently of the five intermediate block posts.

Apart from a solitary LNER locomotive, the LMS Garratts were the only main line examples of their type in the country and spent much of their time working to or from Cricklewood until being replaced in 1955/6 by the standard 9F 2-10-0s. 4988 eases a train of empties northwards through Elstree. *C.R.L. Coles*

9: ACCIDENTS

Providentially the Extension has been spared the major disasters with long casualty lists which have occurred on neighbouring main lines. The names of Harrow, Bourne End and Welwyn Garden City come to mind. The circumstances of some of the Extension's accidents are, however, worth recording. The published reports provide an insight into contemporary conditions and give details, otherwise unrecorded, of day to day operating procedures.

Major Marindin's report to the B.O.T on the accident at St Paul's Road Passenger Junction on 29th December 1884 contains much interesting detail. The 6.19 p.m GER train from Tottenham to St Pancras was on the up passenger line hauled by 0-4-4T No.233 running bunker first. It collided with the 6.5 p.m Midland train from Moorgate Street to South Tottenham which was passing from the City branch to the down passenger line. The Midland train consisted of 11 close coupled carriages hauled by 0-4-4T No.1547 running chimney first. The two engines met right side to right side on the junction; both were derailed and two carriages from each train finished on their sides. The GER fireman was fatally injured but the 20-30 passengers were unhurt. The Midland train was very full and though there were about 100 claims for injury only one case was serious.

Midland block regulations were in force on the main line and Metropolitan regulations on the branch. The St Paul's Road signalman was permitted to accept at the same time two down trains or - as was the case when the accident occurred - a train on the up main for St Pancras and a down branch train. The GER train was approaching under correctly cleared signals, the signals for the Midland train being "on". The signal lamps in the locality were lit by gas at the time. This was before the introduction of the Adlake long burning lamp and lights were important in an area of deep cuttings with steep retaining walls.

At 5.0 p.m, the St Paul's Road signalman, William Bray, noticed "the gas go out" in the Dock Junction up passenger distant. He called for assistance and a gasfitter, Nicholson, and a gasfitter's labourer, Combs, arrived at the box at about 6.0 p.m. Nicholson told Bray that the gas was also failing in the down home signals. Bray gave Nicholson two of the "petroleum" lamps which were kept in the box for emergencies. Bray was very busy and took the lamps, without checking them, from the pegs on which

Though embracing a small engine policy, the Midland inherited the large Whitelegg 4-6-4Ts, which were precluded from working to Fenchurch Street. They found employment on St Pancras workings from St Albans, where they were mostly outstationed. Earlier the class was also used on Wellingborough - Brent coal trains. 2106 is seen in St Pancras in the year of Grouping. *L&GRP*

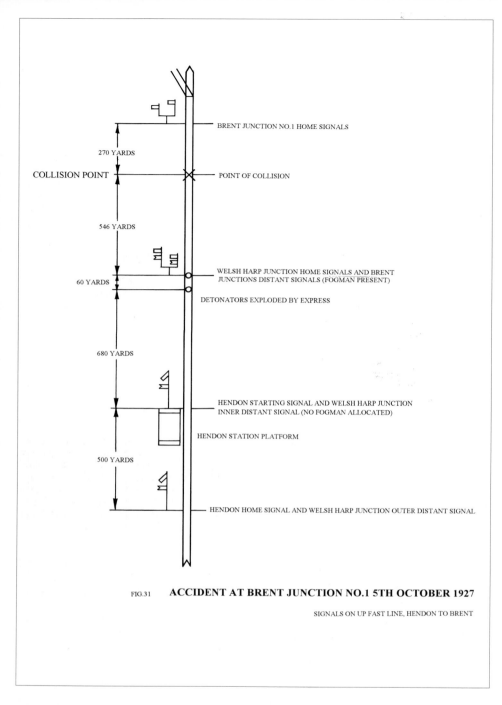

BRENT JUNCTION NO.1 HOME SIGNALS

270 YARDS

COLLISION POINT — POINT OF COLLISION

546 YARDS

60 YARDS — WELSH HARP JUNCTION HOME SIGNALS AND BRENT
JUNCTIONS DISTANT SIGNALS (FOGMAN PRESENT)

DETONATORS EXPLODED BY EXPRESS

680 YARDS

HENDON STARTING SIGNAL AND WELSH HARP JUNCTION
INNER DISTANT SIGNAL (NO FOGMAN ALLOCATED)

HENDON STATION PLATFORM

500 YARDS

HENDON HOME SIGNAL AND WELSH HARP JUNCTION OUTER DISTANT SIGNAL

FIG.31   **ACCIDENT AT BRENT JUNCTION NO.1 5TH OCTOBER 1927**

SIGNALS ON UP FAST LINE, HENDON TO BRENT

those with holes for light indicator expansion bars were usually kept. Painters had been working in the box and the lamps had been mixed up - those that Bray *actually* gave Nicholson had no holes for expansion bars. Nicholson left the box with the lamps already lit. He went with Combs to the down branch home signal and put one lamp on the ballast, unfortunately with the light facing oncoming trains. Combs mounted the ladder with the other lamp, called to Nicholson that it would not fit [through the lack of a hole] and that the gas had gone out.

The Midland driver saw the distant at "caution". On approaching the home signal he further saw two white lights, at the top and foot of the post. Thinking that the spectacle glass had broken and that the white light at the foot was a call forward - green had not yet replaced white as the "clear" signal - he put on steam again. Bray saw the Midland train approaching the junction, put his home signal back to danger against the GER train and tried to reverse the facing points but the GER engine was already on the lifting bar.

Major Marindin found 4 failures:-
1. Accumulation of water in the service pipe causing the gas to fail.
2. Bray gave Nicholson the wrong lamps.
3. Nicholson put the lamp on the ballast so as to show a white light along the line.
4. The driver took the improper light as a clear signal.

He attached no blame to Nicholson and held [rather surprisingly] that the driver's fail-

ure was only an error of judgement. He recommended that a new signal box be provided at the north end of the tunnel on the City branch to protect the junction and also made the eminently common sense suggestion that all the emergency lamps should have holes for expansion bars, thus making them suitable for all signals. His recommendation ultimately resulted in the opening of Lomond Street signal box as described in Chapter 5.

The B.O.T report on the accident at Watling Street on 8th December 1892 is chiefly of interest in its recording of the volume of traffic then being handled and the excessively long hours still being worked by enginemen. Watling Street box had only been open for a few weeks at the time of the accident, the driver of a train on the up goods line was unacquainted with the new arrangements and had "forgotten" the working notice. At 2.55 a.m, his train, the 8.0 p.m from Peterborough, overran the Watling Street up goods home signal. It was possible that he was misled by clear signals on the adjacent up passenger line. His train collided with an engine and brake van standing 50 yards in advance of the home signal and drove them forward into the brake van of the 6.30 p.m express goods from Burton. The Burton train, with 33 wagons and a brake van was in turn driven forward into the van of the 11.40 p.m goods from Bedford which consisted of 31 wagons and a brake van. The Bedford train was standing at the home signal of West End North Junction signal box waiting to enter West End sidings [West End North Junction box was later re-named West End Sidings]. Three men were injured. Although it had no bearing on the cause of the accident, the Inspecting Officer, Major Marindin, commented adversely on the hours worked by the men on the engine of the Bedford train. Their return working was due at Bedford at 7.23 a.m, but it rarely arrived before 11.0 a.m and it had been as late as 2.20 p.m. Driver Hyde's booked duty had been 11 hours 45 minutes for 5th December and 8 hours 58 minutes for each of the following three days, 6th, 7th and 8th. His *actual* times had worked out to 15 hours 25 minutes, 14 hours 20 minutes, 16 hours 10 minutes and 15 hours 50 minutes respectively.

Between 1891 and 1906, there were no less than four minor collisions with the buffer stops of No.6 platform at St Pancras. There does not appear to have been any special difficulty at the location and the sequence was purely coincidental. The first occasion was on 17th August 1891, when No.6 was still the East Arrival. The driver approached the station with only 10 in. of vacuum available as steam pressure had fallen to 80 psi through bad coal. On 12th August 1894, a train skidded into the stops on greasy rails. Surprisingly for the times, the driver was only slightly criticized and the Midland was berated for not enforcing the speed restriction at the entrance to the station. Errors of judgement accounted for the last two occasions, on 17th May 1901 and 3rd September 1906.

Before the introduction of colour light signals and the Automatic Warning System, a thick fog could cause serious operating difficulties. The problems were apparent in a minor collision which occurred at Brent on 5th October

The Whitelegg Baltic tanks were used in the Great War on Wellingborough to Brent minerals, after attempts to sell them to the GWR and SECR failed. 2101 is piloted by 0-6-0 2936 on an up coal train approaching Ampthill tunnel in 1917. *F. W. Goslin.*

1927. At 10.13 p.m, the 5.50 p.m express from Manchester Central to St Pancras ran into the rear of the 3.5 p.m freight train from Burton to London, as the latter was leaving the up fast line at Brent Junction No.1, to enter Brent Loaded Wagon sidings. Fortunately the speed of the express had been much reduced and there were only four minor injuries. The Burton goods was drawn by 0-6-0 No.3656 and comprised 48 wagons and a brake van. The last four wagons and the brake were derailed. The engine of the express was Compound No.1020, with nine bogie vehicles, flanked at each end by a four-wheeled van. The stock weighed 248 tons empty.

The fog had started between 7.30 and 8.0 p.m, the signalman at Welsh Harp Junction calling out his fogmen at 8.0 p.m to arrive at their posts between 9.0 and 9.30 p.m. The fogging post for the Brent Junction No.1 up fast distant was therefore manned. At Hendon, the signalman could still see his fog sighting object at 9.0 p.m and did not call out his fogmen until prompted by the station foreman at 9.15 p.m. The caller-up alerted the underman [platelayer] responsible for fog duty at the all-important Welsh Harp Junction outer distant signal at 9.30 p.m. The underman was in bed, he got up and prepared some food, but he did not report to Hendon signal box until 10.20 p.m, after the accident had occurred.

From 9.57 p.m to 10.10 p.m, the Brent Junction No.1 signalmen [shifts changed at 10.0 p.m] had endeavoured to call the attention of the leading shunter at Brent Loaded Wagon Sidings stage box (or the yard foreman who was due to relieve him at 10.0 p.m.). Permission from the stage box was necessary for the Burton goods, by then standing at the Brent Junction No.1 up fast home signal, to enter the yard. There was a loud sounding bell and a tell-tale indicator at the stage box but both men there were engaged

on shunting movements until about 10.10 p.m. The foreman then entered the box, saw the tell-tale had operated, gave the requisite permission and pulled off the control slot on the directing signal. So the Burton goods had only just commenced to draw away from the home signal when the collision took place.

With the section ahead occupied, the Welsh Harp Junction signalman had accepted the express from Hendon at about 10.8 p.m but

had kept all his signals at danger. So, only the Hendon signals were cleared for the express. After seeing that the Hendon distant was "off", the express driver had moved from the right to the left hand side of the footplate to view the Welsh Harp Junction outer distant. In the fog conditions he did not see it but his fireman called out "right - both off". The driver was uneasy and made a special effort to see the inner distant, but the fog and the glare of the Hendon platform lights prevented this. He reduced speed to about 30 m.p.h in order to see the signals at Welsh Harp Junction, he saw some red lights and ran over a detonator laid by the fogman for the Brent distant and immediately afterwards ran over another, the emergency detonator co-acting with the Welsh Harp Junction home signal. Although realising that the second detonator was an emergency signal, he only reduced the vacuum from 21 in. to 10 in., with the object of "stopping the train in a reasonable way". Speed had been reduced to about 10 m.p.h before the collision. The fireman said that he saw two green lights but admitted that his knowledge of the road was poor and that he did not know to which signal boxes the lights referred.

There were three contributory causes for this accident. The delay in admitting the Burton goods to the sidings, the delay in manning the fog post at Welsh Harp Junction outer distant and the lack of decisive action by the express driver after missing signals and exploding two detonators. Although it was not suggested by the Inspecting Officer, it is difficult to escape the conclusion that the driver's intention was to draw up to the Brent Junction No.1 home signal rather than to stop as quickly as possible. The driver was held responsible for the collision, the dilatory fogman and the men at Brent Loaded Wagon sidings were absolved. The evidence did, how-

The Midland relied for many years on pairs of 0-6-0s to work its heavy mineral service. Locomotive shortage forced the purchase of a number of American Moguls in 1899, the GCR and GNR being forced to take similar measures. No.2515 is at Welsh harp with empty wagons. The engines did not lessen the Company's affection for the 0-6-0. *GWG Collection*

ever, appear to indicate an unsatisfactory situation at the stage box, which would in any case have resulted in a signal check to an important express. The recommendation was made that when the Welsh Harp Junction signalman called for his fogmen, the post at his outer distant should be included, rather than with the Hendon fogmen.

A collision between two passenger trains occurred in the down platform at Luton station on 22nd December 1955. The standing train was the 6.45 p.m from St Pancras to Leicester, booked to stop at Luton for 10 minutes to allow the attachment of vans in front. Some regular travellers used to take advantage of the prolonged stop to have a drink in the refreshment room on the down platform. On the night of the accident, the train had left St Pancras 14 minutes late and, in consequence, the Luton stop had been cut to 8 minutes. When the train moved off, three passengers ran out of the refreshment room, two boarded safely but the third failed in his attempt and was dragged along the platform. The guard stopped the train with its rear coach still in the platform, actually 435 yards in advance of the Luton South down home signal, held at danger by track circuit occupation. Particulars of the three passengers were being taken by the guard and a Police Constable when the train was struck by the following 7.10 p.m express from St Pancras to Derby.

The 7.10 p.m, ten coaches hauled by a Class 5 4-6-0, had left St Pancras 10 minutes late. Two vans had been attached to the 6.45 p.m at Luton, it then consisted of three vans, three corridor coaches and, in the rear, three non-corridor coaches. The latter were steel panelled on timber framing with steel underframes. Although there was no derailment, the last two coaches of the 6.45 p.m were partly telescoped, resulting in the death of one passenger. Twelve more passengers were detained in hospital. The signalman at Luton South had given "Train out of Section" to Chiltern Green when the tail lamp of the 6.45 p.m was about a coach length beyond the footbridge; he was immediately offered and duly accepted the 7.10 train. He received "Train Entering Section" for it about three minutes later, and then saw that the Track Circuit through the down platform was still occupied and that the tail lamp of the 6.45 p.m was visible in the platform. The driver of the 7.10 p.m was in Kentish Town No.3 link and knew the road well but approaching Luton at about 70m.p.h, he was not able to identify the Luton South distant signal among the cluster of yellow lights around the Vauxhall works. He expected a green aspect as he had never been checked at Luton with a non-stopping train. He realised that he had passed the distant when nearing an overbridge, a point about 1,000 yards from the home. He closed the regulator and braked lightly but did not make a full application until he saw the home signal at danger - the express was still travelling at about 20 m.p.h when the collision took place. The report to the Ministry of Transport and Civil Aviation acknowledged that the Luton South signalman was in order in giving "Out of Section" for the 6.45 p.m and in accepting the express. There was no means of judging when a train had exactly covered the 440 yards

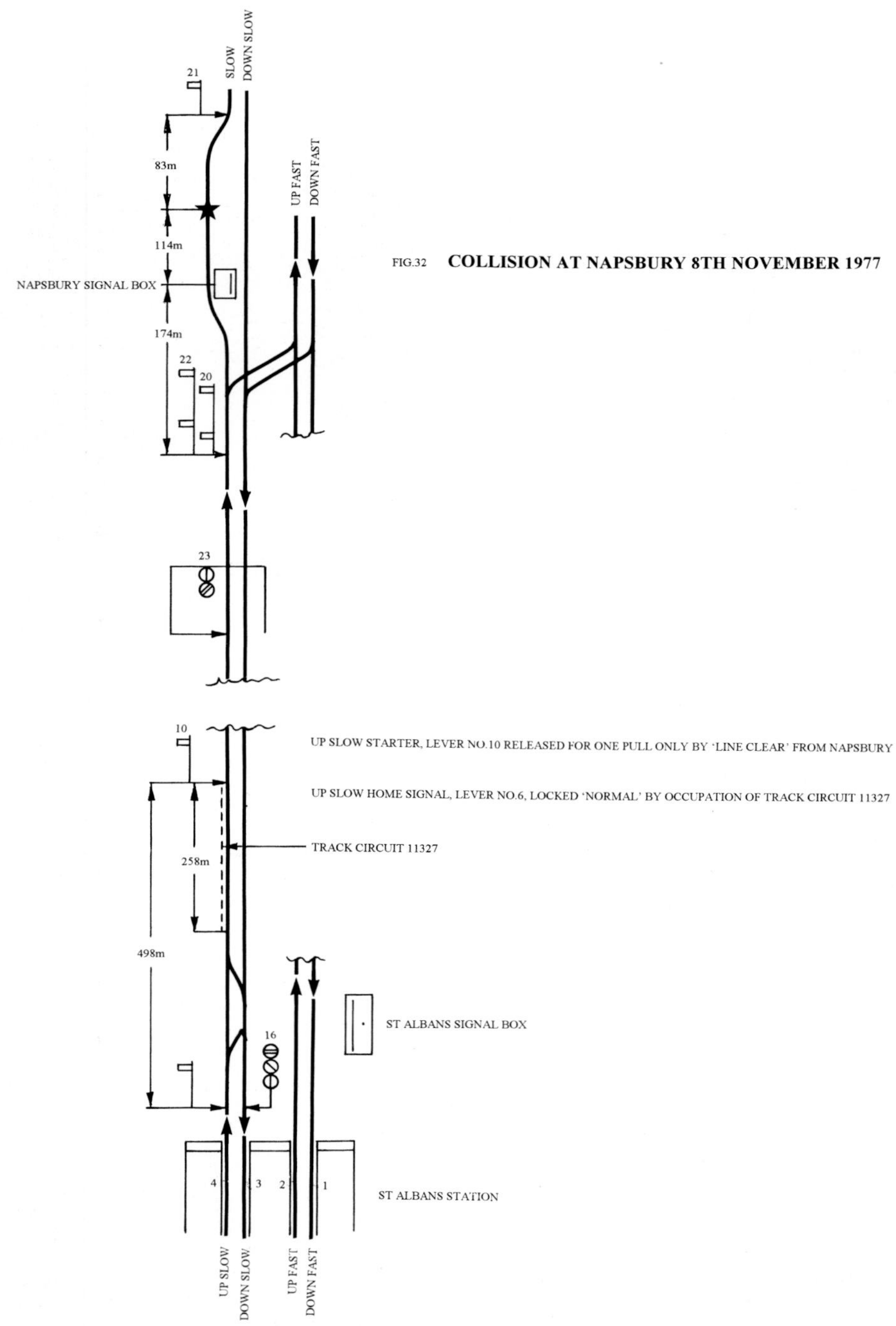

FIG.32 **COLLISION AT NAPSBURY 8TH NOVEMBER 1977**

required by the Block Regulations, and the use of the footbridge, 410 yards from the signal, was accepted as reasonable. A suggestion that the Track Circuit, which extended to a point 512 yards in advance of the home signal, should control the block instrument was accepted. The yellow aspect of the Luton South colour light distant was not easy to identify at first amongst other lights but it stood out clearly at close range. As

a result of the accident, Luton Borough Council and Vauxhall Motors Ltd. took steps to screen their lights and the signal was moved back 310 yards. The point was not made in the report that a green aspect would have been readily identifiable and that the sighting of yellow lights only should have been taken as a Caution indication. It was concluded that the driver of the express made a "serious error" in failing to see the distant signal at Caution and in not making a full brake application until he saw the home signal at Danger.

When the 21.25 train from Glasgow Central arrived at St Pancras on the morning of 23rd December 1966, three passengers informed the guard that ballast had been thrown up under the coach in which they had been travelling. The Carriage and Wagon examiner on duty was duly informed, finding that the trailing end of a brake pull rod of seven eighths inch square section on a bogie of the fourth coach had been dragging along the track. The pull rod transmitted the braking force to the outer bogie wheels via a fulcrum lever to which it was attached by a pin retained by a split pin. The pin was missing and the hole in the pull rod had been worn away by abrasion from the track. Two safety loops, intended to support the rod in case of breakage, were themselves broken. The examiner secured the rod temporarily with wire and notified his foreman so that permanent repairs could be carried out at Cricklewood. The rod was secured when the brakes were "on". The stock of the 21.25 left St Pancras routed on the down fast line as the 07.45 empty coaches to Cricklewood carriage sidings. When the brakes were released, the broken end of the rod dropped. Now pointing downwards in the facing direction, the rod scored the covers of AWS magnets at Dock Junction. At Islip Street Junction, just before Kentish Town station, there was a facing connection from the down fast to down slow line. The points were equipped with an ex-Midland type Economical Facing Point Lock. The rod displaced the cover of the lock and struck the operating crank, reversing the points under the train. The front portion of the train continued on the down fast line and stopped in Kentish Town station due to loss of vacuum. The 4th, 5th and 6th vehicles were derailed and the remainder of the train was diverted on to the connection between

One of the great mysteries of railway operating is why the Midland Railway persisted in working its heavy mineral trains with pairs of 0-6-0s when the rest of the country was looking to eight coupled engines to do the job with greater economy and efficiency. To add to the mystery the Somerset & Dorset - in which the Midland had a stake - ordered six large 2-8-0s from Derby in 1914, some of which, like No.85 above (north of Ampthill tunnel with empties) were borrowed by the larger company during the Great War. *F.W.Goslin.*

down fast and down slow. Despite damage to the structure of the box by the derailed vehicles, the Islip Street signalman was able to put his up fast signals to danger and to send "Obstruction Danger" in both directions. The up fast signals had been cleared for the 07.48 DMU from Radlett to St Pancras, approaching at about 60 m.p.h. The driver saw a green aspect at Islip Street Junction Inner Distant No.1 and then a

single yellow at Inner Distant No.2. He made an emergency brake application but struck the derailed coaches at about 20 m.p.h. One passenger was detained in hospital.

Marks were found on AWS ramps on the up fast line from Bedford onwards and it was assumed that the rod had become detached in that area. The missing pin and split pin were never found - the damage to Islip Street Junction signal box was serious and it was subsequently demolished. The Inspecting Officer concluded that the rod should have been removed entirely at St Pancras or that the brakes on the coach should have been isolated to prevent the rod moving. Instructions were issued for the examination of all safety loops, the replacement of all loops not long enough to avoid wear from the pull rods and replacement, when required, of the square section pull rods by rods manufactured from seven eighth inch round bar.

At Napsbury, on 8th November 1977, there was the rare occurrence of a collision on a section of line controlled by the Midland Rotary Block system. The events which led to the collision, however, were independent of the safeguards of the system. Both the trains concerned were 4-car Class 127 DMUs.

An empty train (5C26) was waiting to return to St Pancras from the down slow platform (No.3) at St Albans. The St Albans signalman decided to give it priority over a train from Bedford (2C65) which had to make stops intermediately. He set the road and signalled 5C26 to run up to the up slow starter No.10. There it would have to wait acceptance from Napsbury where an up fast train was held waiting to proceed to Radlett. It left the platform at about 18.35. The passenger train arrived

Scope for a budding historian. In 1943/4 large numbers of American 2-8-0 freight engines were used in this country; locomotives which disappeared as quickly as they had come with little being recorded about them. Photography during this period was a difficult (and illegal) pastime although one brave soul risked his neck to obtain a print of one of the engines heading through Elstree with an up coal train. *GWG collection.*

Compound 41181 of Leicester starts away from Luton with a St Pancras stopping train in March 1957. The accident of 22 December 1955 took place on the running line to the right of the train in the photograph. *J. Osgood.*

at the up slow platform No.4 at about 18.38. At 18.41, "Train out of Section" was received from Napsbury and 5C26 was offered and accepted. It appears, however, that the starting signal, released for one pull by the acceptance, was not cleared at the time and 5C26 remained at the signal out of sight of the signalman. His neglect of the illuminated diagram, on which occupation of Track Circuit No.11327 would be shown, is inexplicable.

At that time there was a railwayman visitor in the St Albans box and the signalman was also distracted by telephone calls and by having to supervise the first day's work of a new re-

corder. It appears that he was committing to memory the bell signals for entering in the register at an opportune moment. He saw the block indicator for the up slow line to Napsbury at "Line clear" and telephoned the Napsbury signalman to ask the whereabouts of 5C26. The latter replied that he had nothing at Napsbury, whereupon the St Albans signalman said that he had the passenger, 2C65. His Napsbury colleague thought that the priority for the two trains had been reversed and changed the acceptance entry in his register from 2-2-1 (empty coaches) to 3-1 (ordinary passenger). At St Albans, the signalman then attempted to pull off the up slow

home signal to allow 2C65 to depart. He found it locked, in fact correctly due to occupation of Track Circuit 11327 by 5C26. Once again neglecting the diagram, he called the station supervisor to the box by means of the public address system and asked him to tell the driver of 2C65 to pass signal No.6 at danger and the line would be clear to Napsbury. He then, at about 18.44, cleared the starter, the release of which had been obtained by the acceptance of 5C26 by Napsbury at 18.41. Train 5C26 therefore started from signal No.10 and 2C65 followed from signal No.6.

The Napsbury to Radlett section was still occupied by the up freight. 5C26 was brought to a momentary stand at the Napsbury home signal No.22 and then arrived at the starter No.21. The Napsbury signalman, seeing 5C26 approach without lights, changed his block register back again to 2-2-1. The driver of 2C65 passed the Napsbury distant, No.23, showing a yellow aspect. He closed the throttle, speed falling from 35-40 m.p.h. to about 25 m.p.h. Seeing a green light at No.22 (cleared for 5C26 and not restored to danger), he was led to believe that the starter would be "off" so he re-applied power. He then saw the tail lamp and outline of 5C26 ahead, made an emergency brake application and vacated the cab.

For some reason the report to the Minister of Transport was not published until 1981, being dated 24th October 1980, nearly three years after the accident. By that time the signalling involved had been replaced by multiple-aspect colour lights controlled from West Hampstead. St Albans and Napsbury signal boxes were closed on 2nd December 1979. The report acknowledged that the controls on the signalling were adequate and concluded that the collision occurred because the driver of 2C65 was irregularly instructed to pass a signal at danger.

Old habits die hard it appears; the Midland being unable to resist the opportunity to double-head even when the train engine is a Garrett. Hughes-Fowler 'Crab' 42763 of Burton pilots 47987 past Ayres End Lane with a down train of empties on 7 May 1949. It is probable that the 2-6-0 had worked up to London with an unbalanced beer special and was returning via Toton to its home depot. *E.D. Bruton*

10: ELECTRIFICATION

On 8th November 1976, Mr William Rodgers, then Secretary of State for Transport, announced to the House of Commons that it had been decided to proceed with the electrification of the railway from Moorgate and St Pancras to Bedford. The total cost would be £80M. Approval of a programme for route rationalisation and resignalling had been announced earlier in the same year. At 1975 price levels, the cost of the project was:-

Rationalisation and Resignalling:	*£37.3M.*
Traffic and General:	*£0.7M.*
Rolling Stock:	*£21.9M.*
Electrification:	*£18.6M.*
Total:	*£78.5M.*

The announcement presaged a change to the character of the line even more radical than the widenings of the 1890s. The latter, while changing its physical aspects, provided greater capacity for the previously existing pattern of services. Electrification not only gave the line another totally new look but it was also to have a far reaching effect on the eventual pattern and destinations of services from Bedford and the intermediate stations. In fact just how revolutionary a change would be achieved in a few years was not apparent to the planners of 1976.

The full service was programmed to commence in 1982. It was based on an increased

Although this section of the book describes recent developments on the extension, the illustrations concentrate on earlier and more interesting days when almost every train had an individual character and personality. In this scene Jubilee 45694 BELLEROPHON of Leeds (Holbeck) makes a gentle start from St Pancras with the 16.50 to Bradford (Forster Square) on 25 August 1948. The train had an interesting history, starting in 1925 and later being named 'The Yorkshireman'. It was unusual in that it ran to Bradford Exchange via Thornhill, avoiding Leeds. and was further characterised by being the first train on the LMS to consist solely of open stock. After the war the service reappeared but was routed via the orthodox route, calling at Leeds where a reversal was made. The stock in the picture is painted in an experimental cream and brown livery, the engine appearing in apple-green. *E.D. Bruton*

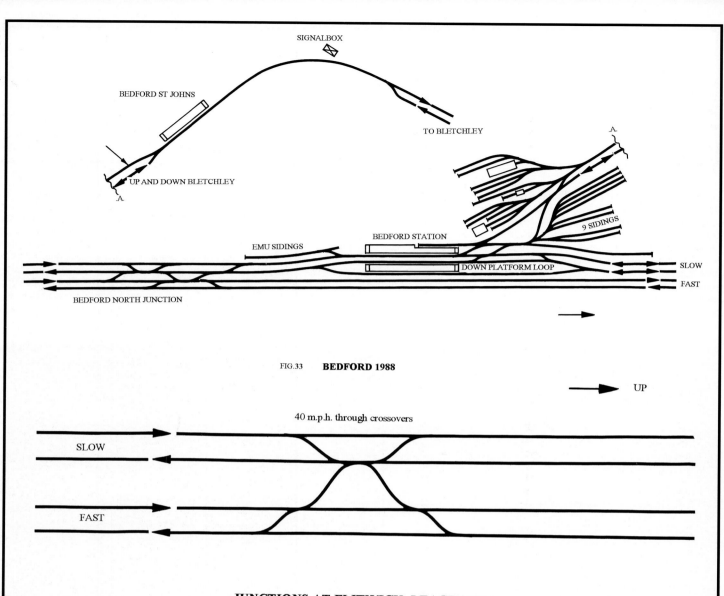

SIGNALBOX

BEDFORD ST JOHNS

TO BLETCHLEY

UP AND DOWN BLETCHLEY

.A.

.A.

9 SIDINGS

EMU SIDINGS

BEDFORD STATION

DOWN PLATFORM LOOP

SLOW

FAST

BEDFORD NORTH JUNCTION

FIG.33   **BEDFORD 1988**

UP

40 m.p.h. through crossovers

SLOW

FAST

JUNCTIONS AT FLITWICK, LEAGRAVE, HARPENDEN AND RADLETT 1983

MP 48.5

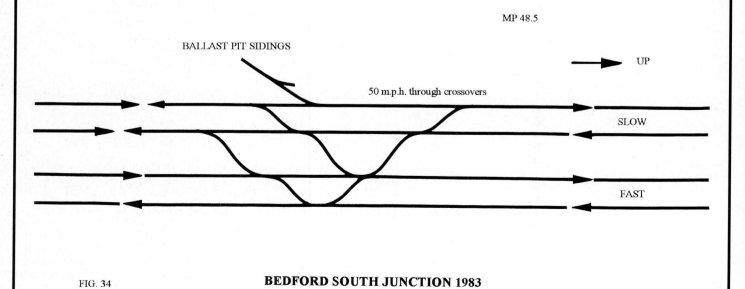

BALLAST PIT SIDINGS

UP

50 m.p.h. through crossovers

SLOW

FAST

FIG. 34   **BEDFORD SOUTH JUNCTION 1983**

use of Moorgate, rather than St Pancras, as the London terminus, and an improved interchange with London Transport at King's Cross. Ownership of the Widened Lines would be transferred from London Transport to BR. The off-peak service would consist of two trains per hour Moorgate/Luton and hourly trains Moorgate/Bedford and St Pancras/Bedford. This was double the frequency of the existing DMU service. The number of trains in the peak hour was to be increased from 10 to 16. Accompanying the improvements to the service would be an increase in line speed limits to 100 m.p.h on the fast lines and 75 m.p.h on the slow lines. Authorisation of the electrification plan did not come before due time. The DMUs, the "last word" in 1960, had not aged well and, with 5 1/2 years implementation to come, it was obvious that they would be long overdue for replacement by the time the new service started.

The traction power supply is transformed from 132kV to 25kV in sub-stations located at Sundon, with two transformers, and Grahame Park, between Hendon and Mill Hill, with one transformer. The total load, at its maximum during the morning peak, is within the short term rating of one transformer. There are track sectioning cabins at Kentish Town, Radlett, Sandridge Road (St Albans), Luton Hoo, Ampthill and Bedford. With 4 closely spaced

tracks on most of the route, headspan construction was generally used for the overhead line equipment. Some additional supports have had to be introduced subsequently at Millbrook, recognised since Midland days as the most exposed location on the line. Booster transformers and insulated return conductors were used throughout to provide suppression at source of interference with communication circuits. Clearances in the tunnels between Kentish Town and Moorgate were restricted, but improved conductor support assemblies enabled the total headroom above the kinematic load gauge to be reduced to only 375mm at difficult locations. The traction power supply system is controlled from the Electrical Control Room at Hornsey, originally provided for the Great Northern suburban electrification from Moorgate and King's Cross to Royston.

The description of the pre-electrification Extension began at St Pancras and ended at Bedford and is appropriate, therefore, to make the return journey when considering the present day railway. The changes due to electrification are most marked at Bedford itself. The completely new station is on a site some 200 yards to the north of the old Midland Road station which has now disappeared without trace. The name became Bedford Midland on 8th May 1978 in anticipation of the change of location. Good use

has been made of previously vacant railway land to provide a station with three through platform roads on an alignment in keeping with that of the adjacent fast lines of the Bedford Curve. The new main building was opened officially on 9th October 1978. The completion of the station was necessarily protracted as the new and old platforms overlapped on different alignments. The new island platform initially had a long temporary extension at its south end so that it could be brought into use before the north end was completed. The latter operation had to await the removal of the lines to the old station.

To the north, the roads through the station continue as slow lines, connection with the fast lines being made by ladder junctions on the north side of Bromham Road bridge. To the east of the Extension, between the station and the Ouse, new stabling and servicing sidings have been laid out. Most of the land was previously unused, and a carriage washer has been installed. An interesting survival is a portion of the side wall of the "old loco", incorporated into a new shed which houses the Civil Engineer's vehicles.

The ex-LNWR branch from Bletchley was diverted at Bedford No.1 signal box from its previous entry into Bedford St Johns station. It now follows the path of the old connection past the sites of the LNWR yard and Bedford LNW

Around 1960 there were strong rumours that the Midland was to receive a batch of Bulleid light Pacifics from the Southern Region, a supposition that turned out to be baseless. The only occasion on which such engines did visit the extension - other than on enthusiasts specials - was during the locomotives exchanges when 34005 BARNSTAPLE worked for a short period between St Pancras and Manchester Central. Here the light pacific sets off with a preliminary run at the head of the 10.15 to Manchester on 14 June 1948. *C.R.L.Coles.*

Also assessed during the 1948 exchanges was B1 61251 OLIVER BURY of Kings Cross which is here seen passing West Hampstead on 10 June 1948 with the 13.50 Manchester Central - St Pancras. *GWG collection.*

Junction box to join the course of the Hitchin branch over the Ouse. A reverse curve brings it to a junction with the Extension at the south end of the new platforms. A replacement St Johns station was opened at the Ampthill Road on the site of the LNWR level crossing and under the bridge which the Midland built so reluctantly. So, 120 years late, a station was at last established at the Ampthill Road. Its single platform, unattended and little used, is in ironic contrast to the joint Bedford station desired by the Midland in the early 1860s.

The diversion into Bedford Midland of the Bletchley trains caused problems with platform occupation at peak hours. In April 1988, a line was laid into the bay platform on the east side, the face of which had been provided in readiness. A difficulty then arose with the plat-

form numbering as the opposite face to the bay was No.1. Rather than re-number all the platforms, the new bay became 1A. If St Pancras had to be deprived of a platform No.1, Bedford could redress the balance by having two!

The crossovers known as Bedford South Junction, which connect the fast lines to the slow lines serving the platforms are rated for 50 m.p.h but their commencement is over a mile from the station. The trailing connection to the Ballast Pit siding has been retained. At the site of Elstow brickworks, a further connection from the up slow is made to a Redland depot. There is also a trailing crossover here between up and down slow lines.

From Elstow, 7 miles of plain track follow to Flitwick where a double ladder junction, with 40 m.p.h limits through the crossovers, is

installed to the north of the station. Exactly similar junctions are located north of Leagrave and south of Harpenden and Radlett.

The original station buildings at Flitwick, Harlington and Leagrave have been refurbished externally and the booking offices have been modernised. The results are commendable. Platform improvements were required at Flitwick and Harlington and two short sidings have been retained on the up side at Leagrave. Limbury Road yard still exists but sees little use.

At Luton there are still five running lines through the station but their dispositions have been changed. The down slow through and platform lines have been combined and the up slow platform is now an island. The changes were made in late 1977, well in advance of the electrification. The main improvement made to the station facilities was the provision of a new travel centre on the footbridge. The connection to the closed Dunstable branch has been severed. At Crescent Road goods yard some sidings are covered by large stocks of ballast. The Vauxhall siding has disappeared. There is plain track between Luton and the crossovers south of Harpenden. The connection to the Hemelite (A firm making building blocks, from fly ash among other ingredients, which used part of the disused Hemel Hempstead branch until BR gave notice that the junction would be severed) line at Harpenden Junction was shown as retained on the first diagrams to be published for the revised track layout, but other counsels prevailed. At Harpenden station the slow lines have been realigned to eliminate the previous speed restriction. Part of the old station building remains in use, now completely dwarfed by a new footbridge which appears to have been sited to suit an entrance which has not been built. The aspects of the old buildings at the country stations north of Luton are pleasant because they dominate the modern additions. At Harpenden, the effect is merely incongruous, preservation without regard to the merit of the result. At St Albans, a new reversing siding was installed between the up and down slow roads at the north end. This required the diversion of the up slow through a span of the overbridge at one time used for a connection to the goods yard. A siding from the down fast at one time used by the Post Office for loading mail was retained, initially. The curvature of the up slow at the site of Napsbury's island platform has been eliminated; the point of divergence of the "St Albans branch" can still be identified and a Redland roadstone depot, very near to the site of the old Parkbury siding, has a facing connection from the up slow.

Radlett station has been rebuilt from platform level upwards but however much the loss of the old buildings is regretted, it must be acknowledged that the new structure is a worthy and convenient replacement. At Elstree, the old buildings on the platforms have gone. Due, however, to previous parsimony with the replacement footbridge and booking office, the success of the new Radlett has not been repeated here. Mill Hill, previously adapted radically to make room for the M1, needed little change for the electrification. At Silk Stream Junction, the limit for the slow lines was raised from 30 to 60 m.p.h. There was room at Hendon for an approach road

Jubilee 4-6-0 45657 TYRWHITT raises some home counties dust as it roars through on the fast line on 29th May 1950. *G.W.Goslin.*

10000, the LMS 1600hp diesel electric, passes Napsbury with an up express on 13 March 1948. *E.D. Bruton.*

and ticket office between the railway and the M1. The new building is small but neat, reflecting the station's reduced status in today's pattern of transport facilities in the area.

Great changes have been made to the Cricklewood/Brent complex. On the down side,

the lines to Acton remain in use whilst the junctions of the Extension with the northern and southern curves to Dudding Hill Junction are now known as Brent Curve Junction and Cricklewood Curve Junction respectively. In the triangle formed by the two curves and the main

line, Brent Empty Wagon sidings remain in situ, now known as Cricklewood Recess Sidings. BR interest in all the land to the west of the Acton branch has been relinquished and the site is covered by buildings occupied by commercial enterprises and a Post Office parcels depot.

On the up side, nearly all of the area previously covered by the old marshalling yards and carriage sidings was taken over by the Cricklewood Maintenance Depot, the spacious layout of which was a sign of a "clean sheet of paper" at the planning stage of the electrification scheme. Subsequent developments have now made the provisions surplus to requirements. Already the large building at the south end, intended for servicing inter city stock, has been demolished following a period of dereliction. At the rear of the depot are the private sidings where rubbish in "Easidispose" containers is transferred from road to rail for the journey to the dumping ground at Stewartby.

The platforms at Cricklewood station have been lengthened and a realignment of the slow lines has eliminated the previous 25 m.p.h speed restriction. There is a double running junction, with moveable diamonds, from up slow to up fast and down fast to down slow at the location termed Cricklewood South Junction. The site of West End sidings has been covered by new housing. Brassey and Barlow are remembered in the names of the roads, joining Campion and Needham, long commemorated in the Midland terraces at Cricklewood. The original electrifi-

Not only have the Garratts disappeared but the coal traffic has gone as well . In steam days, however, sights such as 4973 heading south with a load of coal were so commonplace they they scarcely warranted a second glance. *GWG collection.*

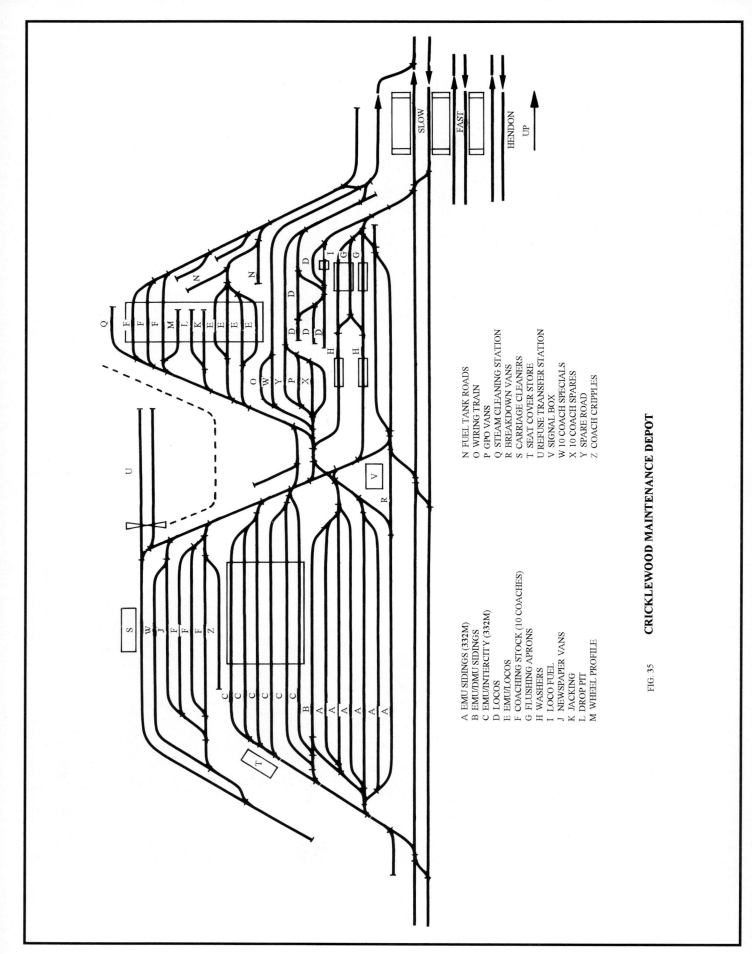

A EMU SIDINGS (332M)
B EMU/DMU SIDINGS
C EMU/INTERCITY (332M)
D LOCOS
E EMU/LOCOS
F COACHING STOCK (10 COACHES)
G FLUSHING APRONS
H WASHERS
I LOCO FUEL
J NEWSPAPER VANS
K JACKING
L DROP PIT
M WHEEL PROFILE

N FUEL TANK ROADS
O WIRING TRAIN
P GPO VANS
Q STEAM CLEANING STATION
R BREAKDOWN VANS
S CARRIAGE CLEANERS
T SEAT COVER STORE
U REFUSE TRANSFER STATION
V SIGNAL BOX
W 10 COACH SPECIALS
X 10 COACH SPARES
Y SPARE ROAD
Z COACH CRIPPLES

FIG. 35   CRICKLEWOOD MAINTENANCE DEPOT

St Albans MPD in 1949 with Fowler 2-6-4T 42334 and an unidentified Jinty 0-6-0 pausing between duties. *L&GRP*

cation scheme included the rebuilding of the up slow platform at West Hampstead with two faces to the south of the West End Lane overbridge. One side was to serve a terminal road, presumably as a turn round point for the Barking DMU service in place of Kentish Town. Although there was some clearance of the site, the platform was not built and the Barking trains were diverted instead to Gospel Oak, possibly due to limitations of line capacity through Belsize tunnels. There is scope at West Hampstead for a comprehensive interchange, linking the ex-Metropolitan, LNWR and Midland stations.

A 50 m.p.h ladder at "West Hampstead South Junction" (Finchley Road to traditionalists) provides for up fast to up slow and down slow to down fast movements. An important change was made here as part of the re-signalling and electrification works. The fast lines, which previously were combined with the slow to pass through the new Belsize tunnel, were transferred to the old tunnel which had been used by the goods lines. The change resulted in much better utilisation of the combined capacity of the bores. At the south end there are further 50 m.p.h crossovers. These provide an alternative to West Hampstead South Junction for transferring trains using the King's Cross tunnel and, therefore, the slow lines through Kentish Town, to and from the fast lines to the north.

The only remaining connection to the Tottenham and Hampstead line is that from Carlton Road Junction. With St Pancras now under-used, the loss of the Mortimer Street to Engine Shed Junction curve may yet be regretted. At Kentish Town, the station has been renovated and a common booking office is shared with London Transport. The interchange with

the Northern Line is more convenient here than at King's Cross but its usefulness does not seem to be widely appreciated. The old up fast line is now a bi-directional carriage line and the old down fast line is a bi-directional slow line.

On the south side of Camden Road tunnels the carriage and slow lines merge to form a third running line to St Pancras in addition to the up and down fast lines. By the churchyard, some roads have been retained as carriage holding sidings. The layout of St Pancras station was simplified. Although it was shown on early scheme drawings, Platform 1, too short for an HST, has not been reinstated. Some slab track had to be provided on the fast lines south of Kentish Town where the level was lowered to avoid disturbing a bridge carrying high voltage cables.

The Moorgate lines descend to King's Cross from Dock Junction North, the new designation of St Paul's Road Passenger Junction. The initial gradient is now established as 1 in

Class 4 0-6-0s 3942 and 3856 on the Hendon flyover with empty wagons on 10th September 1927. These engines, with a grate area of only 21.1 sq. ft., were known without a trace of irony as 'The Big Goods'. Meanwhile large 2-8-0s had been introduced by the GWR, GCR and GNR. *H.C. Casserley.*

55. Speed from here to Moorgate is limited to 30 m.p.h throughout. In April 1983, trials took place with Class 317 EMUs fitted with polystyrene strips to simulate their kinematic gauge. The clearances in King's Cross tunnel, with a 10 chain radius curve at the bottom end, are tight, but slab track (fastenings embedded in concrete, reducing headroom) enables the margins to be maintained.

The old Widened Lines station at King's Cross was completely rebuilt for the electrification. The major works were a new ticket hall with a direct entrance from the Pentonville Road and a pedestrian interchange tunnel to the platforms of the Victoria and Piccadilly lines. The station was initially renamed "King's Cross Midland City" and the newly electrified railway became the Midland City line.

The station at King's Cross Midland City, now King's Cross Thameslink, is built on three levels. On the lowest, the subway from the tube stations terminates with steps to the platforms and an escalator to street level. The platforms, lengthened to 168 metres, are at the intermediate level. Platform B, used by northbound trains is very narrow but improvement is impossible due to the proximity of the outer rail of the Circle line. Some narrow seats are fixed to the boundary wall but the general impression is of sparse facilities with almost dangerous overcrowding at peak times. At the top - street - level, there is the new ticket hall with a footbridge connection to platform B. The old Widened Lines platforms at Farringdon and Barbican were cleaned and refurbished. The cross platform interchange at Farringdon between up trains and the westbound Metropolitan is convenient and useful. The short platform at Barbican remains unaltered, a trap for those in the rear of 8 car trains.

With the earlier Great Northern suburban electrification, the 25kV ac used on the surface was replaced by dc for the section through the large bore tube tunnels to Moorgate. The Midland electrification was at 25kV ac throughout.

A gleaming GER 4-4-0 - the original 'Claud Hamilton' - waits for its next turn of duty - probably a Cambridge train - in St Pancras in 1907. *GWG collection.*

The decision to use ac on the Widened Lines involved the acceptance of reduced electrical clearances and the installation of slab track at critical locations. It was justified at the time by the avoidance of a requirement for dual system rolling stock.

The scheme for re-signalling and route rationalisation was authorised some twelve months in advance of that for the electrification. The new signalling system is operated from a power signal box at West Hampstead, the control area extending north of Bedford as far as Irchester to cover a total of 438 single track kilometres. 618 signals, 370 point ends and 1278 track circuits were required. Relay interlocking was used, West Hampstead box being designed before the adoption of micro-processors. Signalling power is obtained at 12 locations from local electricity supplies. Automatic changeover to a supply derived from the traction system is provided at each site. At West Hampstead, a standby diesel alternator enables communications to be maintained if both power supplies are lost. Four signalmen are required at West Hampstead, working at a console and illuminated track diagram 27 metres long. 13 safety interlockings, linked to West Hampstead by a time division multiplex system, are located in relay rooms at St Pancras, Barbican/Farringdon, Kentish Town, West Hampstead, Silk Stream Junction, Radlett, St Albans, Harpenden, Luton, Leagrave, Flitwick, Bedford and Sharnbrook.

Driver Only Operation (DOO) has required two support systems - two-way radio and closed circuit television (CCTV) equipment. The radio system provides communication between West Hampstead and drivers. A serviceable radio is a requirement for a single manned train. There are four links - one for each area, under the control of the signalman for that area at West Hampstead. 19 lineside base stations were required to ensure complete coverage. The signalman controls the link, trains can be called selectively or a general call made. Drivers have to request communication but have an emergency switch to generate an alarm at West Hampstead. CCTV is installed on platforms which are normally unattended. The hooded monitors are directed towards the driver's cab at the normal stopping position, with cameras providing a view of the platform and train to enable the doors to be closed safely.

The long, bitter, costly and, ultimately, futile industrial dispute over the principle of single manning cannot be overlooked. Its serious effect on services and the electrification timescale makes it a significant part of the history of the Extension. Incredibly, the train sets had been designed and the service planned for DOO without any prior agreement on the subject. The original intention was to commence limited electric services to Moorgate in January 1982, followed

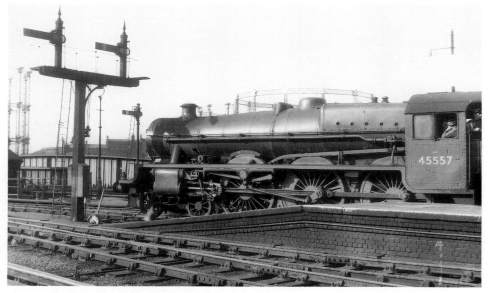

The crew of Jubilee 45557 NEW HEBRIDES relax before heading north from St Pancras on 26 June 1954. *C.R.L.Coles.*

More handsome than a shedful of HST's. Compound 4-4-0 1024 backs away from Kentish Town MPD to work north from St Pancras. *L&GRP*

An unusual arrangement of three distant signals for the up fast line at Kentish Town. The topmost arm is a repeater for Islip Street Junction's up fast home signal. The other two arms are splitting distants for St Paul's Road Passenger Junction. *A. Vaughan.*

by the full service to both Moorgate and St Pancras in May 1982. As it was, the new Class 317 trains were delivered to Cricklewood where they remained idle until agreement was reached on DOO in early 1983. As drivers completed their conversion, services were turned over to the new trains, running in the diesel timetable. More electric services were introduced on 11th July 1983 with the line to Moorgate restored. The full electric service commenced in October 1983, seventeen months later than originally planned.

The eventual agreement on DOO was hailed by Sir Peter Parker, then Chairman of BR, as "The greatest working practice breakthrough in the history of British Railways". In the long term, the overall saving is the cost of the guard's wages less the cost of maintaining them in unemployment, and the cost of the additional safety and monitoring equipment. Less quantifiable is the general loss in passenger amenity. In the short term, during the dispute, there was much loss of passenger goodwill locally as the operators struggled to maintain a service with patched-up and life expired DMUs. It may well be thought that Sir Peter was overstating his case.

The first complete electric service had an off-peak frequency of four trains per hour on the section between Kentish Town and Luton. There were two Moorgate/Luton trains per hour, alternate trains running non-stop from King's Cross Midland City to Mill Hill. A further two trains per hour ran between St Pancras and Bedford, not stopping south of St Albans. A weakness in the service was the low frequency (once per hour) of trains at Hendon, Cricklewood, West Hampstead and Kentish Town. The last two of these stations are useful interchanges, at all of them there was little inducement to patronage in an inner area with such long intervals between trains. The frequency was eventually improved to two trains per hour by changing the Moorgate/Luton service so that all trains stopped at every station. In the 1985/6 timetable, the Moorgate/Luton timing was 50 minutes. St Pancras to Bedford took 54 minutes, including an 18 minute sprint to St Albans.

The complete change in the suburban service was accompanied by an equally radical revision of the long distance services from St Pancras. From May 1983, the locomotive hauled expresses were replaced by High Speed Trains. The change achieved a great simplification for the operator and a high standard of excellence for the customer. The 1985/6 standard timing was 73 minutes from St Pancras to Leicester. Given the characteristics of the route, it is doubtful if this could be bettered significantly by any conventional train. Luton and Bedford were served by a fair number of HSTs. In the down direction, the Luton departure times were 23 minutes after those from St Pancras. There were 8 down trains making a first stop at Bedford, taking 36 minutes for the journey. Bedford also had 9 up non-stop HSTs. Most were allowed 42 minutes to reach St Pancras, providing a generous recovery margin.

The freight service on the Extension in 1987/8 comprised Company and Merry-go-round trains. Oil, roadstone, coal and refuse were the loads carried.

The advent of electrification brought about a revolution in rolling stock which as radical as the change from steam to the Class 127 DMUs. 48 sets of Class 317 Electric Multiple Unit trains were produced specifically for the Extension - unlike the Class 127 DMUs, they were designed to be compatible with the restricted clearances of the City route. The 317s introduced not only the general improvement in comfort and convenience always associated with electrification but also features such as power operated doors which had not hitherto been provided on stock making journeys as long as 50 miles. Power doors were of course a necessity for the intended Driver Only operation. The large vestibules for the doors reduced the area available for seating and, despite the omission of the guard's compartments, the number of seats provided fell from 352 in a 127 unit to 295 in a 317. Necessity, in the shape of the long tunnel sections on the City route, was the mother of invention; the two toilets provided in one of the trailer cars were of the retention type, a big step forward for British Railways.

The Class 127s had a power rating of about 6 h.p per gross ton weight, compared to a very approximate 4 h.p per ton for a steam suburban train. The 317s increased this to over 8 h.p per ton, with a consequent improvement in performance, not only in top speed which was increased from 70 to 90 m.p.h, but also very markedly in acceleration. A common body shell was used, with two sets of pneumatic sliding doors per coach. The doors were passenger operated with driver override. It was possible to walk through the complete train to reach end doors for emergency evacuation. Internal fittings included a pressurised heating and ventilating system and a public address system. Externally, disc brakes and Tightlock couplers were fitted. Up to three units could be operated in multiple but in practice only two were coupled due to platform limitations.

Two way radio and various safety provisions in the control system were intended to facilitate DOO. However, the train sets were built with first class accommodation, but with no provi-

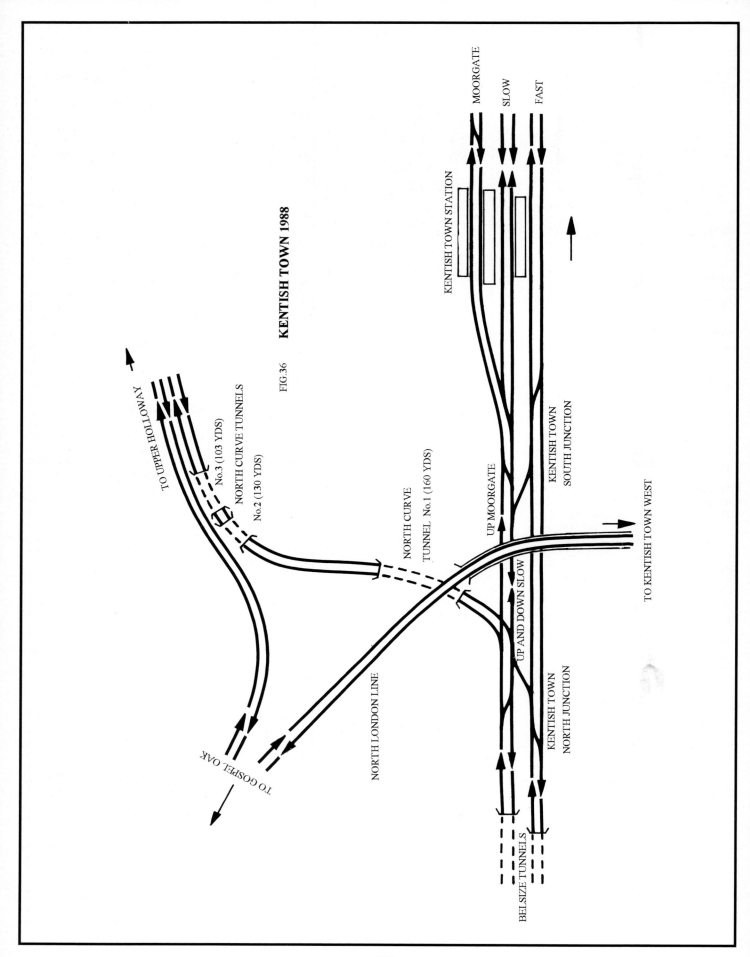

KENTISH TOWN 1988

FIG.36

MOORGATE

SLOW

FAST

KENTISH TOWN STATION

UP MOORGATE

KENTISH TOWN
SOUTH JUNCTION

TO UPPER HOLLOWAY

No.3 (103 YDS)

NORTH CURVE TUNNELS

No.2 (130 YDS)

NORTH CURVE
TUNNEL No.1 (160 YDS)

TO GOSPEL OAK

NORTH LONDON LINE

UP AND DOWN SLOW

TO KENTISH TOWN WEST

KENTISH TOWN
NORTH JUNCTION

BELSIZE TUNNELS

Prior to the advent of six-coupled engines, the London sheds possessed almost sixty 0-4-4 tanks for suburban and ECS workings, 1385 being seen at Kentish Town during the first decade of the grouping. *Lens of Sutton.*

sion for guards to maintain its integrity. They entered service as one-class trains and the seating accommodation in the erstwhile first class section was in some cases revised. The units encountered teething troubles on entering service, for the fleet had previously covered little more than the mileage required for driver training. It was claimed that lack of trial running due to the manning dispute had prevented the troubles from being detected earlier. It is not certain, however, that additional time for proving trials would have been available within the original programme. The initial difficulties with the 317s included problems with the traction motor smoothing chokes and some embarrassing platform overruns, some of sufficient length to necessitate obtaining permission from West Hampstead to set back. The most serious fault was, however, the unacceptably bad riding of the power cars. With all axles motored, these cars were the equivalent of a 1300 h.p electric locomotive. In fact, the riding was so bad that it led in some cases to failure of the mountings for the main transformer. At one stage, up trains from Bedford were stopped short of the platform at Luton for a visual check of the brackets before being allowed to continue. Rectification included the fitting of extra dampers for which the trains had to be sent back to works. During the ensuing shortage, seven Class 313 units were borrowed from the Great Northern suburban service. They ran on the Extension without their shoe beams but were not passed for the City branch. On occasions, three Class 313 units were coupled to form a nine car train, something not seen on their home ground. Relief trains of refurbished Mk 1 corridor stock were also provided; these were hauled by Class 45 or 47 diesel electric locomotives.

"When the bold step was taken of re-opening a Victorian railway tunnel across the City of London last year, no one realised just how successful the new Thameslink service would be'. So read a BR publicity pamphlet of July 1989.

Although not wishing to begrudge BR the natural pleasure of putting a rare success story on record, the wording does give rise to doubts about the efficacy of their market research. Thameslink has, however, been a remarkable venture, perhaps the most radical change to a large scale service that has taken place in recent years. The possibility of re-opening the Snow Hill link from Farringdon to Holborn Viaduct was first mentioned at the end of 1984. Approval of the scheme was announced in July 1985. Eleven months later, railway operations in eastern and southern England were integrated by the formation of Network SouthEast. An incidental effect of this change was the smoothing of the inauguration and subsequent operation of the new service.

For years after the withdrawal of the initial passenger services the Snow Hill link had been well used by transfer goods trains. In the 1960s the freight traffic declined and finally ceased. The line was closed in 1969 and the track lifted in 1972. The re-opening involved reinstating the junctions at Farringdon and Holborn Viaduct and laying track between them on the old alignment up the steep bank in tunnel. Electrification from Farringdon was on the Southern Region's 750v dc system. Direct access to the electrified network south of the Thames was thereby achieved.

It is certain that a connection to the southern lines was not considered when the original Midland Suburban Electrification was planned and implemented. Much effort was expended in civil work to provide clearances for 25kv throughout to Moorgate. If Thameslink, with its requirement for dual voltage stock, had been foreseen in 1976 there is little doubt that the dc system would have been used between Kentish Town and Moorgate. But, compared with the vision of the Victorian railway planners, the present funding of projects piecemeal by a reluctant Treasury prevents a long term view and, in the end, costs more money for a given result. So, within five years of electrified services commencing on the Extension, the specially built Class 317 units were transferred away, to be replaced by new Class 319s.

The 319 units were provided with a power system capable of operating from either a 25kv 50Hz overhead supply, on the original Midland lines, or from a 750v dc third rail, on lines south of Farringdon. When operating from the overhead supply the secondary of the main transformer feeds a bridge rectifier to produce a dc voltage equivalent to that obtained from the third rail. The current in each of the four motor circuits is controlled by two Gate Turn-Off thyristors, fired alternately by a chopper control system. Gate Turn-Off devices of the required

One of Bedford's compound 4-4-0s, 41044, heads for home through the Hertfordshire landscape at Napsbury on 4 August 1950. *E.D. Bruton*

The Britannia Pacifics were, until 1957, a rare sight on the Midland extension although tests run with members of the class in 1953 fired expectations of an allocation. As it happened the tests were connected with the running of fully-fitted coal trains; the third of which was witnessed by the photographer at Chiltern Green on Sunday 1 February 1953 with Longsight Pacific 70030 WILLIAM WORDSWORTH. Similar tests were later run with BR 5MT 4-6-0s. *E.D. Bruton*

The Midland compounds were one of the most successful designs seen in this country and from being introduced in 1902, successive batches were built including a large number by the LMS in 1924 which came close to becoming the standard express passenger locomotive on the system. In post-war days, ousted by the Stanier designs, the compounds were relegated to lesser duties - although some survived into the 1960's - such as the 18.52 St Pancras - Bedford seen here at Napsbury on 24 July 1950 behind 41009 of Bedford which was one of the 1905 variety with 7ft driving wheels. *E.D. Bruton*

rating had only recently become available when the units were designed and this was their largest application to British rolling stock at the time.

To the Extension passenger, the change from 317 to 319 units was a welcome improvement. Much seemed to have been learned in the short time which separated the two designs. Seating, decoration and the heating system were all improved. The air doors of the 319s are more reliable than those of the 317s and the audible warning of closure is appreciated. More importantly, they have passenger operated emergency releases. There are arguments for and against this provision. In minor incidents, passengers may detrain unnecessarily and imperil themselves on adjacent running lines. It is essential on the 319s as there is no connection between units. But on the 317s the end doors had to be used as emergency exits. This appeared to be totally inadequate for a major accident. With the front of a peak hour train involved in a collision, evacuation of some 700 passengers would have had to proceed unsupervised through eight coaches and the likely location of casualties would be as far from the one useable exit as possible. When it is remembered that some 317 services ran with the rear Driving trailer loaded with mails and locked, it is understandable that some regular travellers felt more at ease when the 319s were introduced. From January 1991, Class 319/1 units were introduced on the Bedford services. The major change from the original 319s was the provision of a small first class section adjacent to one of the driving compartments. This appeared to prompt an increase in

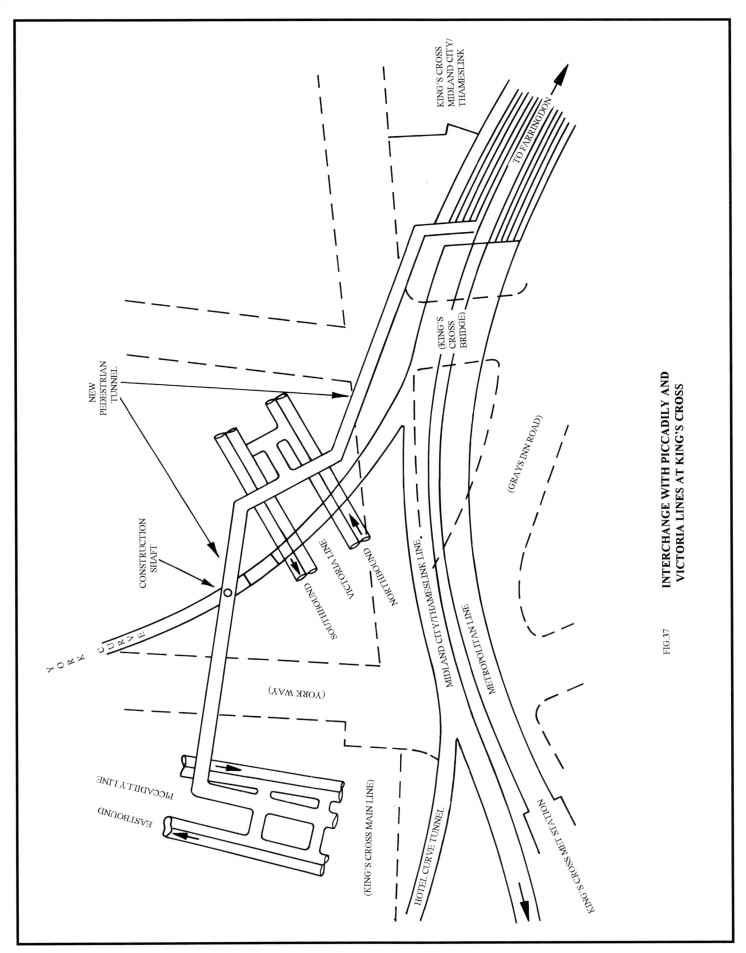

YORK CURVE

NEW PEDESTRIAN TUNNEL

CONSTRUCTION SHAFT

VICTORIA LINE

SOUTHBOUND

NORTHBOUND

(YORK WAY)

PICCADILLY LINE

EASTBOUND

(KING'S CROSS MAIN LINE)

HOTEL CURVE TUNNEL

MIDLAND CITY/THAMESLINK LINE

METROPOLITAN LINE

(GRAYS INN ROAD)

KING'S CROSS MET STATION

(KING'S CROSS BRIDGE)

KING'S CROSS MIDLAND CITY/ THAMESLINK

TO FARRINGDON

INTERCHANGE WITH PICCADILY AND VICTORIA LINES AT KING'S CROSS

FIG.37

on-board ticket inspections - a dilution of the DOO principle. The 319/1s are borrowed for a variety of services south of the Thames in the course of which the train sets are often turned round. Hence the first class traveller on the Extension, joining at a thirty second station stop, can find that his very limited accommodation is four car lengths from where he expected it to be. The centre of the train would probably be a more convenient location although complaints might be raised concerning other passenger walking through.

The riding of the 319s, both power and trailer cars, is irreproachable. There are prominent dampers connected between the bogie frames and body sides. The flanges sing a song of protest on sharp curves giving rise to the thought that good riding qualities have been obtained at the cost of high flange wear. Inevitably, criticism of the stock appeared in the local papers published along the route. Usually this was of the "seats are too small and there should be more of them in each car" category. Once, the 319s were described as "the crawling Thameslink", an unfair title for 100 m.p.h trains. Two suggestions for improvements to future designs come to mind. One welcome change would be the provision of air conditioning to permit the elimination of the opening quarter lights. When the latter are opened on hot days the interiors become very noisy at even moderate speeds

and almost intolerable at full speed or in tunnels. The increase in amenity in winter due to the quieter interior is very noticeable. The second improvement would be the repeal of BR's apparently fundamental law that the relative positions of standard class seats and windows should be arranged without considering the passenger's outlook. Having put the criticisms on record the balance must finally be redressed. Suburban stock with the standard of comfort and performance of the 319s would have been inconceivable only a few years ago. There is also the aspect of the general convenience of the Thameslink service, a product, not only of a fresh look at a derelict route, but also of the train sets which brought BR's bold step to an everyday reality.

In contrast to the Extension, the crossing of the Thames provided access to a wide variety of destinations, either via Elephant and Castle or London Bridge. The latter is reached by the spur from Blackfriars to Metropolitan Junction which now includes a section of single line. From London Bridge, Gatwick Airport was an obvious goal. The 319 units are maintained at Selhurst, reducing the functions of Cricklewood despite the comparatively recent investment in its facilities.

The new service commenced on 16th May 1988. Some changes were made to the names of stations, King's Cross Midland City became

King's Cross Thameslink and West Hampstead Midland was similarly changed to West Hampstead Thameslink. Bedford Midland and St Albans City became plain Bedford and St Albans respectively although the former regains the Midland suffix in the Bletchley/Bedford timetable to distinguish it from Bedford St Johns.

The initial off-peak service was arranged as follows:- Two trains per hour; Bedford to Gatwick Airport with alternate trains extended to Brighton. Two trains per hour; Luton to Purley with alternate trains running via Streatham or Crystal Palace and taking 92 minutes overall. Two trains per hour; Cricklewood to Bromley South via the Catford loop, with trains continuing alternately to Orpington in 66 minutes or Sevenoaks via Otford in 79 minutes.

Trains terminating at Gatwick Airport ran non-stop from St Albans to King's Cross Thameslink in 24 minutes and called only at East Croydon after London Bridge. The Bedford to Gatwick Airport time was 106 minutes. Trains continuing to Brighton called at all stations after Gatwick Airport, taking 148 minutes overall. The remaining services called at all stations, thus providing Cricklewood, West Hampstead and Kentish Town with a welcome four off-peak trains per hour instead of only one when electrified services commenced in 1983.

Major changes were made to the Snow Hill link in 1990. The line was diverted through

Lacking any signs of steam or smoke, 9F 2-10-0 92083 works silently between Luton and Leagrave with a train of empties for Wellingborough.
Photomatic.

The most numerous of the Midland express engines were the 2P 4-4-0's which, although overshadowed by the compounds, first appeared in 1882 and were perpetuated - with much rebuilding - until 1932 when the number in service amounted to no less than 298 locomotives. Like the compounds they were well dispersed over the LMS system and they survived until as recently as 1963. In this view 535 stands at Cricklewood MPD on 7 July 1937. *H.C.Casserley.*

a new station, St Pauls Thameslink, (City Thameslink from 30th September 1991) built in an underground box in replacement of Holborn Viaduct terminus. Entrances were provided from the City thoroughfares of Holborn Viaduct and Ludgate Hill, between which the new station is situated. By a slight encroachment at the north end into the old Snow Hill tunnel, the platforms are capable of accepting 12 car trains.

A dramatic change of level of the route was necessary. The old formation climbed from Snow Hill to join the lines from Holborn Viaduct and pass over Ludgate Hill. The change from below to above street level was concentrated by the diversion into the relatively short distance between Ludgate Hill, at the south end of the new station, and the bridge over Queen Victoria Street at the north end of Blackfriars station. The gradient was critical to the extent that the lowering of the Queen Victoria Street bridge by 300mm was undertaken. The resultant 1 in 29 incline provides spectacular views from the northbound Blackfriars platform of trains making the ascent. The project was funded as part of a large office development scheme, the latter made possible by the closure of Holborn Viaduct station on 26th January 1990 and the

abandonment of the above ground railway. The line was severed between Farringdon and Blackfriars from 14th to 28th May 1990 inclusive. In that remarkably short interval, the diversion was completed and St Pauls Thameslink was opened with the new line on 29th May 1990.

By May 1990 the Thameslink services had undergone two years of evolution. The timetable which commenced on 29th May 1990 introduced some changes which reflected that development. 15 trains passed through Kentish Town to arrive between 08.00 and 09.00. The off-peak Bedford to Gatwick Airport and Brighton service was virtually unchanged from the initial timings of 1988. The Cricklewood/Sevenoaks trains were extended to Luton and the Luton/Purley trains were replaced by a service between Luton and Guildford via West Croydon and Epsom. Trains on the new service ran non-stop between Mill Hill Broadway and King's Cross Thameslink and called only at Effingham Junction between Leatherhead and Guildford. With all services running at half hourly intervals, the net result was an additional two trains per hour in each direction for all stations from Luton to Mill Hill inclusive. The increase in frequency from two to four trains per hour for Radlett and

Elstree was especially welcome. On the other hand, calls at the interchange stations of West Hampstead Thameslink and Kentish Town were halved from four to two trains per hour.

The great advance made by Thameslink is that, with negligible effect on the commuter as nurtured by the Midland electrification, it offers new possibilities to the casual user. In particular, the direct service to Gatwick Airport and the ten minute interval Luton Flyer coach between Luton station and airport are tempting many car users back on to trains.

Dependability is the keyword. For every flight missed a customer is lost. The development of the new services has resulted in a change to the character of the Extension. While continuing to play host to the HSTs from Sheffield and the through freight traffic, the emphasis is now on internally generated business and the new connections to the south. Bedford, one of the limits of Network SouthEast, is taking on the semblance of a frontier post. It is remarkable that the Extension, still with some of its original features, has adapted so well to such a radical change of pattern of service.

APPENDICES

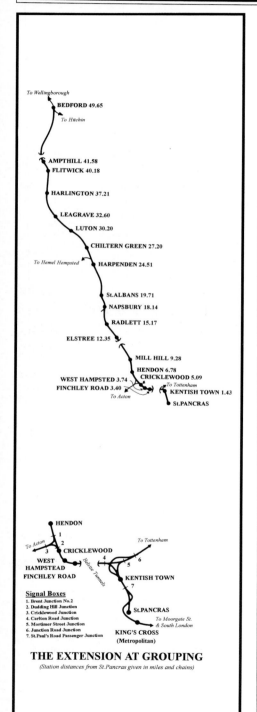

THE EXTENSION AT GROUPING

(Station distances from St.Pancras given in miles and chains)

Signal Boxes
1. Brent Junction No.2
2. Dudding Hill Junction
3. Cricklewood Junction
4. Carlton Road Junction
5. Mortimer Street Junction
6. Junction Road Junction
7. St.Paul's Road Passenger Junction

STATION	PASSENGER TRAFFIC 1873 - 1922 PASSENGERS BOOKED						Receipts (£)
	1873	1883	1893	1903	1913	1922	1913
BEDFORD	116613	143696	180929	226652	229023	230808	49499
Ampthill	14279	20472	24900	22356	24220	20825	2366
Flitwick	11234	14275	17999	22500	31212	28298	3205
Harlington	10794	14764	15729	18813	22297	20012	2030
Leagrave	6856	20468	19843	31006	24948	22533	1035
LUTON	86965	136857	147482	200063	263385	259871	44122
Chiltern Green	4295	7908	7379	7368	4189	3728	149
Harpenden	29678	41522	63684	97661	136638	104771	14847
ST ALBANS	55468	77530	108239	171034	208444	197498	30502
Napsbury	-	-	-	6875*	5209	13200	172
Radlett	16776	20295	25830	50936	74571	79438	7702
Elstree	19225	24353	34900	50096	60069	66538	5276
Mill Hill	11555	16083	23934	43003	76883	81014	7173
Hendon	63384	106241	184625	298974	132015	70742	7898
Welsh Harp	23246	25455	16621	5063**			
Cricklewood	20251	60799	111728	167593	56939	56893	2552
West Hampstead	13146	27827	72448	88115	27207	17888	1285
Finchley Road	52770	58302	81515	78936	20613	5870	1018
Haverstock Hill	179837	110803	106951	118613	23530		374
Kentish Town	344107	402369	448745	501913	196087	134714	10295
Camden Road	246967	209229	166616	182896	24676		813

*: total for 1906 (first full year). ** Total for 1902 (last full year).*

Gradient Profile

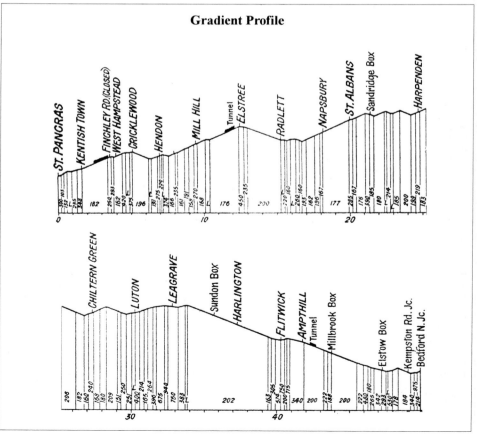

ENGINE ALLOCATIONS

Engine allocations 1920-59

Class	Kentish Town 1920	1945	1959	Cricklewood 1920	1945	1959	St Albans 1920*	1945	1959	Bedford 1920	1945	1959
7P 4-6-0	-	-	4									
5XP 4-6-0	-	12	15									
5MT 4-6-0	-	18	16			9						6
LM4 2-6-0					2	5		1				
BR4 4-6-0												6
BR9 2-10-0						5						
LM8 2-8-0						12						
4P 4-4-0	16	3	-								8	
3P 4-4-0	14	-	-								2	
2P 4-4-0	7	2	4							11	3	
4-2-2	13	-	-							7		
2-4-0	4	-	-	7						11		
0-6-0	16	17	12	21	29	12		2	3	27	19	12
4-6-4T	-	-	-	8								
2-6-4T	-	7	-					8	9			
2-6-2T	-	15	20		13	1		2	6		3	4
0-4-4T	40	4		16	2						5	
0-6-0T	43	27	15	56	38	10		2	2	2	2	3

Sub-shed of Cricklewood until 1934. All Cricklewood 4-6-4T's and some of the 2-4-0's were based on the sub-shed

BEDFORD ENGINE ALLOCATIONS : 1892 – 1959

TYPE	TOTAL	ENGINES
		1892
2-4-0	4	193-6
	9	821-9
	2	151-2
	1	1088
4-4-0	4	1742-5
4-2-2	1	37
	1	34
0-6-0	20	830-49
	42	
		1914
4-4-0	6	551-6
2-4-0	10	53-7,61-2,94,229-30
4-2-2	9	616-8,24-6,40,2,660
0-6-0	20	2473,97,2709,95,6,9,2800-3,21, 2949, 3103,70,95,97,8,3427,34,3707
0-4-4T	3	1242,52,7
0-6-0T	2	1723,4
	50	
		1933
4-4-0	16	549-553,719,20,50,3,5,60,2-5,7
2-4-0	4	115,79,88,267
0-6-0	18	3112,9,57,95,3217,3329,3428,74,7,3707,8,68,76,85,3909,10,4228,9
0-4-4T	5	1239,60,72,3,1369
0-6-0T	3	1665,1780,8
	46	
		1950
4-4-0	11	762,41007,9,38,44,56,70,91,4,41198
2-8-0	1	48177
0-6-0	18	58149,43174,43222,58241,43428,74,58305,43721,66,77,85,43876,88,43910,23,67,71,44582
2-6-2T	7	40141,65,41209,69-72
0-4-4T	1	58091
0-6-0T	3	47223,52,47549
	41	
		1959
4-6-0	12	44984,45137,45139,45221,45267,45342,75040-44,55
0-6-0	12	43428,40,74,43529,31,65,43665,43766,85,43808,43829,58214
2-6-2T	4	40020,41271,80,84005
0-6-0T	3	47264,79,47549
	31	

TRAIN LOADINGS

EXPRESS PASSENGER LOADINGS 1920 (WEEKDAYS)

TRAIN	DESTINATION	WEIGHT (TARE)	COACHES (APPROX)	ENGINE CLASS	COMMENTS
00.00	Manchester	215	8	2	
02.30	Manchester	259	9	3	233 from Leicester with class 2 engine
07.55	Nottingham	200	8	3	Class 2 from Leicester
08.15	Manchester	189	7	3	186 tons ex Nottingham with class 1 engine. 163 tons from Derby with class 2 engine.
09.00	Carlisle	252	9	4	
09.30	Leicester	174	7	1	105 tons from Bedford
10.15	Manchester	253	9	4	240 tons from Derby. 188 tons from Chinley.
10.40	Sheffield	175	7	3	Class 2 from Nottingham
11.35	Derby	218	8	2	Class 3 from Leicester
11.45	Carlisle	185	7	3	
12.15	Manchester	272	10	4	
13.30	Manchester (Vic)	196	8	2	
13.37	Leeds	243	9	3	
14.15	Manchester	216	8	2	
15.20	Leeds	193	7	3	
16.15	Leicester	267	9	3	
16.22	Nottingham	164	6	3	
17.00	Leeds	217	8	4	
17.35	Leeds	192	7	3	
18.15	Manchester	280	10	4	
20.00	Derby	249	9	3	
20.50	Carlisle	226	8	4	
21.05	Carlisle	249	9	4	
23.30	Carlisle	177	7	3	
23.40	Leeds	186	7	4	

Note. Midland coaches averaged approximately 25 tons; the weight being used as a basis for column 4

PASSENGER TRAIN LOADINGS (tons) 1954
ST PANCRAS TO LEICESTER AND BRANCHES

Timing	Class of engine					
	2	3	4	5	6	7
XL limit	-	-	220	255	300	340
Special limit	200	245	270	310	350	405
Limited load	225	270	300	345	390	450
Full load	255	305	340	390	440	495
H.Hempsted bch (up)	60	120	150	-	-	-
H.Hempsted bch (dn)	60	100	120	-	-	-
Hitchin bch	190	260	-	-	-	-

GOOD[S TR]AIN LOADINGS (loaded mineral) 1913
BEDFORD TO LONDON

	Class of engine					
	UP			DOWN		
Engine class	1	2	3	1	2	3
Bedford - Leagrave	35	42	50	35	42	50
Leagrave - London	42	50	60	35	42	50

Notes
3 loaded goods = 2 loaded mineral
4 empty wagons = 2 loaded mineral wagons
5 10t wagons = 6 ordinary wagons
Double headed loads = Double train up to 90 loaded mineral or equivalent
Maximum number of wagons = 100 (70 Bedford to Leagrave in the up direction).